SECRET LIFE OF A SPOOK
BY

PETER PAGET

SECRET LIFE OF A SPOOK

Based on a True Story

By PETER PAGET

© Peter Paget 2016

All Rights Reserved

peterpaget2012@yahoo.co.uk

ISBN-13: 978-1540485120

ISBN-10: 1540485129

Contents

Contents 5

Biography 7

Acknowledgements 9

Preface 11

1. Before the Beginning 13

2. Early Days 38

3: Areas of Enquiry 56

4. Into The Unknown 77

5. Undercover Endeavours 121

6. Things get serious 142

7. Matters More Domestic 164

8. Osama bin Liner 179

9. Times they are a changin' 195

10. A Very Serious Character 217

11. Over the hills and far away 245

12. Sunsets & Sails 251

13. The Great and the Good 263

14. Exposure 274

15. Epitaph? 290

16. In Retrospect 292

EPILOGUE................... 297

Other books by Peter Paget........... 311

Biography

Peter Paget was born in London just after the end of the Second World War, a baby boomer, he grew up in London and the West Country where his intelligence was noted at an early age when he advised The Cabinet Office Chief Scientific Advisor at the age of just seventeen years old, by donating free of patent or royalty a technological technique to HMG. This was later bought and taken up by BP Oil and distributed World Wide.   Peter was co-opted into the British Intelligence Community shortly after this and has worked undercover on various tasks and assignments for the past fifty years, while also leading a double life as author, lecturer, therapist and international adventurer.

Peter has been both a researcher and programme contributor to the BBC, ghost written books for Granada, made educational programmes for students and the British Army Schools and written under a pen name where his two paperbacks have sold in both the English language, French and Spanish translations over half a million copies. Peter was trained as a professional sub-Editor and script Editor and some of his family members are currently engaged full time in the media. Peter was a Full Member of the Royal Television Society in 1995 as a Researcher.

Acknowledgements

Many faceless friends have contributed to this book. They cannot be identified but they all know who they are and they understand my deep gratitude to their contributions to the safety of the United Kingdom over the past fifty years. I owe my life to more than a few of them. I would not be here but for their loyal efforts to those who in honour quietly serve in the shadows.

Some of these dear friends are now no longer on this mortal coil. I have still retained their names, places and identities to protect their families. My own family has been very supportive but even they will learn of things unsaid, which they have not been allowed to know during the course of my lifetime in service to HMG. Some of my relatives have been much braver than I. They were more exposed, more vulnerable. I have had the relative luxury of being under cover and so long as that was maintained the enemy did not have sight of me. I still have to stay under cover, under radar to certain parties who would happily do away with me without a second thought. I afford my mates and colleagues the same protection as was given to me.

My thanks also go to post production helpers with the polishing and editing of the work you are about to read. In particular, to Tania Tirraoro without whose endless technical help and editing this work would never have been seen here today. Also to Lloyd Canning for his kind permission to use his wonderful art work for this book cover, and indeed the works to come, old and new.

Advice has also been actively sought from both American and United Kingdom security agencies to ensure the OSA is not at any point breached. Certain things need to be known now before everyone has passed on and taken their secrets with them.

However, for those who have mistaken me for a whistle-blower, no, I am not, this is just to set the record straight where mistakes need to be acknowledged in order that they are not repeated in the future. A brave new world, one hopes better than the past.

My Eternal Thanks,

Peter

Athens 2016

Preface

The Sun streamed like a golden tube through the oriole window of the master suite of The Penthouse, overlooking Southampton Ocean Terminal.

South Western House was my temporary home, the place I had chosen to deliver my manuscript before my quiet and unobserved departure yet again undercover into the grey world of the double agent.

The building seemed appropriate, its baroque period features reminiscent of a grand but faded past. The building where they say the gentleman and lady passengers of Titanic had spent their last night before sailing on that ill-fated voyage.

I sensed this voyage of mine would perhaps also be my last. That sense of foreboding and destiny, which had urged me to put into print the unthinkable, the unacceptable and the bizarre episodes which had led me to this place.

Yes, I had been careful, certain names dates and places had been changed, sanitised, obscured where the few, now retired, individuals, - they say you never leave the service - would potentially be at risk.

The others were beyond danger. They were already dead, some gallantly, some tragically, most without point or reason, but all unrecorded by history other than in the odd glimpse of a doctored news report or piece of media-distributed misinformation.

Ah! The art of information management, or as it had been put to me, a lie sandwiched between two truths or a truth sandwiched between two lies. This was not the cavalier world of Fleming's James Bond. Yet at times it seemed even more dangerous, more surreal, perhaps beyond the realms of reason. Acted upon by more than the hand of man, perhaps by the fates themselves.

So we are, "Still here", as the American banker had said, stumbling away from the Twin Towers on that fateful day, covered in dust and blood. He, like so many others, just innocent victims along the way.

My job, over the years, had been to contribute to the effort to being, "Still here".

At the beginning, in fact before the beginning, my life had been, like all of us, influenced by my upbringing and parents...

1. Before the Beginning

Wide Eyed Youth

My father was a pacifist, insofar as during the Second World War, he elected to join the London Fire Brigade because he did not wish to be in the British Army and killing people.

He was originally from Canada, but had been in the United Kingdom for many years and had married my mother, a genuine Cockney. Born within the sound of Bow Bells, she was the seventh child of a seventh child in a family of nine. An Aries, was always moaning about her lot in the world. You might say she was a balanced person; she had a chip on each shoulder, but my mother was convinced that the world was an evil place and agin her at every turn.

People were to be avoided as they bade you no good fortune and she watched them with a suspicion bordering on the obsessive.

My father was an outgoing man, got along with

everyone and was very popular.

Originally a piano teacher in London where, while during his wartime duty in the Fire Service, he had some near misses. Once, a German V2 rocket had fallen right beside a Nissan hut in which he and his mates were playing cards. The missile had fortunately fallen into soft clay, penetrating down many yards before exploding. The blast had travelled right over the curved roof of the hut without harming it at all but had demolished three houses on the other side of the street, killing two occupants outright.

My father certainly led a charmed life; perhaps the same angels that seemed to sit on my shoulders at times also looked after him. He was highly thought of by people he came in contact with, but suffered from a nervous disposition and on occasion would stammer, a characteristic my mother professed to have knocked out of him when they married. She claimed she had made him the man he was; a claim I didn't believe. But he had missed a number of chances in life, which was a shame really, because they were opportunities of considerable merit. In the early days of radio and crystal radio sets, his cousin had identified this new innovation and suggested to my father, John, that they open a shop selling these new toys. My father was not so sure, questioned that they might be just a nine-day wonder, and had declined the free fifty percent partnership his cousin had offered. So the shop opened without him, did rather well and went on to become a national chain; which is still there today.

His cousin was not the only one to notice my father's integrity and intelligence. Another contact of his had noticed that the working folk were now taking it into their heads to travel down to Brighton from London to the seaside and he elected to purchase a charabanc. We would call that a coach or bus these days. Again my father was offered a free fifty percent partnership if he wished to help form the company. Nerves again took hold and my father turned down the offer. This company became Grey Green Coaches and later went national in its operations.

The final turn of my father's monetary ill-fortune was surely a product of both human meanness and mischievous fates at work in his life in so far as for three years he had been a member of a little football pools syndicate, each week putting his shilling into the pot for their group bet on the outcome of the Saturday matches. This one week my father was going on holiday and he had forgotten to proffer his shilling into the pot. The syndicate won £3,000, a small fortune in those days, and cut my father out of the winnings, as he had not contributed that week.

Perhaps out of a sense of desperation, need for comfort or sheer stress, at the end of the Second World War my father had an affair.

My mother was working as a switchboard operator at the ARP control centre and her shifts rarely coincided with my father's Fire Service schedules, so they were not seeing much of each other. My father took up with a friendly lady in his control centre and this relationship continued after the war before he was de-mobbed.

My father desperately wanted children, a breed of being my mother despised. Many decades later, after his death, I came across my father's love letters to my mother, sent during the war when they were apart. His need for children was passionately expressed in these touching and emotional notes. After the war, even though the affair was still alive, one did not get divorced in those days; my father gave my mother an ultimatum. "Children, or it's over."

My mother grudgingly gave in and I was the result, a fact she would remind me of many times throughout my childhood. I had only arrived to save the marriage and she had suffered much pain during my birth, so she never allowed my father to make love to her again. The amazing thing is they stayed together for the rest of their lives. How times have changed.

In the course of lectures on the evils of sex mother confessed that when my father and she had first got married she had fallen pregnant and was so terrified by the whole process that she had not made any preparation for the birth and refused to go to hospital when labour commenced. She was only rushed to the maternity unit in a taxi at the last moment. The baby, a girl, had been born on the waiting room floor and had died shortly there afterwards.

I always kind of missed my former sister, even though that had happened before I was born, but it was a backdrop to my upbringing as a single and only child.

My early childhood was one of isolation. My mother hated children, so no contacts were allowed of younger folk. My early recollections and the few black and white photographs of that period, record that I was growing up in North London in a house with a walled garden, around which I drove my pride and joy, a little blue pedal car. At the end of the garden was a summerhouse and this was my private domain and personal retreat. A place of peaceful sanity away from the rather terrible rows my parents had when mother wished to have a go. Being an Aries by definition she was always right, no matter what.

Sometime in the summer of 1952, a car travelling in the street outside one night ploughed into our front garden, demolishing the wall and killing the driver. My father promptly decided he had had enough of London and elected to move to the West Country. I was pleased at this thought as only the September prior I had been entered into primary school and had a rather rough reception. Upon my first day the older boys in some twisted school ritual had dragged me into the boys' toilets pushed me on the floor and urinated on me. I know not why, apparently new boys were all treated thus, one presumes to have them understand their place in the order of things.

The ignominy was compounded by my class teacher telling me off when I returned to the classroom, after the "play-time break" for wetting myself and my dishevelled appearance. I sobbed quietly at the back of the classroom, wondering if my mother's views on the outside world were indeed correct.

My parents raised capital and bought a hotel in Torquay. Odd, I thought, as my mother disliked people so much. It was a kind of forerunner to "Faulty Towers", the comedy in which "Basil" also hates his guests except when sucking up to anyone perceived to be of an upper class or profession.

My mother was proud of her common roots, good working class stock I was told, although her father was actually a marine electrical engineer engaged in the construction of large vessels on the Thames. He had contracted TB in his middle years and passed from this mortal coil leaving his widow to struggle to bring up their nine children. Perhaps this was the cause of my mother's aversion to normal family relations.

My father had been the ninth of an even larger family of thirteen. Originally of English gentry stock, the family had apparently lost its money at the hands of a profligate son who gambled the money away in the late Eighteenth Century, since when the family had been engaged in trade. I was told my grandfather was a musician and had a liking for good alcohol and an even greater liking for the ladies; a roving eye, as they say.

My parents were as chalk and cheese. I got on well with my father; he was very clever and invented things all the time in his workshop. He also had a great interest in Astronomy and had fine optical instruments made of brass on mahogany tripods, all of which my mother considered a complete waste of time.

Does one get the impression I did not get along with my mother? Then again she did not get along with anyone, so it was only fair. My mother's strength was discipline; everything had to be ordered, in its place and without fuss. Illness was considered a sign of weakness and not tolerated. Education was the big thing; you had to be better than your peers, no prizes for second place.

Perhaps out of all the contradiction of that, at the age of ten, my body decided to pull some fuses. My school was a mile away from the hotel, downhill and I would run to school, easy downhill, and then as my mother would not pay for school dinners, a mixed blessing, I would run home at lunchtime, bolt my food and run back to school again. You might think that would keep me fit, which it did for a while, except in winter. I was having some trouble at school again, I was moderately clever, which somewhat upset the duller boys. Sometimes my books would be sabotaged and I would get the blame again for not doing work. Also, I spoke with a middle class London accent and that didn't go down very well in Devon in those days, the other kids accused me of being a snob, when in fact I was just trying to keep my nose clean and keep out of their way.

This all came to a head one day when the head bully, there always is one, a sort of primary alpha male, cornered me in the playground and accused me of showing him up in class by answering first. Pulling a penknife from his pocket he pushed me back against the wall and stabbed me in the wrist. Holding my thumb over the oozing wound I duly attended assembly and attempted to sing along with the morning hymns while the hall walls slowly started to rotate around me. I collapsed in a small but suitably dramatic pool of blood, which had flowed down my hand.

I woke up in the school medical room with my wrist bandaged and the school did what all good schools do, they covered it up, and I was accused of provoking the attack, kept in class to the end of the day and sent home with a note to say I had been the unfortunate victim of a minor accident. My first lesson in, 'official information management.'

So it was not too surprising that under a certain amount of stress my body produced a series of childhood illnesses, one after the other, which kept me off school for most of the year before the eleven plus, an examination which determined your intellectual place in life, either Grammar school, secondary modern or something else in the great scheme of things.

Next door lived two incredibly aged sisters, one an ex-headmistress and the other a former English and History teacher.

The eldest was 89 and the younger, a "mere gal" of 86. They became my Governesses for that final year and strict instructresses they were too. Homework was never ending, tasks were demanding, involving research and field trips to the local woods to locate and collect samples. Birds to be identified, whole histories of British campaigns to be learnt and remembered by heart. These ladies were traditionalists at their best and missed the eminent careers they had once enjoyed. I was their sole pupil and I was going to carry their torch in a final declaration of their talents.

Three weeks before the eleven plus my mother fell out with them over a minor matter of fees, however their work had been done by then and my brain had been rearranged into a finely tuned instrument of investigation and focused intent.

Also at this time a curious and magical episode had occurred. In the walled garden, where I was confined during my off time hours a magpie had arrived. Nothing unusual in that, except this one was no regular bird. It came for food, would eat from the palm of my hand and even cracked a few simple jokes, learnt like a parrot. It actually did say, "Pieces of eight, pieces of eight" as it looked at me with its head slightly on one side. My mother declared it must have been someone's pet and been trained before it escaped back into the wild. Magpies are members of the Raven family and can imitate speech much like Mina Birds, who are proficient talkers.

About this time and over the course of feeding my

newfound friend I got better and was in a fit state to attend and sit the eleven plus examinations for the County of Devon.

Some several weeks later a letter was sent home summoning my parents and me to attend a meeting with my primary school headmistress, a Miss Fleet. A lady in her middle years, of military countenance and known in school as 'The Dragon.' My father was too nervous to attend, he knew the wisdom of keeping your head below the firing line, however the letter gave no indication of what the meeting would be about. It just had a decidedly ominous tone.

On the due date I, along with my mother, sat outside the office of the Headmistress. It was a sunny afternoon. The door creaked open, and filling the space was 'The Dragon.' She wore a plaid skirt, a pale green cardigan and a tie, yes a tie. We entered like obedient sheep and sat down. There was a pause. The Dragon eyed us over half- rimmed glasses. An older gentleman sat in the corner - we were told he was a school examiner.

Without wasting time, 'The Dragon' addressed my mother, "So how did he cheat?" she quizzed with an icy stare. My mother froze, absorbing the accusation before she exploded into a defence of this unheard-of slander. 'The Dragon' had met her match.

"He's only ever been in the middle of the B stream," declared 'The Dragon', "And now this!"

"What?" queried my mother?

The older gentleman in the corner seemed now moved to calm the atmosphere. "Your son has come third in the whole of the County of Devon Eleven Plus exams," he declared. "He has answered one question using mathematical calculus. The school does not teach this to Primary school children."

My mother glowed. "Well, he has been off school ill and we have had to have him have some private tuition from my neighbours." 'The Dragon' softened, a disgrace now had become a different situation, one from which the school might take some credit.

The older gentleman smiled, a wry smile, "Oh! That would explain it," he said.

"Under the circumstances we have considered that if you agree, the Education Authority would like to offer a grant to allow him to attend a special school. A school which is part of a new government scheme for gifted children." My mother looked smug; finally, her efforts had paid off in a most unexpected way.

"You see," continued the examiner, "Your son seems to be quite exceptional."

The following September found one very small boy, newly-equipped with stiff grey shorts, black blazer with a galleon crest emblazoned on the breast pocket, neat cap, over-long raincoat and a new leather satchel, entering this red brick and rather awesome environment, staffed by teachers in flowing black gowns resembling a murder of crows circling their new-found prey.

At the first assembly the Headmaster said, "We have been charged to create scientists to take this great nation of ours into a brave new world. You boys have been selected as the best of your year. Examinations will be held annually. Our expectations are high. Any boy not making the grade will be invited to attend a lesser institution and make way for a more suitable candidate. You are an elite. Do not let me down."

The school was a resurrected creation, a former school now equipped with new engineering workshops, new labs, all new staff, and all experts in their field. We were not the only ones under pressure, the staff were expected to produce results; impressive results or their own careers could suffer.

One interesting and delightful anomaly remained. The school had formerly been co-ed, both boys and girls. It says much about the prejudice of the era that this new school was for boys only. It was shamefully presumed that girls could be left to do what girls do best, needlework and cooking, such was the limitations of some schools of thought in the 1950's.

However, it had been agreed that the Sixth Form Girls of the original school should be allowed to stay on to complete their A level courses. So, with this all new intake of 11 and 12-year-old boys, the Prefect and Monitor positions had been allocated to these seventeen and 18-year-old goddesses in their smart white shirts, neat ties, black stockings and legs halfway up their backs. To an 11-year-old they were like Amazons, intellectually our superiors, physically aloof, honed in the arts of grace and style and amazingly adult.

They treated us like shit. We were the newbies, the greenhorns, prepubescent kids who they had to put up with for the last two years of their education, while we hung around them debating how to get into trouble and then be sent to detention after class. Where we eyed them with immature yearnings while our unfulfilled manhood sought some kind of fantasy as to what they might do to us in the sports storeroom next door. It never happened, well only in our imaginations. Happy days.

The school had among its academic talents what might only be termed some 'characters'. They say genius is ever so near to insanity and the school had assembled a number of geniuses. I suppose the arch-villain and most unpredictable boffin was Sammy, the Chemistry Master. His lab was a dangerous place.

This was long before the nanny state health and safety obsessions of modern day education. Sammy delighted in being dramatic. I think he took the view that such episodes would help the scientific data lodge in the virgin brains of his charges. He was also an expert shot with the blackboard eraser, a felt and wooden implement of no minor weight.

If caught lacking attention, Sammy could hurl the missile with deadly accuracy from his slightly-raised podium and score a direct hit on the head of any child given to looking out of the window. You never took your gaze off Sammy; he did not take prisoners.

On one fateful day a foolish and inappropriately rebellious boy let off a stink bomb at the rear of Sammy's lab during class. The Spanish Inquisition was immediately resurrected and Sammy demanded to know who the guilty party was. We never split on each other, so Sammy produced a large glass flask, some dire looking ingredients and a small lecture on the dangers of toxic acids. Fumes emitted from the flask and flowed like a heavy fog around the room. Every boy in the room vomited. Having made his point, Sammy opened a few windows, the local birds in the trees outside flew away and class proceeded uninterrupted by any further "stink bombs".

Physics was my favourite subject however and this was presided over by Hank. He would construct his own lab gear and experiments and we delighted in the wave machines and the Van de Graff generators, gadgets capable of producing minor streaks of lightning at will.

I did rather well at Physics and won the school Physics prize four years running. On the last year, I was asked to accept a special prize instead as it was getting a bit depressing for the other boys who knew they did not stand much of a hope of winning it off me.

One mid-winter, Hank fell ill and was off for several weeks. In the interim, his classes were taken by the headmaster, who had a M.Sc. in Chemistry but was no whizz at either physics or maths. He would stand at the blackboard with his chalk in his left hand and the corner of his teacher's gown in his right hand, licking it occasionally, as this was his eraser for the constant mistakes he would make in his calculations and formulas. I would usually see these immediately and up would shoot my hand.

I can understand that this must have been somewhat irritating for the headmaster and not a little challenging, so I was summoned to his office where, behind closed doors, we struck a deal. I would be seated in future at the extreme front and right of the classes he would take. He could see me out of the corner of his eye. Thus, in future the protocol was that if my hand came off the desk by a few inches he would pause, his frame obscuring the current calculation from most of the class. The right hand, armed with the dampened corner of his gown would casually and slowly move to the offending figure or symbol and erase it, correcting the error before anyone else noticed. He both respected and hated me all at the same time. It was an understandable sentiment.

The other notable character of the school was "Ticky" the senior mathematics master. Ticky could easily be distracted from the academic theme of the hour and moved onto his favourite subject - gambling. Many an ill-spent school hour was enjoyed, not wasted, we felt, on the details of various gambling systems, both for football pools, dogs and his favourite - the horses. I am sure some of the boys could have gone on, not to be scientists, but very successful bookmakers after Ticky's master classes in calculating the odds on the outcome of any given sporting event or race. We noticed he was always absent during Cheltenham Week.

There was only one female teacher on the staff, her subject History, and her name, Miss Gass. No youngster, this poor soul was the butt of every practical joke in the book from our crew of merciless and ambitious boys. One day a sleeping bat was retrieved from under the eaves of the school outbuildings. Needless to say, with great care and consideration the bat was transported to the History classroom prior to the next lesson. Suitably made up around its mouth with a little red poster paint from the Art room, the bat was positioned inside the teacher's desk. It was almost inevitable that the good lady would open her desk for something during the lesson, a book, and another piece of chalk perhaps.

The suspense was palpable, never had she had such an attentive class on the subject of Julius Caesar. And then the moment came, in full flight on the demise of Caesar at the hand of Mark Anthony, she half-opened the desk top, out flew the bat, which became lodged and entangled in her hair. Her screams were heard several school-blocks away.

We all got hours of detention for that one but it was

well worth it.

We took our GCE O-levels early; I achieved 13, but only just scraped through in English Language, so it was decided that I, along with five others, would re-sit the exam the following Christmas. There was no time in my curriculum to take extra English lessons, as we were all loaded up with extra Physics, Pure and Applied Maths. Remember, the school was tasked to produce scientists, so at the same time I had to drop Art, which, I really enjoyed, and Woodwork in which I also excelled, as these were considered of no practical value in the world for which we were destined. So to improve my English I decided to start a school magazine. Prophetic really as this was the first creative writing and editing of other submissions that I had undertaken. The magazine was a simple affair, produced on the school's primitive Banda printing machine, just text and the odd cartoon, one of which caused me some trouble. One of the boys had drawn a simple sketch, innocent by any reasonable standard, but I was hauled into the headmaster's office and accused of publishing pornography. The crime, the depiction of a member of the opposite sex, with two suitably located bumps. Breasts apparently were not acknowledged nor allowed at that time in a respectable school magazine.

It was about this time I was introduced to Chris. My father had decided that it was about time I had a friend and at fifteen my father selected a similar aged boy attending a nearby public school. Chris was also an only child and came from a New Zealand family of Danish descent who ran a small chain of high class photographic shops selling Leica, Nikon, Canon and other top makes. The family was friends of my father and they, too, were concerned that their son was rather an isolated individual.

With so much top range photographic gear around we were allowed to borrow whatever we wished from the retail stock and go off on shoots whenever we liked. Hence I was introduced and schooled over the next few years in the world of professional photography, mostly 35 mm and some home movie work. Chris's other great interests were stamps and also guns. Everything from antique weapons right though the Wild West up to the modern day. How exactly this collection had started was unclear, but it surely had something to do with Chris's detailed and obsessive knowledge of British military history, from the English Civil War onwards.

One of our rather mad episodes was being arrested by the local plod for discharging muzzle-loading Arab muskets across a piece of Dartmoor where, unbeknown to us, there was a public footpath. A quick call to the local firearms officer soon got us off with only a warning.

Chris's collection was quite something. He was the youngest registered antique gun dealer in the whole of the United Kingdom and the annual inspections from Devon and Cornwall Constabulary always brought gasps of admiration. One time the Inspector stated, "You boys have got more armament and ammunition than we have in both counties!"

Not only was Chris an expert on the history of guns (you could give him any piece and he would give you bible and verse on the maker and when and where used) he was also an expert in the mechanisms of weapons, everything from a Blunderbuss to a modern automatic, of which he had several. This gave him a detailed knowledge of the microseconds it would take to pull the trigger on any given firearm and its inclination to shoot high, low or off-target. Thus, unlike the modern cult of guns whereupon some hood pulling out a piece sends everyone into a panic, shouting, Chris would immediately know what the characteristics of that weapon was, what ammunition options it might take and even by the way it was being held by the operative, how expert or not was that person's knowledge and ability with it.

We used to play this game. Safety-conscious, with weapons loaded with blank used shells (it is not good for a gun to be triggered unloaded), one of us would approach the back of the other. Either in direct contact or at a given distance, the victim would have to instantly identify the gun, maybe by seeing its reflected image in a mirror or glass window pane. Then spin, turn and disarm the assailant before he could discharge the weapon or tackle him in such a way that the "shot" would miss.

You would be surprised how much time it takes to pull the trigger on a standard weapon not fitted with a hair trigger. If the safety catch was on you have seconds, bags of time to disarm.

Do not try this at home as some of the techniques involve breaking the arm or wrist of the assassin, while at the same time using the leverage of the weapon itself as an aid to the defence. The point about this training was that guns held no fear; they were merely machines. There was no chemistry of panic or feeling of submission to the bearer of arms.

The other great interest we shared was everything Japanese from martial arts to their medieval history. Chris even acquired a full Samurai suit of armour, beautifully made with hundreds of bamboo platelets, chain mail and full headgear. Neither of us could get into it; the Japanese were a lot smaller in those days.

We also practiced with Samurai swords, the real thing, incredibly sharp and flexible, being made from many folded laminations of finely-hammered steel according to an ancient tradition of craftsmanship.

We also built radio-controlled boats and planes, from component parts, not just off the shelf. We built everything from the transmitters to the servos. We would then take them to the local boating pond and have battles, sometimes involving sinking other kids' boats. We would buy fireworks and chemicals from the local pharmacy and construct or adapt rockets. One scale model motor torpedo boat we built could actually fire its own firework rockets at "enemy" vessels on the lake.

It was very much the time of the space race between America and Russia and we were all taken up with it. I built rockets. These were so powerful they had to be launched from a small gantry made from Meccano and fired by a homemade simple device that rotated a match, struck it, which lit a Jetex fuse and fired up the rocket. Sometimes they blew up on the pad if the mixture was wrong. Over time, we moved onto two-stage rockets, but we never succeeded in perfecting three stages. The last one launched, rolled over onto a horizontal trajectory and flew straight through my parents' bedroom window. I was not too popular to say the least and all future launchings were confined to the outskirts of the local golf course when the players had gone home.

Launchings were more spectacular at dusk or in the dark but we saved our best constructions for Guy Fawkes Night. We would over-fly a local kid's bonfire party, sometimes succeeding in dropping bangers from winged rockets, which had a timed release fuse to drop the payload. We saw no harm in this. No one got hurt; we were not intending that they should. It was just a competition in which we all engaged.

I had learnt to drive from the age of thirteen off-road on campsites. My father had an Austin A30 first off with a clutch like a Kangaroo. Later he bought an Austin A35 Estate car and I passed my test early in my seventeenth year, the same year I passed my A-levels in Physics, Pure and Applied Maths, a subject in which I gained some merit for an exceptional result.

I had saved some money from little jobs and bought my first vehicle, a second-hand grey minivan. Chris had more family funds and bought a 1934 Bentley Tourer with huge headlights which he duly refitted with over-bright bulbs. He was also dating girls; more pulling power than my minivan. We both joined the Young Conservatives, not on a political motivation, but because they had the best looking female talent and the best parties. Chris took up with Miss Torbay, a girl he would eventually marry.

My success with girls was much more limited. I was rather shy about the opposite sex and we did not seem to have much in common. I needed contemporaries who could discuss really important things like space, the universe and was there life on Mars. Alien girls were thin on the ground.

I suppose you would say in modern terms I was a bit of a geek. Computers were virtually unheard of at this time so amusements were all of the practical kind. The bedroom was not only for sleeping but was also my lab. My mother gave up on cleaning it as the entire surface area was covered in half-constructed planes, boats, rockets or other gadgets, some of which worked and some not. 'In development', as they would say at the MOD. Which means they are crap.

My father and I had formed The Astro-Research Society and this small, but intense, body of folk met every month to debate the latest space developments, astronomical findings and everything weird and out of the ordinary. My father was an ardent Spiritualist and from the age of seven I had been taken along every Sunday to the local church, where I had witnessed every type, shape and level of medium, clairvoyant and healer, ranging from the amazingly talented to the complete fake.

I got to be able to tell the genuine from the fake as much from the patter of the probing open questions, for example, "I've got a George, somewhere here on the left of the chapel?" A hand would always go up, everyone had a George somewhere in their past. However, some practitioners were remarkably adept at coming up with obscure and random data out of the blue, which the recipient would confirm with some startled amazement.

I began to develop these techniques myself, both from reading people (this was long before Neuro-linguistic Programming or NLP), and from inner intuitions that I could not explain. I just believed you had to feel it. The mind was not involved; it was deeper, more primitive than that, something really primordial. This would come in handy in later life and often saved my skin. A kind of real-time remote viewing.

One of the members of our little society was a Commander Bond, no relation to the fictional character; Bond was a fine upstanding character of long and eminent military history. He was also a great raconteur and humourist who threw parties and loved to play games. His service to the state had commenced in the First World War when he was the commander of a squadron of observation balloons flown over the British lines in some of the darkest battles of the war.

He recalled a tricky moment when his balloon's tether had been shot away by a German shell and he drifted ever closer to the German lines. Ironically he was saved by an act of desperation, as apparently the balloons were regularly shot down by their own side as the British infantry knew they would give the German artillery a ranging distance to fire at. So indeed this occurred again, as a hail of British bullets punctured the envelope and Bondy, as he was known, floated down just before no man's land. A close call.

He was a dedicated naturist and every weekend, even at the delicate age of his late eighties, would be found sunning himself completely starkers at the local health farm along with various ages of nubile female and gentleman members. He invited me along there and I recall upon entering the rambling estate seeing some members, completely nude, attacking a thicket of brambles with machetes in some group gardening exercise. It looked a dangerous sport.

Bondy was to be significant in the next big development of my life as he had friends in high places and could open many doors. I had been doing some thinking on keeping the pristine beaches of the Devon coast free of tar and oil, which occasionally came ashore from moored cargo vessels that periodically cleaned their fuel tanks and bilges by pumping sludge into the English Channel. Not a very environmentally friendly thing to do. So when one afternoon I was alerted on BBC radio that Torrey Canyon had run aground off the Cornish Coast, I was immediately moved to assemble all my research into design structures that might assist in this potential disaster.

The ship, we later learned, had gone aground while on autopilot, set wrong, while the crew were asleep. So now firmly stuck on the rocks she was losing crude from her tanks and was slowly breaking up under the battering of wind and waves. As the situation escalated, the press ran appropriate shock-horror stories of what could happen to the sea life and indeed to the tourist industry if all her cargo was lost. I was a member of The Shore Patrol Club in Torbay and knew the effects could be long-lasting and very messy.

I knew Bondy was the right man to get my data and research into the right hands. Yes, he agreed, this would be very helpful. My inventions amounted to an advanced form of boom made up of long sausages of rubber, held together with links that were flotation control chambers. Thus it would form a floating dam around the ship and contain the spilling oil. Then skimmer barges would scoop up the oil and recover it back into a usable product. All of this could be simply made from existing kit and hung together to save the day.

In the meantime, the Ministry of Defence had been asked to apply their expertise to the crisis and their idea was to bomb the vessel with napalm to set the oil alight. Napalm is banned under the Geneva Convention; they had tons of it down there in 24-hours and bombing commenced. It didn't work; any chemist could have told them oil needs a wick like element to make it boil before it will ignite in water.

The press and public were going mad. This was the first disaster involving a super-tanker, small by today's standards but big then, and solutions were in short supply. Bondy said my research had to be taken to the highest level. He knew Sir Solly Zuckerman, the Cabinet Office Chief Scientific Advisor. "We won't send it to The Cabinet Office," declared Bondy, "That is for petitions and public stuff. Solly has an office at The Admiralty. We will send it there." So off my stuff went by courier to The Admiralty.

A day later an emergency meeting of the Cabinet was called to discuss the situation. Sir Solly of course was to attend. He walked in with my papers under his arm. I had given him a disclaimer to any patent or royalty and he had taken the concept under his wing. It was funded, a simple version built and flown down to Cornwall. It worked. I received an official letter of thanks from the cabinet office, one of three in total I received when a year later, the government sold the concept to BP Oil for a quarter of a million pounds. It is to this day the industry standard first defence for oil spill containment. Neither I, nor Bondy had mentioned to Sir Solly that the inventor was only seventeen years old at the time. However, although too young to be an 'official' government advisor I was now "on side" and getting noticed having been for this short period a 'Special Government Advisor'.

John Reedman was a dashing sort of fellow. He stood out and when he came along to a monthly meeting of the Astro-Research Society one felt he was there with a purpose. He did not say a lot but he listened intently. We were discussing the Russian advances in the space race at the time and this was indeed a subject of great interest. On some pretext of a trip to Cornwall to view wrecks, he invited me to take a day's expedition to review my research.

He drove very fast; I had not travelled at a hundred miles an hour before across straight and mostly empty Cornish roads. He lit a cigarette, paused and launched into a few anecdotes about the Second World War. He had been a major in the British Army, in Signals. I did not understand the significance of this at the time, and had undertaken some interesting missions. He moved onto having been commissioned to undertake some intelligence test on The British Army, all ranks, German Prisoners of War and the American Land Army, with whom we were working as allies. According to Major Reedman, the British Army and the German were about the same in IQ, he had found, but he had been surprised that the GIs had not come anywhere near in their IQ test results compared to the Europeans.

I felt he was going somewhere with this ploy. "You are a clever young fellow," he continued, "We don't find too many like you."

"Signals?" I enquired, "Is that something to do with communications?" "Sort of," replied Reedman, being cagey. "It's more like MI5. Military Intelligence." I sensed he wanted to say more but was debating internally how to phrase it. "You are too young to be accepted into the regular selection process."

"What selection process?" I quizzed. Was the Major offering me a job or what? He went on - I felt he knew he had my interest now, "Well, there are other groups, other bodies that work as advisors and give some thought - looking at difficult problems.... Would you be prepared to take some tests?"

"Yes of course!" I replied. "Who will be running them?"

The Major's gaze glanced away from the road for a moment, "You don't need to know that," he replied.

2. Early Days

FIRST FLIGHTS OF FANCY

More and more "interesting" people started to come into my life. This first commenced in the general area of my education. First to contact me was an Oxford Professor. He invited me to help crew his 12-ton yawl sailing out of Brixham. The Prof drove a "woody", the estate car version of a Morris Minor, and would set off from Oxford for one of his regular long weekends afloat.

He would be accompanied by his girlfriend, quite a bit younger than he, and along the way he would pick up a couple of hitchhikers (they were about in those days) on the seduction that, 'would they like a free weekend on his yacht?' Few refused, but little did they know that his boat had been built in 1908 and was a very heavy affair needing considerable manual labour to sail her.

I was the "Mate" and would meet this crew on the

dockside. As soon as we set sail, the professor would take a course directly out to sea. As soon as land disappeared over the horizon, Captain Blythe would appear as he worked and schooled his new found deck-hands through hours of hand-blistering and character-building toil. Buoys would be launched and man overboard exercises would follow to pick them up using only sail, wind and tide. If you didn't get it right you did it again, and again and again.

The unwitting hitchhikers would sometimes be in tears begging him to put them ashore, but of course the wind was always in the wrong direction and they would have to stick it out until Sunday evening when amazingly, suddenly, the wind blew fair and we would sail back to port.

I sensed this was one of the 'tests' that the Major had referred to, as the professor had just appeared in my life with virtually no clear connection; just one day he turned up and invited me to sail his boat.

Then came Doug. He was an ex-RAF fighter pilot and along with his 'mates' ran a newly-formed and very, very small aero club. There were just six guys and they had acquired a mothballed Percival Prentice Trainer, ex-RAF, which had been built in 1946 but never flown.

The guys had each put one hundred pounds into the kitty. I was invited to join for thirty quid. They had leased an ex-wartime emergency landing field on the edge of the moors between Exeter and Torbay from a rather mad, hippy type who lived on the land in a caravan. We set up shop. There was a small shed which was equipped with the airfield coms, radio, genny etc. and landings log book, a wind sock was erected, the grass mown on the diagonals and we all walked the runways picking up any flints and stones that might damage tyres.

There was only one problem with the field. When it had served in the Second World War it had been on open moor. Since then, the Forestry Commission had taken over all the land around it and grown fir trees in regimented rows. These now rose straight as an arrow to around 30 to 40 feet high. Fortunately, slightly offset to the diagonal lines of our field were firebreaks, cleared trackways designed to inhibit the travel of a forest fire should there be one.

Some careful calculations were made as to how to operate our new airport. I think the term 'barnstorming' would cover it. These guys were all experts, former Bomber and Spitfire aces who knew exactly what they were doing and had flown many a dodgy mission during their flying careers. Only two were not RAF, one ex-Navy and the other a civilian who declined to say very much about where or how he had learnt to fly. There were mutterings of South America but that was only rumour.

We needed a fuel store, so various old galvanised water tanks were acquired, cleaned and set away from the comms hut close to where the aeroplane was to be parked. This was equipped with some tie downs, chocks and called the dispersal by the old hands at this game.

Stories were told of cutting airstrips out of virgin jungle and other exotic places around the world wherever they had been needed. So now we had to figure out how to get a considerable quantity of aviation spirit out from our nearest stockist, Exeter Airport, a distance of some 20 miles.

As with all such innovative crews, there was a

maverick; a term meaning a finder, the guy who always found exactly what you needed. Thus after a little research time by our maverick, our fuel tanker duly arrived.

We set a large domestic house-sized water tank, uncovered, in the now gutted interior of a Mr Softy ice cream van, complete with musical warning chimes all intact. Our civilian pilot muttered with a smile, "Perfect cover."

That afternoon, having been made airport safety officer, I set off for Exeter with the maverick and couple of other chaps for moral support, to collect fuel. I don't believe vehicle insurance, tax disc or any other such technical details were considered very important. We wanted to fly, we needed fuel and we were off to get some.

On the return leg, fully laden, we discovered that we'd been rather ambitious about how much fuel could be carried in an open tank under normal driving conditions and we had to slow down as aviation spirit began to slop over the edge of the tank and we were all hanging out the windows to breathe.

Rounding a corner, the passenger in the front shouted a warning to Maverick, "Fuzz!"

There indeed was a police car sitting parked on the side of the road ahead. Maverick was unphased.

We slowed a little, "Sing!" he commanded. "What?" went up the cry? "Rule Britannia!" came the command, so we all broke into song. As we passed the squad car, Maverick sounded the ice cream chimes. The coppers smiled. Lesson two, I noted, hidden in plain sight.

Being Airport Safety Officer had perks. My minivan

was made over, pimped, as we would say these days. I had a hand in designing what was needed. The roof top was painted yellow, amber warning beacons were fitted - blue ones would have needed a permit and we were not into paperwork - sirens adorned the roof and two imposing notices fitted front and rear, declaring 'EMERGENCY CRASH TENDER'.

Inside was fitted out with various fire extinguishers: CO_2 and water for different classes of fire, chisels, hammers and axes. As Maverick said, "If I belly flop, I don't fancy my chances with you hacking into my cockpit with that lot."

We did not equip the fuel tanker with an extinguisher. We figured if she caught fire the only thing to do would be run, very quickly.

The great day came and Doug and his co-pilot ferried the Prentice to our field, circled a couple of times and made a long and gentle approach into the wind for our small postage stamp of grass.

We watched with baited breath. Binoculars were passed around, the radio crackled and our controller of the day offered whatever information might be useful. Wind SSW about 12 knots.

The tiny image of the plane grew larger; surely she was too low? On a direct path to the best diagonal, into the wind she approached almost at tree top height. At the edge of the trees, down she dropped like a lift descending. Doug pulled her out, she was down, one small bounce and now would she stop in time before the grass ran out? Yes! All OK!

"I wouldn't try that on a wet day," declared Maverick. The small dark green plane turned and taxied over to the dispersal. We waited for the engine to die and the prop to cease rotating before we all ran over to the plane cheering like kids at summer camp. Our baby had arrived.

I had to wait a couple of weeks before I got a flight in our plane. Take-offs had to be perfected and also engine start procedures. The first time Doug restarted the engine the prop rotated a few times, she sputtered and stopped. A few jets of aviation spirit had spurted out of the exhaust onto the grass at the dispersal site and we could smell it.

Doug fired the starter again, she fired and a jet of pure flame shot out of the exhaust, setting fire to the splashes of fuel on the ground. It was standard procedure that when on the ground and in taxi, the cockpit cover was always pulled back, an old Navy technique just in case you had to get out in a hurry, so Doug was in shouting range as a cry went up, "Fire!".

"Chocks away!" yelled Doug as he gunned the engine and dragged the plane away from the burning grass. The back draft of the prop had partly blown out the fire and we all ran forward to stamp out the burning grass. No point in wasting an expensive fire extinguisher charge on a bit of grass. We were ready for that next time and had some buckets of sand nearby to assist in dousing any pyrotechnic antics.

So by my first flight, the procedure had now been run several times and we all felt confident we could manage it without disaster. I sat in the co- pilot's seat and was instructed to lightly touch both the foot and stick controls and just mirror the movements during take-off. My eyes were to be glued to the air speed indicator and I was to read off that speed constantly to my instructor, Jerry who was kind of vice chairman of the club and honorary instructor, as he was very patient.

"Tighten your seat straps," instructed Jerry, "As tight as you can."

We taxied out to the extreme corner of the field, turned into wind and stopped. After an engine power check, we ran up the engine to a deafening roar.

The wind screamed past our ears, temperatures and oil pressures looked good and on Jerry's command

I pulled the cockpit canopy shut, off came the brakes and at maximum throttle we rolled towards the far corner of the field. 10, 20, 30, I called off the airspeed in 10 knot increments. The far side of the field was hurtling towards us. There were no X and Y points on this airstrip, these are markers where in theory you can abort the take-off. You either took off or probably died.

The aeroplane did everything at 70 knots in theory. It took off, flew and landed at 70 knots. The Prentice had been built to mimic a laden bomber to train pilots in the characteristics of those rugged old planes. She was by definition underpowered and had a ponderous rate of climb. However, she was quite sturdy in construction expecting to be beaten up by rookie pilots.

50...55..., it was now getting a bit critical. In smaller increments I now called off the airspeed, 56...58…...now or never.

"Rotate," muttered Jerry and off we staggered, clearing the Irish bank, a substantial earthen rampart which formed the boundary to the field. Directly ahead of us now were the 30-foot pine trees. Jerry slightly turned the Prentice to starboard without dropping a wing and we entered the fire break track and climbed steadily with the pine trees whisking past our wing tips, clearing the trees we headed off North over the moor. Jerry gently wagged the tail as we carried out these procedures explaining that if you were going to stall, one wing would stall before the other and when you felt it start to drop you swung that wing forward with the rudder, picking up its airspeed and countering the stall. It all sounded good physics and good aerodynamics.

My father asked later that day about the flying. "Is it dangerous?" he enquired. "Not at all," I reassured him. He seemed content, so I did not elaborate. I think he was concerned because his cousin had died in a pilot error-induced crash over Croydon just before the war. Falling out of the sky was one of my recurring nightmares, but I did not intend to have it happen. After all I was only 17 and you are invincible at that age.

A small enamel plaque affixed to the instrument panel of the Prentice stated, in red, AEROPLANE DOES NOT SPIN, JUMP OUT. As we did not carry parachutes the instruction seemed a little academic.

Over time I got to handle the Prentice with some confidence. She had been equipped specifically as a trainer and was fully-instrumented, much as a larger and more complicated aircraft. The scariest procedure for a trainee involved donning green goggles, which turned the surreal, deep amber of the cockpit canopy jet black. The two sets of amber and green filters allowed no light from outside to enter my eyes. You now had no horizon and had to fly only on the instruments in front of you. "You're dropping the nose," corrected Jerry, an instinctive thing to do, to always be well up on the airspeed. Stalling at low level was not a desirable option.

"Straight and level, straight and level," Jerry's voice coaxed me through the terror of not being able to see a damn thing through the cockpit canopy.

Coming back on the glide path, I again mirrored Jerry on the controls. As we flew over the carpet of pine trees, the field came into view. It looked even smaller from up here. At the last minute, as we cleared the last tree, Jerry dropped it down like in a high speed lift. My stomach came up into my mouth and then we flared out, a bit of a thump and we were on the ground.

On went the brakes and we slued to a halt well before the end of the field. A small bead of perspiration ran down my face. We taxied to the dispersal killed the engine, set all controls back to normal and jumped down making sure we only stood on the piece of the wing strong enough to take our weight.

"Your job," commanded Jerry, "Is to pick those bits of pine needles out of the wheels and under cart. I brushed the trees on the way down." He continued, unemotionally, "Oh, and go and find some tape. There's a small tear in the fabric on the edge of the wing."

"Does it have to be Ministry approved tape?" I teased.

"Do you know the definition of a good landing?" he quizzed.

I looked blank... "One you walk away from," said Jerry with a smile.

On another occasion I flew with Maverick to deliver the Prentice for an airframe check and engine service. The booking had been made and although the weather wasn't perfect Maverick decided to chance it.

We took off and flew under the relatively low cloud base towards our destination using visual navigation and the chart on my lap. As we proceeded, we encountered more low cloud and then fog. Dead-reckoning our direction as best we could, Maverick figured we must be near the airfield we were heading for. The radio was on the blink and he couldn't raise the field. Maybe the weather had something to do with that, but he decided to drop down and get under the cloud to take a visual looksee for the airfield.

"Look out for its white flashing beacon," said Maverick as we carefully dropped down through the fog, his eyes glued to the altimeter. It started to get bumpy, a sign you are getting nearer the ground as you pick up turbulence. We emerged from a fog bank, Maverick's gaze still on the altimeter.

"Power lines!" I shouted. There right in front of us at a few hundred yards on the nose hung the sagging cables of overhead high tension power cables. Maverick reacted instinctively.

There was no time to think in these circumstances, automatic responses kicked in. Maverick dipped the nose sharply and we flew under the power lines. Dropping off height was a lot quicker than trying to gain it. We were now about 20 feet above ground, the farmland streaking past us. Ahead lay a long meadow and to the right a farm.

"Where the hell are we?" shouted Maverick and took a snap decision. "I'm putting her down," We had both been aware that the fuel level was getting a bit problematical and we couldn't cruise around in the fog forever.

The smoke from the farmhouse chimney angled in our direction; we were heading into the wind. "Those bloody bullocks had better keep out of my way!" observed Maverick as the steers in the meadow stampeded off to the side of our descent path. We prayed there wouldn't be any holes in the meadow, which might flip us over. Thump, thump, we were down.

Maverick's professional bush experience again kicked in as we slowed. He turned the little plane around, followed his own tyre tracks and ran the aircraft back to the beginning of the meadow so we could take off again into the prevailing wind.

We stopped, checked the engine dials and switched everything off. A puzzled farmer headed in our direction accompanied by his sheep dog.

Maverick hailed him like a landed alien from another planet, "Good Morning Sir. We are looking for the local airport. Got disorientated in the fog." The farmer looked at us like we were completely mad. "It's over there, half a mile away. You boys are damn lucky, you could have hit my bullocks," he scowled.

Maverick muttered a similar word under his breath, but not wishing to antagonise the locals retorted, "Thank you my good man, we shall not trouble you anymore." Without further ado we restarted the engine, took off along the now well-worn grooves in the meadow and followed the now visible main road to the airport. Flying low past the control tower we waggled our wings and made suitable sign language, probably not visible by the controller who now emerge and launched an approving flare. We landed and were greeted in rather abrupt manner by the Airport Manager.

"Why can't you idiots follow procedures?" he moaned. "You have had us all worried; radar indicated you had gone down. Had the Police out looking for you. Not good form at all!" Maverick looked bashful, "Yes dropped under radar I'm sure. That weather front put the altimeter out - Could have been killed." If he was looking for sympathy, he did not get any. "I shall have to make a report," grimaced the Manager.

"Bloody Bureaucrats," muttered Maverick.

My flying continued, but my attention was also drawn – guided - to another flight of fancy. Into my life came Father Wysocki. Outside a local market town was a Polish displaced persons' camp, folk, whole families, left over from the Second World War who had nowhere to go. His proper title was Monsignor Peter Wysocki, indicating he was more than your regular priest.

He came to a meeting of The Astro Research Club and we were all rather amazed that here was a fully ordained Catholic Priest earnestly engaged in the investigation of the supernatural. Yes, he did do exorcisms, but there was a lot more to the good priest than met the eye.

He invited me out to the Polish refugee camp many times and on the safety and security of his home turf, he conveyed many an intriguing story. He was Jewish, I think he changed his name after the war, and his father had been a brilliant physicist.

Before the Second World War in Poland, Wysocki Senior had been a student of the work of Nicola Tesla and had a fully equipped lab wherein he would experiment with the concept of anti-matter.

As a child, the Monsignor recalled his father

producing pea-sized glowing balls of electricity, a sort of miniature ball lightning, which would bounce along his father's lab bench without coming nearer than a centimetre from its surface, a truly strange electrostatic effect. Then they would fall off onto the floor and vanish with a peculiar popping sound.

In the early days of the German occupation of Poland the Wysocki family had been visited by the Gestapo. His father was taken to work for the Germans in a secret project near the German/Polish border. Sometime later in the only communication he had ever received from his father, smuggled out under great risk of reprisals, his father had apologised to his son for this cooperation, but explained that his family had been threatened with execution if he had refused.

In the letter, he had indicated to his son that the Germans were trying to develop some kind of secret weapon, a wingless flying machine using Tesla-based technology and the work of Victor Schauberger.

Shortly after the arrival of this communication, the family was visited again by the occupying German forces and they were all put on a train in railcars heading towards what they were told would be labour camps for the duration of the war. Peter Wysocki was a teenager at this time but pretty savvy on what was going on and had, as he put it, a very bad feeling about this train journey. His family did not agree with what he did next. The train was lightly guarded so he jumped off as it ascended an incline and found that he was within a few days' march of the advancing Russian army. Deciding this was his best option, he headed in their direction but this radically backfired.

He was taken by the Russians, accused of being a German spy and promptly sentenced to be shot in the morning. Ingenuity inspired him again and he escaped overnight, only to be captured by the nearby German forces and accused of being a Russian spy. Knowing where this would lead he confessed to being an escaped Jew from the passing trains and was the next day put back on the cattle wagons heading to the death camps.

Life was not looking too bright for young Wysocki, but again sensing the weakness of the security on the train–Germany could not spare many troops for such duties—he once more jumped off the train. This time he did not escape unnoticed and a guard winged him in the leg as he ran away.

Nursing his leg in a local hay barn, he was discovered by a sympathetic farming family and nursed back to health, but he could not stay as troop movements were all about the area. It would only be a matter of time before he was discovered, putting the supporting family in danger of reprisals.

He chose a brave and courageous strategy, setting off walking East, not West. He survived for six months living off the land right across Asia, smuggled himself onto a fishing boat and arrived just as the Americans were accepting the Japanese surrender. He located the US Command in Japan and was liberated to the United States. A while later, he became a Catholic Priest, returning to help his people in the British refugee camp for the displaced Poles.

The calm courage of this Priest was an inspiration and lesson to which I could never aspire. He had taken what little he had of his father's work to the Vatican, where he had found there was a much deeper interest in this area of research than he had expected.

He became a member of a working party delving into

the inner workings of the universe; a group headed up by a Jesuit cardinal and attended meetings at the Vatican's private observatory.

"There is an inner enclave," he told me, cardinals who have a very deep and profound understanding of the world. This was not the public face of the Catholic church at that time, maybe it is more now when they acknowledge the likelihood of alien life.

The good Father had a fun side as well; despite his vows, once a month he would get me to pick him up as his chauffeur. On this monthly day off he exchanged his priestly robes for casual clothes and looked quite the country gentleman.

We would stop by and pick up his girlfriend, well, let us say a 'lady of the night'.

Then we went off on a gentle pub crawl around the district, maybe some food and then back to her place, need I say more. I liked this guy; he was human.

During this time, I was in my gap year and earning money in any way possible. I bought a Triumph Herald and kitted it out for driving instruction. I passed the Ministry of Transport Approved Driving Instructors test, although at only 18 years of age, I must have been one of their youngest instructors.

Regulations were more lax then, these days I am sure you would have to be older. I also used that car for a bit of private hire, also unregulated at that time, hence my sorties out with my friendly priest.

My driving instruction was not without incident over the course of teaching 220 people to drive. One girl was adept at selecting reverse when she needed third and that led to some interesting emergency stops as the back wheels locked and all you could hear for several yards behind us was other traffic frantically hauling up to avoid a collision.

Encounters also came in other dimensions. One client needed a refresher course having supposedly been off the road for a few years. I arrived on time and found the client to be a very attractive woman in her 40s, blonde, and wearing a very short and somewhat alluring dress.

She drove quite fast and I asked her to slow down more than once. She smiled and quipped "Oh! I'm a fast lady." All went well and a second lesson was booked. Upon the return to her country house home, she offered to show me her husband's collection of classic cars. I politely accepted and we walked to a large garage where indeed were lined up a grand display of Morgan motorcars. She turned, looked meaningfully into my eyes and sighed, "I get so bored up here. You must be hot stuff. I'm wet."

My mind blanked, "It's humid today," I stuttered, "I expect it's condensation." Wishing the ground would open up and cover my embarrassment, I made my excuses and left. Driving down the lane I thought, "Damn, that was a dead cert fuck!" She did not rebook; I had blown it...

About this time, I was trying to date girls, without, I have to say, very much success

I had a little contract to take home late-night staff from a couple of local clubs. Live entertainment was much more in evidence in those days and both of these clubs not only supplied live music but also scantily-clad waitresses catering for both a truly male and hip audience. Taking the strippers home never proved a problem, these girls knew exactly what it was all about and I was not in the running at any time.

However, one of the clubs, The Blue Angel, was run by its owner/chef, who went by the nickname of 'Greasy'. It was three in the morning and I was on for taking home the waitresses. Greasy took pity on this socially-gauche teenager.

"Hey son," he beckoned, "If you fancy one of them, drop her off last." They were all attractive and these were the days of the permissive society and the club was a very laid back venue, gambling, jazz, and dim lighting. I must admit there was one girl who kept giving me the eye, so accordingly she was indeed the last drop.

She had been in one of the rear seats. As I let out her co-worker, she slipped out and jumped in the front passenger seat.

"I get a bit car sick in the back," she said. My heartbeat took a skip and a jump. I wasn't sure if I could handle this. We arrived at her house. She turned, snuggled into me and kissed me on the cheek. "My husband works nights and won't be back to the morning. You can come in for coffee if you wish!"

I felt the panic rise in me. Was it the contradiction that she was married, was it the thought of being party to a very sexy, up-for-it cheating wife? I don't think morals came into it; I was just out of my depth.

"I'd love to," I said. "But I have to go on now for another job, The Manor Club is expecting me."

I was lying; I had already done the Manor Club an hour ago. I remember being very red in the face. I really had the hots for this woman but heck, her husband might be a tag-team wrestler for all I knew.

I drove away feeling both elated and depressed all at the same time. I saw her six months later in the local supermarket; she was heavily pregnant. Blimey, I thought, that could have been mine. My mind had very mixed feelings. Perhaps that had been another close call.

3: Areas of Enquiry

MORE THINGS IN HEAVEN

The Astro Research Society's area of enquiry was principally the supernatural, any subject where we were at the edge of human experience. I teamed up in research with a Trans-Atlantic organisation based in California, The Borderland Sciences Research Associates, headed up by a guy called Riley Crabb. He had taken over from a former director, Meade Lane, who had asked some profound questions about the human condition and our experience here in this life.

He had produced a number of notable papers including "The Coming of the Guardians", a privately published thesis exploring the interaction of the third dimension, the here and now, with the fourth and fifth dimensions, which Meade Lane saw as intimately involved with human existence.

He claimed that the correlation of these other realms

explained all manner of supernatural phenomena including religious experiences and spiritual events.

The concept involved the idea of resonance. Just like on the octaves of the piano keys, matter has frequency. We live in the third dimension, in this physical spectrum of awareness, outside of which we were surrounded by realms that are invisible to us.

We were born as souls out of these ethers and into those other planes we returned upon physical death. This is clearly shown by regression memories of people recalling their previous lives and indeed the existences they had between incarnations. What Lane and Crabb maintained was that communication existed between these levels and even physical translation of both beings and material things occurred.

Now in these studies, we were definitely in the areas of investigations, which fell under the general heading of Unidentified Flying Objects or UFOs

Much controversy has surrounded this subject for the past 70 years and the one consistent factor in all sightings, reported landings and contacts, is they appear to be transient events, rarely occurring on the ground or in the sky for much longer than a few minutes. When people have claimed longer experiences, they occur in a situation where they say they have been "taken" or abducted during which periods of absence have been reported lasting from hours to even days.

In an attempt to get a historical perspective on all this, I engaged in reading every single thing I could get my hands on both in the UFO, psychic, natural phenomena and the occult worlds. I was surprised that some of the material I ordered from the public library had to be sent down from The British Library and was stored in secure sections for which one actually needed approved permission to even have sight of. I was always granted this; after all I was, "on side".

I delved back into the writings of the nineteenth century, the works of Madame Blavatsky, the founder of Theosophy and that wonderful collector of the odd and unexplained Charles Fort, whose sense of humour I loved, and many other tomes. These included an account of our cosmic history entitled *Oahaspe*, which detailed the supervised evolution of the Earth races for many millennia past written in the late 19th century.

Although it seemed almost an affront to modern science and discovery, it seemed that there had been a discourse between mankind and these other levels of existence throughout known and indeed pre-written history.

This appeared to vary over time, sometimes it appeared to be interpreted as a religious event, at other times psychic or supernatural and in some of the more UFO-type reports, a very physical communication sometimes even involving transport and abduction of the witness for some bizarre purpose of procreation towards hybrid or alien children.

The Earth appeared to be in some respects a kind of experimental lab and a gene stock for related species of humanoid. Whatever the explanation, neither the alien 'interlopers' nor those involved in some way with it, were talking much. It was, as one researcher had coined it, "The Greatest Story Never Told!"

I came to know a number of key witnesses involved with these supposed events. One lady named

Elizabeth, claimed to remember being taken aboard an alien ship from her country cottage home in East Devon.

These events are chronicled in my books *"The Welsh Triangle"* (Granada/Panther) and *"UFO-UK"* (New English Library), written in the late 1970's and currently out of print although folk still appear to seek them out on the second hand market. I am republishing them as eBooks soon, so they will be available again.

In précis, Elizabeth appeared to have had at least one "phantom" pregnancy and during her alien experience, it was implied that this foetus had been extracted from her on a previous occasion and was now a living child existing "on high," was the term used, which may mean in the stars or on another planet.

Elizabeth was a 30-year-old woman, of striking appearance with the most piecing blue eyes, as were her husband's, a milkman then working outside Totnes in Devon. She did not understand her memories and few believed her, so she never spoke of it in public.

In the same area, a man I had the good fortune to come to know later was unwittingly thrown into the spotlight when his children discussed his "contact experience" at school, having overheard their father disclose the story to his wife.

Arthur Bryant was a gardener at HM Prison, Prince Town, Dartmoor, Devon, when he had one afternoon been taking a country stroll on the edge of the moor.

This took place within 12 hours of the death of George Adamski in New York, a famous UFO contactee and author of a number of books including "*Flying Saucers Have Landed*," which he co-authored with Desmond Leslie from Ireland.

The gist of the account was that Adamski had returned in a new body, what appeared to Bryant to be, a 13-year-old boy wearing a space-suit too large for his modest frame. The boy conveyed in broken English, a message both for Desmond Leslie and indeed, for the whole world.

It amounted to a warning that we had been visited by beings from a planet of *Epsilon Eridani* for procreation purposes. This did fit with other information I was receiving at the time.

Some decades later in the year 2000, astronomers confirmed that this star is not only a similar orange colour temperature to our own Sun, but that it has at least two planets and two asteroid belts in its orbit. as commented upon recently in astronomical papers.

However, Bryant himself was no Sci-Fi buff or UFO enthusiast. In fact, he was a very simple man, modest and not particularly well-educated. Public exposure had been forced upon him; he did not seek it and it did him little good. He was visited by a thick-set American who basically told him to keep his mouth shut or else.

Bryant and I became casual friends. I visited him a number of times with my school-friend Chris. Bryant opened up on a number of important points that he had struggled to retain, as his encounter with the alien ship, a classic saucer shape, had lasted over half an hour and it was a bit of a blur.

One phrase he recalled, was when he asked how the craft was driven; "Adamski" and two cat-eyed aliens with him, had stated it was driven by, "*ideo-motor movement*". This roughly translates as 'mental power'; an interesting concept and one I would explore later in life.

Two years later, Bryant died in hospital after a short illness. Chris and I visited him during his final days. He thanked us for our support during a stressful period of his life when he had lost both the support and understanding of his wife and family for bringing them into ridicule in the local community. An intriguing fact was that Bryant was physically the spitting image of Adamski and they were both of distant Romany stock, a racial group known for their psychic abilities.

At his funeral on the moor, I was the only person to attend from the paranormal research world. The only other attendees were his close family and a few villagers. He was buried in an unmarked grave in the churchyard near his former home at Holme Church near a 'Holy Brook'.

Little did I know then that much of these early areas of enquiry would form the basis of two books that I wrote in the 70s and 80s. They both sold well and were later translated into both French and Spanish as well as being serialised in Paris Match Magazine.

In the course of my investigations, I met many credible witnesses of the paranormal with sometimes incredible tales to tell.

One such fellow was a retired helicopter design engineer, nobody's gullible fool. One evening, as he turned his car into the driveway of his Wiltshire farmhouse, its headlights illuminated the hovering form of a semi-transparent dome-shaped craft, a few hundred yards away, over his meadow of long grass.

Startled, he quickly backed up and shone his headlights again into the field, but the craft had vanished. The next morning, he walked down into the meadow to find an incomplete crop circle impressed in the grass. One of the very few unfinished glyphs ever to be found; he reasoned that he had disturbed the process of its construction when he had arrived home the night before.

Other paranormal events had occurred with this chap. He almost felt at times he had an invisible companion and a spirit with some interesting tricks.

While working at home on bits of machinery he would on occasion put down a spanner or other metal tool right in front of the job. Upon reaching forward to pick it up he sometimes found it had mysteriously vanished. In frustration he would often exclaim, "Oh! Come on, give it back", and some minutes later he would find it had returned, sometimes in the same place or just nearby.

Another characteristic which he shared with some well-known inventors, Nicola Tesla for one, was going to bed with some technical problem on his mind and waking in the morning with the complete engineering solution, even drawings of mechanisms that he would quickly have to write down before they passed from his mind.

Was he too receiving a little mental help from other realms or was it all from the diverse regions of the brain or subconscious? As this chap was responsible for much of the engineering of some very complicated modern helicopters, you could hardly rate him as some demented nut. Those choppers flew very well and still do.

My own educational development led me to be

accepted into Birmingham University, where I studied and worked in the main computer research department. This had recently been equipped with an English Electric KDF 9 computer with the aid of government funding at a cost of £3 million, back when that was a lot of money.

It took up the entire basement under the main hall and was entered through air locks. It had humidity and temperature control and of course one had to be vetted and issued with security passes. This baby was approximately third generation after the Bletchley Colossus and had transistors, vacuum tubes, three miles of wire and a permanent shift of two technicians sitting in an adjoining office waiting for it to break down, which it did often.

It ran 24-hours a day, seven days a week, worked on input via punched tape, some of the first electric teleprinters by Friden and early IBM machines. Huge reels of wide magnetic tape held data storage to drive its thorough but ponderous workings. Programs could run for eight hours or more and we did work for some interesting parties other than the in-house budding Ph.Ds. frantically preparing their theses before someone else published a similar idea.

We did much work for CERN looking at bubble chamber tracks, which showed the paths of decaying sub-atomic particles. In those days, we were still chasing mesons, sub-atomic particles, rather than musing on God particles, and their spiralling paths were always intriguing to examine, disappearing up their own anus, as we joked.

Other studies were less abstract. We did work for The Vatican, analysing the books of the New Testament in their earliest forms and found that any one book had multiple authors or scribes. You can tell by the recurring style, some had up to five scribes. Early English to French translation programs were a challenge and often gave amusing results. "A traffic jam," would be "Une confiture de circulation," instead of, of course, "un embouteillage."

In the wall of the main computer hall was a large triple-plated, glass viewing window. While in the middle of some huge and tedious program we had little to do. Our protocol was that I would be sitting at the main control desk, usually with my feet up, reading The Times newspaper into which I had cut a small hole so I could keep an eye on the viewing window.

When any visiting dignitaries, often groups of Japanese businessmen, were seen heading our way, a secret signal went up. We would immediately busy ourselves loading and unloading magnetic tape reels that were not in use at that moment and hold impromptu technical huddles, making exaggerated gesticulations pretending to solve some amazingly complex problems.

They couldn't hear us; in fact, we would tell jokes. Suitably impressed, the visitors would move on convinced we were at the cutting edge of current science. The all-clear would be flagged and we would return to our lazy pursuits or completing the crossword puzzle.

The head of the department was a rather mad genius who loved tennis and would invariably turn up for work in tennis shorts, no socks and plimsolls. We tried to keep him out of sight of the be-suited Japanese; he was just too wacky.

We also carried out some classified work. Britain was

still trying to build long range missiles that proved outrageously expensive. They were usually scrapped before completion at a cost of several million pounds a punt to the unsuspecting tax payer. Many a dedicated Ph.D. student could be found drinking away his sorrows on being told the last three years of his work had just been flushed down the government toilet courtesy of some annual budget cuts.

It was during my long sessions babysitting 'the beast', as we called the machine, that I was surprised to find I would often sense when it was about to fail. This was not very predictable as many programs did fail on start-up or it could run for minutes or hours, find a glitch and crash. These were the early days of programming and the VDU was a thing of the future; we were working in machine languages back then.

I would get a feeling, divert my attention from the newspaper and study the many flashing lights that sat in display units atop the sentinel-like computer cabinets. Lo and behold, the lights would stop; she had jammed and the technicians would emerge from their coffee drinking, scratch their heads and begin analysing what the beast had done.

Sometimes hours later, she would either carry on or more than likely that day's work was lost and the programmers would be told to go back to the drawing board. To this day I have a profound distrust of computers, as they say, "Junk in, junk out." On more than one occasion, I wondered if I had somehow interacted with the beast and messed up her mind for those few critical micro-seconds, or was this just wishful thinking?

Indeed, people I met later in life could do that very thing, sometimes at will, including Uri Geller, whom

I learnt later had been tested in some hush, hush military research that they later called PsyOps.

I studied Business Studies in parallel at Aston University, down the road, and also Work Study. Very boring, but useful later when I would run some of my own operations.

While at Birmingham, I had moved into a bungalow owned by the widow of a deceased former colleague of mine at The Astro Research Society. I did not wish to reside in the city and the daily journey through the countryside was worth it.

Stan had died of stomach cancer the year before and we had been close friends. He had been an active member of The Royal Observer Corps and had shared some confidences about our country's measures at that time in case of nuclear attack. I have been fascinated ever since by bunkers and secret places, of which many still exist. Dorothy and I had become quite close after his death and she was very supportive in my early days away from the family hotel.

During my university holidays, I travelled to Glastonbury and met with Tudor Pole, an author and gentleman of some means who had been highly instrumental in setting up and restoring the Chalice Well, a research centre and guest house built by the site of an ancient Roman Spa. Sited at the base of Glastonbury Tor, it was a magical place and attracted all kinds of thinkers, mystics and would be seers.

I became very interested in the earthworks of the area and the old formations, which appeared to depict a Babylonian ten sign Zodiac laid out over a very wide area surrounding the Tor. Only later it seemed, did twelve signs become the norm for astrological depiction. The original ten signs seemed to show a sky configuration dated to before the great flood, which appears to have been a major world catastrophe referred to in many religions and mythologies.

While at Glastonbury, I became friends with a learned mathematician and teacher at one of the public schools in Marlborough. He had done some in-depth work measuring the units used to construct stone structures from different periods. Thus he could determine exactly whether a church was Saxon or Norman.

In his studies of Egyptian monuments, he could also ascertain if the chambers inside were royal or for access to the common people. The units of their dimensions would either be the royal or common cubit; thus determining exactly their role in the order of things. Hence I became very aware that in the structure of ancient buildings and their sites, much was encoded in their layouts. Literally books in stone with hidden messages only for access by the adept and initiate. Later, I would learn much more about the significance of these measurements and their connection with the science of sound.

While at University I continued my work with The Astro Research Society, which included astronomy and many sky watches for both meteors and UFOs. One warm August night, this was rewarded by a startling and potentially dangerous event.

On the edge of the horizon of a clear and starlit night, a huge orange ball appeared and moved across the sky, leaving a dense green smoke-like trail on either side of it. This intensified and then faded, intensified and faded and in this action, like a skipping stone on water, disappeared over the opposite horizon.

I was so shaken I did not even attempt to take a photograph with the 35mm camera which hung around my neck. This was no UFO, but a huge bolide, a very big meteor entering the upper atmosphere. Unbeknown to me, if it had been much bigger and on a lower trajectory I could have been toast. I felt very grateful to be safe and alive.

Another near-miss also occurred that year. My father, being a bit of an electronics nut, had erected a huge VHF and TV aerial array clamped to the top of the rear "stink pipe", a thick metal drainpipe running up the rear of the property to which the bedroom waste water pipes were connected. These were made of copper; it was before the days of commonly using plastic, so it was an excellent earthed conductor.

My bedroom was near this pipe and I had a wash-basin in my bedroom connected to it. One quiet summer's night with no particular weather in evidence, I was standing washing my hands at this sink, which was full of warm water.

A man's voice said very distinctly in my right ear, "Move to the right." It was a commanding tone, a tone you did not question, and you obeyed. I did so a couple of feet. Immediately I was clear, lighting struck the array and there was a vivid blue flash as electricity jumped from the wastewater to the cold water supply tap. I sat down on the bed shaken. There had been no one else in the room when the warning command had been given and I was not in the mood to question where the voice had come from. I was alive and that was good enough.

My father entered the room and asked what the bang had been, had I dropped something? I told him what had happened. He didn't believe me. I remember not caring much at the time. It was very real for me. I was grateful for whatever help had just come my way.

While staying with Dorothy in Evesham, her daughter flew over from Switzerland. She was married to a Swiss-Italian and had two young boys. She was about 24 and we really hit it off, partly on the basis that her father and I had been such close friends.

At the end of her two week stay I was again put in a very tricky position. She declared she had become very fond of me and things were not going well for her in the marriage over there. If she left her husband, could we make out together here in England? Heck, I was attracted to this girl, older than me, but quite a stunner.

However, I was still at University struggling with my part-time jobs to pay my way through. I had no reliable income and to take on a ready-made family with the needs of two youngsters was a big ask. My emotions said yes but my mind got the better of the debate and I shuffled sideways saying we should write and see how we felt when she got back to her home in Switzerland. The relationship faded over a few weeks and I always have wondered what might have come of it, as I did really like her. To say it was love would be far too soon; chemistry may be?

I was still working with Birmingham University and driving my "pimped" grey minivan, all decked out as the airfield crash tender when on a wet and grey morning in Birmingham, a Ford driver piled into the back of me at a traffic light. Fortunately, the beefed up bumpers of the minivan prevented me being killed, but I was pretty shaken up and bruised and battered enough to need time off Uni and return home to Devon until I recovered.

This gave me the opportunity to catch up on my other research. I traded my battered minivan for a beautiful Riley 1.5 RME with sweeping front wings, red leather seats and a walnut dashboard. My popularity with the opposite sex somewhat improved.

Chris, and I continued to explore the wild and weird worlds of the unknown fringes of human experience. He had a UFO encounter he claimed, a sort of close encounter of the second kind, but did not want to talk about it much. We were moving in circles of local high society and such matters were not considered politically correct unless you were over 80 and waiting to meet your maker sometime soon.

After a period of working for the Rank Organisation, during which I was trained as an internal accountant (which really meant bending the figures to fit the company profile), I started my own endeavours in electronics, gained a good knowledge of acoustics and, perhaps spurred on by the family traditions of Chris and his father's photographic shops, I started my own Hi-Fi business.

This was in Torquay and I soon had three shops in my little chain. Unfortunately, these were troubled days in the land and Edward Heath was Prime Minister, in a time of serious dispute with the coal miners' unions.

Shortly after I opened my third shop the Government announced a three-day week. Streetlights were being turned off and the public urged to save electricity in any way possible. This was not the time to be running electronics shops and I pretty much crashed in flames, not actually bankrupt, but very near.

During this commercial period of my life, I married a local girl whom I had known for some years. We both needed to break free from the confines of our respective families. Was it love? I don't think so; more a common need to escape from a very restrictive existence.

I helped to run a small housing association, thus furnishing myself and friends with similar needs with some nice apartments overlooking Torbay.

My wife had given birth to a baby daughter, Melissa, and we lived with our two Siamese cats within sight of the hotel where I had grown up in Torquay. I got involved with making audio visual material for schools and colleges, including the British Army Schools and became skilled as a script editor and writer having produced over twenty AV units.

Chris, with his intense interest in history, elected to buy a rundown stately home near Totnes, Devon and offered a fifty per cent share in it to me if I could raise the money. I chickened out on that one. It was a huge place and the roof repairs alone looked awesome. In the end, it took Chris ten years to restore the place, before he opened it as a photographic museum and spooky house with 'find the ghosts' tours.

It probably really was haunted as it's said to sit on six ley lines, supposed psychic energy pathways. Chris told me that over the years, he and other guests had seen 38 different ghosts from various historical periods in full 3D and colour. Chris may have been larger than life, but he had no need to tell lies. He exclaimed in philosophical muse, "I wonder if they see each other?"

The hooded monks seemed the most strange as they would walk right through one of the visitors. At that moment the unwitting soul would feel an intense cold sensation, often associated with psychic phenomena.

Occasionally ghosts would appear on photographs taken at the house or as strange areas of light or orbs.

For a while later on, the place became a spa, under different management and later still, it was turned into residential accommodation for a spiritually-orientated community. The "ghosts" were considered a bit of an embarrassment and consigned to history, like many other things we cannot easily explain.

In the middle of the 70s, having lost my three electronic shops and with the country in disarray, we left for France. I put myself into The Université de Nice and lived under canvas for six months through the warm summer weather with my wife and young child. Life was fun in the student environment in which we resided.

Prior to getting there, a journey of economic exploration had occurred.

I first stopped in Holland, where I stayed for two weeks in the home of Calvinists, but the strict regime and bland diet soon got the better of me. From there, I moved over the German border, which proved far too expensive in day-to-day living costs, so I headed south to the French border.

Having expected to be taking up residence in Holland, my money was all in Dutch guilders (this was before the days of the Euro) and I knew you had to declare taking money into France to get it out again legally. Hence I duly stopped in the line of "Items to Declare" at the French border and waited in a line of trucks. When my turn came, I waited outside the Border Customs Office wherein a blazing row was going on between the French official and a sweating, irate truck driver. When that ended it was my turn to be processed.

The perspiring official, very stereotypically French, sat in his undone waistcoat, perspiring, his classic moustache drooping, reflecting his mood. He eyed me with distain as I explained I wanted to declare some money I was bringing into France and that it was in Dutch guilders. My French was broken and I am sure, an insult to his long standing civilisation.

"How much?" he asked me abruptly. I indicated the amount, about £4,000 in sterling equivalent.

"How long are you staying?" he barked at me in French.

"At least two weeks", I replied, hedging my bets. At this point an interesting equation took hold in his mind. This well-dressed young Englishman was going to stay in his beloved country for about two weeks and potentially spend about £4,000, a small fortune in those days.

He excused himself. I could see him in the anteroom via a small wall mirror. He combed his hair; he straightened his drooping moustache, he donned his jacket and returned and sat down. "Yes, sir!" he said in a modest tone, "How may I be of assistance?"

I noted another lesson in life: Money talks.

Life at Université de Nice was interesting, the corridors often smelled of grass, though not the cricket field variety. The students all drove beaten up 2CVs that hadn't seen their canvas roofs for some time and had dilapidated deck chairs inside. Seat belts occurred only in a galaxy far, far away.

They seemed to be able to corner at the craziest angles of yawl without turning over and they defied death on a regular basis. Life was good; life was cool.

The American students had been sent over by rich daddies to take a degree in English, because it would be easy to pass. Wrong! They didn't realise American English was not going to be acceptable to the ex-Oxford Don who ran that department. They should have stayed at home and taken Cosmology instead, it would have been an easier ride.

Unfortunately, while I was there, the British government chickened out of the first Channel Tunnel construction mid-term, when the French were somewhat ahead of us. So in typical, and of course entirely reasonable, revenge, the Corsican students burnt down the English Department. We Brits stayed off campus for a couple of weeks until passions cooled down. No point in getting beaten up!

Perhaps out of a combination of contradictions, being in a foreign country, getting short of money, little chance of a job in France; France is for the French, difficulties with the language. I thought I spoke French, the French knew I didn't; my marriage in France collapsed and I returned to the UK alone, leaving my wife and child in our apartment in Nice.

I'd been offered a super job teaching English as a Foreign Language to European businessmen and millionaires from a Swedish Airline company, SAS. This allowed me to support my family for a while, but the relationship had become strained and divorce was the agreed logical outcome. I gave her everything I had and moved on. The new job was great; company mini-bus, cash in hand from Sweden and an expenses account to take out these folk to high-class venues so they could use their English in situ. Plus, my boss fancied me, a tall older Swedish lady called Erica. I was on the beach!

Erica was fantastic for me at that time. My confidence had taken a blow with all the UK company troubles and while my French experience had widened my horizons, it had exhausted my funds. What remained of the marriage finances went to my wife; the divorce was quick and painless on both sides. We were both still young and she swiftly remarried.

I started again from scratch, something that was to happen a number of times in my life ahead. Paradise, they say, is a passing phase...

Driving back to Torquay from Heathrow airport, having dropped off a couple of my wealthy businessmen students, I was coming through Wiltshire at dusk. It was a deserted section of road and there on the grass verge were a couple of students thumbing a lift. I picked them up and we got chatting. It was getting late and we got to talking about the supernatural.

They told me the cottage where they lived was haunted and asked if I would like to stay the night to see for myself.

My schedule was flexible so, intrigued, I accepted their offer.

The ancient village of Mere sits in the heart of Wiltshire next to a most remarkable bowl shaped enclave, which for all the world looks like a Moon crater. Their cottage was probably 17th century. Mike was an antique furniture restorer and his companion was his girlfriend.

They did not mention his cousin, Jane, also lived at the cottage in Mere. Jane would be the next big episode in my life as I was to learn the moment I saw her sitting by the fire in that ancient 17th century setting.

She rose, smiled at me in absolute delight, and said, "I dreamt of you last night and now you are here. It has been a long time. You are sleeping in my room tonight!"

Jane and I were to be together for a classic seven years. Part of me loves her still; we are and were as brother and sister, a connection we felt that had occurred over several lifetimes. She says Egypt, Rome, even earlier in ancient times, the days of the great flood, we both recall being on ships, great sailing ships. And we remember our deaths, her falling down some stone stairs in Egypt, myself being assassinated along with others in Rome for trying to tell the truth. 'The Truth will set you Free'. Maybe, it often gets you killed, but more of that later.

Back in Torquay, Erica had found a rich Swedish businessman and we agreed that as I had found Jane, it was time to part. It had been a great seven weeks. Erica hired me, she fired me. No problem, time to move on again. Wiltshire beckoned.

4. Into The Unknown

EVEN MORE WEIRD

The military town of Warminster in Wiltshire, southern England, has been the home of various sections of the British Army for many years. It's also the location of the School of Gunnery with its nearby ranges on Salisbury Plain.

Whether it was this or other, more subtle, factors that may have had a bearing, during the 1970s, there was an explosion of UFO-related and strange unexplained phenomena that hit the headlines. Arthur Shuttlewood, a local journalist, brought the occurrences to public attention in newspaper reports and the "Warminster Thing" became daily news for a while.

Fascinated by these happenings, Jane and I sought to establish a research centre in the town to serve as a focal point for the collection of information and stories that could shed some light on these amazing events. At the time, it was the cutting edge of paranormal research and it was logical that we should gravitate to this UFO hot spot location as we were both obsessed with the subject. By some miracle, we managed to buy a run-down small manor house in the town and set about restoring it, mostly by our own hands, as we could not afford outside craftsmen.

We renamed the manor, "Star House" and it opened as "The Fountain Centre" where we accommodated fellow researchers when they were in the area. We also published an ad hoc magazine entitled "The Fountain Journal" which is still available online. It detailed the month to month reports of UFO sightings and what it all might mean. It was a fun time and we got to meet people from all over the country. Star House became the focal point of intense discussions between UFO and paranormal researchers and 'experiencers' as they had become known.

As I intimated earlier, my connections to British Intelligence had never gone away and I had been asked to consult or offer insight and information on numerous occasions. Let's say our contacts were occasional but ongoing. Additionally, the subjects of this involvement was always – and still is – sensitive, so, up until now, I have just omitted reference rather than make for a stilted memoir.

However, from here on, they became more pertinent to the story, so I will include them with, of course, due respect to national security regulations.

Until this time in Warminster, my involvement with British Intelligence had been on a lull, but now resumed. American Intelligence had a rather unexpected interest in the UFO happenings and, via

Hans Holzer, they requested my help as a point-man for their data-gathering on the issue. Thus, Star House became something of a cover for Intelligence acquisition for our partners on the other side of the pond. This is partly covered in Nick Redfern's book *In search of the saucer spies.*

While the visiting researchers may, in the light of these revelations, feel rather upset at my double role, I felt it was in the general interest of understanding the UFO phenomena and would like to emphasise that none of their private lives were of any interest to anyone else. The only thing the Americans were interested in was the accuracy of the UFO reports.

On the part of the British, as it appeared that the off-world entities were infiltrating Army establishments, naturally British Intelligence also had an interest in being in the loop so my information found its way back to them, via the Americans.

What do I mean by infiltrating? In one or two instances at the Warminster ranges, a UFO would zoom in at low altitude and cause the electronically-controlled training targets to go haywire. We speculated that the pattern of the interference on the targets held any digital messages. We didn't come to any firm conclusion.

Since the original approaches with Major Reedman (no, it is not his real name, but a play on the term 'straw man' – as the Intel community likes such jokes and puzzle clues) I had been accepted into a lateral NGO (Non-Governmental Organisation) known obscurely as NAIG. This stood for 'North Atlantic Intelligence Group' and consisted of a number of loosely associated acting and retired intelligence people and military officers who had been inspired and originally instigated by the actions of the first US Secretary of Defense, James Forrestal.

A brief outline of the beginnings of NAIG and Forrestal will set the scene for what has occurred later over the past 66 odd years: -

Forrestal was formerly the Secretary to the Navy, when there were also parallel posts for the Army and the US Army Air Force. In 1949 they came under the newly created single post of Secretary of Defense. One of his major achievements was uniting the three commands under one authority as prior to this, and to some extent to this day, there was a fierce competition between the three commands. However, as in the UK, the Navy was always considered the Senior Service. So it was logical that Forrestal should be promoted, by President Harry S Truman, to head up the Defense of the whole of the USA.

Forrestal was a notorious workaholic and had his hand on everything. Nothing got past Forrestal and he was a highly ethical man, a devout Catholic of Irish descent, who believed in the responsibility of honesty within government, subject to the usual security protocols. Forrestal was an Aquarius, 15th February 1892, which seems a long while ago now, but he was a progressive thinker with a long foresight into the future.

He advocated and achieved the complete racial integration of the US armed services and lobbied against the partition of Palestine, a stance that did not win him any friends in the Jewish community in Washington. Forrestal is quoted as saying, "....no group in this country should be permitted to influence our policy to the point it could endanger our National Security," in a comment to J. Howard McGrath, the

US Senator from Rhode Island.

The death of Forrestal in 1949, by a fall from the 16th floor of the Bethesda National Naval Medical Centre, was attributed to suicide. But the full reports on the suspicious circumstances surrounding his demise were not released until April 2004. There seems no reason why the matter was considered one of national security, unless there were details that were not politically correct or would have raised suspicion at the time. The full report revealed that broken glass had been found on his bed and signs of a struggle. The fact that this occurred on the very day that he was due for release and his brother was on the way to the hospital to pick him up leads to grave suspicions that he was in fact murdered. Why?

Was it that he had antagonised the Zionist, Jewish lobby in their attempts to establish the state of Israel, or for some deeper reason other than the internal conflicts between factions of the US government over the military budget and readiness for war in which Forrestal found himself piggy in the middle?

What is known is that Forrestal would, as Secretary of Defense, have carried the highest security clearance available at that time, and was fully briefed on the events at Roswell where much evidence has emerged that an unidentified aerial craft had crashed along with diminutive occupants, most of whom died on impact. Forrestal is accredited with establishing Majestic 12, a select committee of the brightest minds to examine and exploit the technological fall out from this crash landing.

America was just post the Second World War, was divided in government on being in war readiness against future threats and dealing with the rising power of Russia. It was not one unified command of common authority and purpose or foresight on a very uncertain future. The last thing in the World they wanted to deal with was the implications of some exterior communication with a technologically advanced civilisation that might make the efforts of man look like little more than the aftermath of the stone age. Forrestal wanted to declare to the world what we knew, others did not. They prevailed.

In this confused and contradictory environment of policy and planning, the first beginnings of NAIG emerged as an unofficial cooperation between experienced persons who feared for the outcome of those days.

President Eisenhower, in his final address in January 1961, warned against the predominance of vested monetary interests in the military industrial complex taking over the policy and direction of US policy. He knew as Supreme Allied Commander during the final months of the Second World War, that opportunities to end the conflict earlier had been passed by. The purpose of wars, after all, is to endure, not necessarily to end them or win at the earliest opportunity, because wars make profits, BIG profits.

NAIG, along with many other associations and organisations, tries to maintain a rational debate within, not protest without, and to bring a common sense rational for the good of all parties towards resolution.

Unfortunately, the controlling cabals that have always held the real power within and outside of governments, manipulate politicians and the blinkered electorates via the mass media, into motivating the general public to focus on military adventures. These are sometimes disguised as "peace-keeping missions" to control resources, thus maintaining, in effect, the same colonial influence that existed in the days of Empire.

The only difference now is that the sovereign governments play front of house to their administrations, while owning their own debts. They do not necessarily own many of their own resources. Similar to after the US civil war, the former slaves were now free men, but they were now economic slaves just the same. Power hangs on to power. It is the nature of things.

The UFO crash at Roswell was a technological windfall to emerging technologies worldwide. Through the careful management of Col. Phillip J. Corso and Lt. Gen Arthur G. Trudeau of the US Army Research and Development (Overseas Resources Division), items of advanced technology were salvaged from the crash. They were sent to various corporations and establishments under the cover that they had been recovered from a foreign power, which in fact was the remit of Col. Corso's department. This leap-frogged many areas of technology, that today we take for granted. We may have had the beginnings of these things, but for example the English Electric KDF9 Computer that I worked at Birmingham University, with its miles of wires and post war technology, was light years behind the microchips that emerged later.

In recent years, an interesting hypothesis has emerged in the Inner Keep, (code for the Intelligence inner circle) that Roswell was not an accident! The occurrence of UFO crashes is extremely rare. The technology involved has few or no moving parts, being mostly of a plasma field technology, which constantly renews itself, hence the 'flashing light effects' displayed in UFO sightings. They do not break down. The materials of which they are made, shown from recovered craft, are extraordinarily resistant to heat, wear and tear, erosion and have a high-voltage capacity, which qualifies their ceramics as superconductors.

Most of the "crashes" are deliberate. Humans like to steal things; it is in their DNA. They would rather steal something than learn something as that has impact on their delicate egos and they strongly resist that input. But give them something to steal and they drag it away with relish and make it their own. So why would this systematic crash policy be in place?

Consider this: These craft technologies were far, far in advance of the human level of understanding in the 1940s. Yet sightings of alien craft over the period of the last 70 years indicate that they have greatly evolved as early craft appeared to be much more of a nuts and bolts affair. Then came Roswell, a type of craft rarely observed after that time with its semi-circular rear profile, loaded with bits of technology which we just about understood, Corso says, about 20% of it, up to the time of his death in 1998.

It is unreasonable to assume the civilisations operating these craft were evolving at such a speed themselves, as they seem to have had the more advanced level of crafts many, many years ago, even in ancient times. So why would they be operating antique craft and allowing them to crash on a few selected places around the Earth? The Roswell crash for instance was within a few miles of America's only operating nuclear armed air force squadron at that time. Hence, an identified area of human high-end technology and activity and the craft were staffed in the main by robots; advanced biomechanical robots that were 'expendable'. These are known in UFO circles as the small 'Greys' that appear to have very limited abilities, do as they are commanded and have little or no emotions or imagination. They act and appear to be purely, pragmatically functional.

A very advanced civilisation encountering a planet occupied by tribes- big tribes- of insecure, aggressive primates, with limited understanding of what or who you are, would need extreme patience to educate them to a point where communication might be possible. Or perhaps, even, for the primates to become a useful work force.

Say your interstellar expedition size is quite small, so you must devise a method by which the primates will educate themselves. So why not leak information and technology to them and allow them to figure it out as and when they can.

 Perhaps the advanced visitors wish to temper the indigenous population's "wilder" side. Why not build in systems to manage this as part of the technological evolution. Then there's the numbers game. How many primates should the planet reasonably support? Now that's the '$64,000 question', as they say.

Do you see where this is going? Can you comprehend how a very advanced civilisation might view you? Looking at you as one might study a colony of ants and trying to implement environmental controls when the off-planet "expedition" force may number but a few hundred while the planet population numbers around seven billion?

The events at Warminster consisted of many UFO sightings, landings, close encounters and strange sounds and vibrations on the roofs of startled residents of the garrison town.

So what were the incidents at Warminster all about? God only knows. There were interactions with the gunnery school ranges and staff. There was some procreation activity but mostly it seemed to be psychological testing.

By psychological testing, I am wondering if the point of the visitation activity was to determine and observe the response of the soldiers to it. For example, what is their threshold of fear and curiosity? On the ranges the servo controlled targets went up and down of their own accord. What was that all about? Some kind of message? Can one bring to a focal point, open-minded people and seed them with ideas; principles that they can take away and play

Around the same time, and still continuing, the phenomena of crop circles began appearing in fields. It has become an evolving programme of mathematical and symbolic glyphs, which every year are religiously photographed, sent around the world and analysed. Many do not realise they are mainly subconscious messages or theorems yet to be fully deciphered. (See "Crop Circles Revealed", a photographic book to which I contributed and edited – US Edition)

All of these events were monitored and fed back to US Intelligence via friends of mine to whom I refer in my previous book, "The Welsh Triangle". These included Hans, my mentor, sponsor and handler who was also a prolific writer. It goes without saying that Hans was of course another member of NAIG.

The incidents at Warminster also threw up the inherent divisions in UFO, Crop Circle and paranormal researchers, a characteristic they share with conventional science, insofar as they all want to own the events and phenomena they are investigating.

It means they get bogged down in petty arguments and rivalries between themselves and mostly miss the point of what they are doing. Into this soup intermixes the naysayers. Those who by dint of a critical disposition, along with professionally paid PsyOps saboteurs and just plain bloody-minded folk, shoot down everything that is not in their comfort zone. This 'trouble at t'mill' keeps a lot of the good information confused, obscured, undiscovered or covered up quite successfully.

Like in so many ET to Earthling communication operations that I have observed and reported on over the years, they run their course and then end, either because they have achieved whatever they can or ET or the humans give up on the situation. One communication link was apparently kept going for 12 years between a group of civilian spiritually-minded folk and ETs via television communication beamed directly into their house using the American English language which seemed to be computer-generated. The ET end eventually shut it down with the statement that the group was a lot slower on the up take than they upstairs had imagined would be the case. The main complaint from the Earthling group seemed to be that they had not made any money from the communicated information. Need I say more? ET does not use money, so why should such a concept be on their agenda?

When briefed on the ET situation, their craft, style and what one could deduce of their philosophy, US Secretary of Defense Forrestal had asked rhetorically, "Are they communists?"

Forrestal had a bit of an obsession about communism, with it being the post Second World war era. Well, that is unanswered at this time, but the latter day influence of other ET origins, appear to be several sources, according to a former member of the Canadian Government, it would seem that the United States has gotten under the influence of what would appear to be much more of a capitalistic element of off world thinking concerned with exploiting the American people just as a resource. Like attracts like one presumes. This connection they say dates back some sixty odd years.

Those of you not familiar with these wild and obscure assertions may think they are the ramblings of the alternative fringe, the conspiracy theorists. I assure you they are not, these are the thoughts of senior military officers, insiders and those who qualify for the 'need to know'. Those who have security clearances like 'Ultra', 'Cosmic' and such. They include people who have had their hands on that nuclear switch and are trusted to be responsible and sane. I have known several of them personally. Can't name them here at this time, at least while they are still alive.

After Warminster had died down somewhat, I was again deployed by the Americans, via Hans to West Wales, to investigate, what became known as "The Welsh Triangle" and RAF Brawdy on St. Brides Bay. The tabloid press was full of close encounter stories and UFO reports; it made headlines.

I was tasked to go down for several months to try to find out what the hell was going on down there. My cover was that I was writing a book and indeed, I did write a book, having been offered a generous advance by Granada books for a six-month investigation.

Although it did not tell the whole truth, it still had enough in it for the British government to buy up over 70,000 copies and burn them. The publisher just reprinted. Burning books belongs in a George Orwell Sci-Fi novel or Communist China, not in the UK; it's just a little pointless, like banning "Spy Catcher" the book Peter Wright, by the former MI5 scientific Officer. It just makes everyone want to get their hands on it.

Jane and I sold Star House in Warminster. While the UFO activities hadn't disappeared completely, things had gone quiet and we found ourselves once more in the thick of weird happenings. Again, it was my job to become involved with local witnesses as UFO researchers. This was not too difficult a task as both Jane and I were both intensely interested in the subject and wanted to authenticate and protect the local people from accusations of it being a hoax. We knew it was not, other the Americans would not have paid for us to go.

So what's the real story behind "The Welsh Triangle?"

First some basic facts. At that time, the Americans had put in place a number of sonar underwater listening stations in the North Atlantic, to monitor enemy submarine movements, something that now happens worldwide.

One was on the southern tip of Greenland and another was within RAF Brawdy, which sits right on the cliff edge at St. Brides Bay. Heavy gauge cables run out for miles and miles under the sea to sonar microphones that listen to the very low frequency vibrations of the propellers on subs and other ships. Each one has its own signature and from this information you can triangulate the position, course, depth, revolutions and status of the boat or ship. You can also listen to whale song via the same system.

The US listening station was running under the cover of an Oceanographic Research Station, supposedly operated by civilians—not so—and commanded by a US Navy Captain. Staff were not allowed to wear military uniform or drive any Yankee cars and would be shipped home in disgrace if they got so much as a parking ticket.

The amusing thing is of course, the Russians knew all about it and duly upgraded St. Brides Bay to first strike status in the event of nuclear war. So the good people of West Wales would get fried first, courtesy of unwittingly hosting the American presence.

Brawdy, however, was also picking up other mysterious movements in the North Atlantic, mostly off Iceland. The objects detected appeared to be capable of 150 knots underwater, just a little more than a British nuclear sub could manage, which was then about 48 knots flat out. Usually though, the subs just drift with their reactors shut down, as you can detect the engine cooling water from any good weather satellite.

An exercise was held to try to corner some of these objects, but some dived to great depth, while another just surfaced and took off into the sky, not a known submarine capacity.

However, it seemed to bring some counter-surveillance by ET back home onto the American listening stations including the one near Shag Harbour, in North America and at Brawdy. I went into the old surface station there on the cliffs when the MoD dispersals unit was trying to flog it off years later. It has triple fences, watch towers, guard rooms—all the usual junk associated with a high security base.

Almost like a scene from a movie – and I can hardly believe it myself even now - I rummaged around in the former COs office and found, dropped down behind a filing cabinet, a complete list of secret US bases! I sent it on to British Intelligence who (after a close perusal, of course) returned it to the US with a curt note about sanitising procedures. They don't like being caught out. Happens often, so I am not too popular in some circles. Bless!

This ET counter-surveillance activity was being picked up by the local population and reported in the national press much to the chagrin of US Naval Intelligence. These included things like, "UFO sightings", space-suited beings on the ground scaring the locals when they happened upon them near the base and strange computer failures in the facility, even ghost images appearing within the system.

Where do you hide a tree? In a forest of course. ET was seen to have deposited some kit in rock formations nearby to monitor the base and divers getting too close would hear a strange underwater hum. One claimed to have been attacked underwater by a machine, escaping with rips in his wet suit and very shaken. None of this information made it into my book, *The Welsh Triangle*, as it was far too sensitive at that time.

RAF Brawdy, also known as RNAS Brawdy, served multiple purposes at this time as it also accommodated the US Navy controlled submarine monitoring station. The American part of Brawdy had the highest security requirement of a US overseas base. Not even the British were allowed in; it was a piece of American soil. The Americans extended the airstrip to facilitate landings of heavy transport planes. Across the bay from the airstrip, local farmhouses experienced power surges causing electrical failures. These were reported to MoD London and were investigated by visiting RAF officers who couldn't determine their cause.

The witnesses were experiencing a gamut of occurrences including UFO sightings, evidence of UFO landings in the form of burnt circles in the meadows, electrical surges and bizarre, mystical dreams. Some even reported seeing seven-foot-tall aliens wearing white space suits outside their properties. Brawdy later tried to dismiss this as personnel performing a hoax, but as the base was supposed to be top secret, there would be no reason for staff to draw attention to the area; quite the opposite.

I myself was present when a whole herd of cows was somehow 'teleported' out of a closed and locked barn to a field a mile away. The barn was still locked afterwards and had they been let out and herded to the field, they would have had to pass by the window where we were sat, drinking coffee. The cows were unharmed. I expand on this mysterious incident in *The Welsh Triangle*.

There was also damage to local property at the Fort Haven Hotel, St Bride's Bay, at the end of whose land was a Royal Observer Corps bunker (not part of the Brawdy base). The owner of the hotel saw a UFO land by the bunker and from the vehicle a beam of light emitted in her direction, though not at her. It hit, instead the hotel roof and set ignited a small fire, quickly extinguished. I felt was significant as a lot of the American facilities were underground and this may have been part of the ET surveys. Perhaps the light was to warn the woman away, although this is just my speculation.

American PsyOps also seemed to get involved discrediting witnesses. The main reason you hide things from the local population is not security, it is embarrassment that you cannot control the situation. One cannot admit to being impotent to something over which one has little or no control.

The base was infiltrated on a regular basis by 'beings' who could run rings around the Navy's defences. And then some. Damn it, these guys could fly around, get through any security, take down computers and security systems at will and the craft they flew could not be tracked on radar. Hardly reassuring to a unit that was considered front line to national security.

Even while I was there for my official visit, I took a few snaps on my 35mm camera, and when developed, there, lo and behold, on the cleared-out podium of the main computer hall, were the luminous violet silhouettes of two tall beings, just looking at me. I did not see them at the time. The film was UV sensitive and just picked them up.

Brawdy eventually officially closed its submarine surveillance operations, although some say it just buried itself underground where it would be less vulnerable to a first-strike Soviet attack. When I went there some years later, it was in-part home to a unit of British Army Signals, say no more, that's code for Intelligence.

After the remit to West Wales ran out, we headed off to Swanton Morley over in Norfolk. We took up breeding Anglo-Arab horses and Jane had a stallion called Hebron Dancing Light, who answered to "Taffy" as well as a few mares, including the niece of the famous Arkle named "Permissive Society". She answered to the stable name of "Ginger". She was a 16.4 hand chestnut and I had bought her injured and nursed her back to health, although she never raced again. The money from "The Welsh Triangle" bought more horses than was wise. Norfolk was the cheapest place to buy land in those days for rearing animals and we were very green in both senses of the word.

During this time, my two paperbacks were published. In 1979 *The Welsh Triangle* came out, followed in 1980 by *UFO-UK*. The second book was more of a grand tour of the UFO scene in the UK at that time and Intelligence used me to interface with UFO researchers wherever I found myself lecturing or attending meetings. I spoke kindly of them when I could.

The fear was that some of these folk were seriously anti-establishment and were sniffing around government installations looking for any conspiracy they could find. There were also the anti-nuclear people; these focused more on Greenham Common and the like. Some of this is covered in the book, "*On The Trail of the Saucer Spies*", by Nick Redfern, in which I believe I am mentioned, albeit under cover.

Around then, the famous Rendlesham Common UFO incident occurred. There was much more to this affair than has formerly surfaced in the press, as I will explain here.

Right across the whole of the USA, Europe and the Soviet Union, nuclear warheads were being mysteriously defused. This involved aerial ET craft, usually three, beaming some kind of penetrating energy device into the warhead bunkers and physically removing the plutonium triggers. Without this they will not go bang, even though the other fissionable compounds remain.

It seemed that whoever was doing this, with their very precise high-tech gear, had a method of modifying the electron shells of the dangerous plutonium and converting it to pure iron, although some residual radiation was present for a while in the by-product.

The operating craft were not inclined to take this iron "home" and in both Russia and the West, the craft would either land or come in very low and deposit the iron on the ground, either as a slag united with a green ceramic substance - green indicates uranium (I have examined and analysed this stuff), or as a fine ferrous dust, as at Rendlesham forest. This dust was all over the nearby pine trees and the Army and the Forestry Commission had to come in, cut them down and dispose of them. Also in similar incidents in Russia, where the slag remnants had been deposited, nothing ever grew again.

Sometimes the former fuse, now iron, was deposited down a small hole in the ground just to keep it contained. This activity has been going on for some time and was a National Security secret, because if your enemy knew your "deterrent" was a dud, then you had no deterrent at all.

As it was, the ETs seemed to be doing this to both sides and it was not until much later that the Soviets and NATO realised that this was an equal opportunity enforced disarmament. However, one could not be sure at any one time which warheads might be "live" and which might be disarmed, so a regular programme of maintenance had to be carried out to keep the "deterrent" in place. Replacement and upgrading occurs even to this day, hence why they have to make new ones. Tragic.

Other activity noticed in the US was ET craft fooling around with the gyroscopic and computer guidance and control systems on Minuteman missiles and their bunker control systems. Whole squadrons of missiles would go down and in one incident, a missile was made live and running ready to fire. A rather disquieting thought, as it may have been re-programmed in its trajectory flight path.

In the past, UFOs have been known to down military jets and transport aircraft if they get too bothersome. Sometimes they just take them over in mid-air and set them down in the jungle, as happened a few times in Vietnam. They did not crash; they were undamaged but I am sorry to say, the crews were dead. My source is top-line USAF Intelligence. The process the ETs used is not kind to the human body and both airframe and bodies were riddled with micro-fine holes. It was almost as if they had encountered an advanced meson weapon, like a laser but fires high-powered, sub-atomic particles. Simple physics really, you can look it up.

For those folk thinking of Nicola Tesla's "Death Ray", no, it's not quite the same. The UFO craft can generate them simply with their drive mechanism, hence in early times of the 1950s, when US jetfighters dived under a UFO in mid-air, they just got shredded. It seemed not to be an act of aggression but an accident. The UFO craft could not turn off its antigravity drive system otherwise it would have fallen onto the aircraft underneath it and you cannot discharge that amount of EHT (Extremely High Tension) without a lightning strike and a bit of a bang, so it is a no-win, no-win situation.

I have known several RAF pilots who have been buzzed by UFOs or "foo fighters" as the little robot ones were nicknamed in the Second World War. One of my chums, a Squadron Leader (another NAIG Member), had a foo fighter fly in through a gaping hole in the side of his bomber made by a passing German shell, fly down the fuselage, turn round and fly right back out again. The crew called for their brown trousers on that one, but declined to report it for fear of being sent to the funny farm and grounded.

Any serious military reports of close encounters always get classified until maybe recently in some countries in South America. The Soviets have also been more open to such reports and even Belgium and France have opened up a bit. But the egos in the USA and UK have a lot of difficulty in admitting that there is anyone around smarter than they are.

Generally speaking, normal military personnel, pilots, squaddies, chaps up to the rank of Major, are very pragmatic and will speak of these things. When society has put someone in charge and they must be seen to be in control of matters, Colonel and above, incidents outside of the comfort zone get suppressed. Politicians are even worse as they have to be seen to be re-electable, so must information-manage a lot more; that's generally known as telling porky pies: an acceptable lie.

The military hierarchy will just clam up or use some polite phrase like, "We can neither confirm nor deny", which is code for, "You are damn near the truth but we are not going to admit it."

While at Swanton Morley in Norfolk, Jane and I got married. We had been together since the Mere and

Warminster days and we had appeared in a full page article in the former Sunday tabloid, *News of the World,* on the phenomena.

Jane was a fantastic psychic and astrologer. She was seen by several people, at a distance, outside of her physical body in full 3D colour, looking as real as you or I, a characteristic of Shamans. She could also stop car engines at 30 miles away, so long as they were petrol and had electrical ignition systems. Uri Geller could do similar things. I met him in France when I was a student at Université de Nice.

Jane couldn't visit supermarkets as she always set off the electronic tag detectors at the doorway. It can get embarrassing explaining to the store staff that you haven't stolen anything, you just have a very high tension electric field (aura) that people can feel when you walk into a room. You can measure these things. It is real and although low wattage, runs at about 40,000 volts. Enough to pop most detectors into a hissy fit. Geller could also make computers malfunction as could Jane. I have been known to do the same, but only intentionally.

Popping electric light bulbs, especially upon waking when you turn them on is another psychic's characteristic, especially if one is a bit fired up. The initial surge in the filament is enhanced and it simply overheats and melts. I first noticed my interactions with computers when running the English Electric KDF9 at Birmingham Uni.

While at Swanton Morley, I also had a part-time job with BBC TV East with producers Doug Salmon and Michael Cole. We produced a weekly magazine programme entitled, "Weekend" and it did rather well. We won the Royal Television Society's Award for Regional Television and my role as researcher and occasionally director, was to dream up ideas for the programme and get them filmed for the show by the end of the week. Lots of fun!

We did stories on all sorts of wacky stuff and Jane got a weekly spot doing an astrology look-ahead for the coming week with a big round map of the star signs in the sky and the alignments. The first time she was to appear she had stage fright and I had to carry her to the car screaming, "I can't do this, I can't do this!" She did it and brilliantly. One time when in the studio doing her thing, Michael Cole walked in having been watching it on his monitor in the BBC tower block next door. "I've just come down," announced Michael rather obviously, "Never knew you had 'ascended'," quipped Jane.

Also around this time, with Jane's encouragement, I had become involved in alternative medicine and qualified in acupuncture and other techniques including laser therapy. I worked in Norwich and those skills have always stayed with me. I also worked in London, just off Harley Street, Wimpole Street to be precise.

While I was away, Jane and one of my best friends became rather close with their joint interests in horses. The nags were the black hole in my finances; we had eleven at one time in a menagerie of 48 animals that included a cow, two goats, four dogs and many cats, I believe 15 at one time. One neutered tom called Louise was sweet, but 'two sandwiches short of a lunch' and a great source of amusement. One sunny afternoon he was asleep in an apple tree when a sparrow flew into his arms. Louise flapped about and lost the sparrow, but spent the next three weeks in the same tree waiting for that sparrow to return. He would also wait for hours outside a rabbit hole expecting the local population to oblige.

One day in the horses' food store, I noticed a rustling in a horse nut sack. Quietly, I ushered all the cats into the food store with a dish of cat food. Putting the food on a shelf, I gave the sack a huge whack with a stick and up shot a rat like a jack-in-a-box. "Oh! Shit, cats!" thought the rat and did the most amazing high speed circumnavigation of the walls of the room with 14 cats in hot pursuit. The door blew open with the wind and out shot the rat across the stable yard with the pussy posse in pursuit. Louise remained in the middle of the food store looking puzzled. "I am sure that must have been a rat," thought dear Louise. He returned later and sat there for a few days.

Money ran low and we were forced by dint of circumstance to move to a smaller property. Those were the days when you could grab a bargain property. I usually bought them from banks when they were 'distressed', lived in them, did them up and flogged them for a reasonable profit. It was all quite legal and tax-free as it was one's main residence and so long as you did not make too much of a business of it, the taxman didn't complain. Ah! The days of high inflation, good news for some. Always see the advantage, never the downside; glass half-full not half-empty.

After a couple of years, Jane and my chum got quite a bit closer and we parted amicably, but there was a problem. She had these animals to take care of and they were broke, so I went to see a grand local gentleman, Lord Walsingham. Driving up the road that runs across his estate to his stately home, nearly as big as Buckingham Palace, the front mews came into view. His secretary, a retired Army Major greeted me. "His Lordship is in the library. He's expecting you."

There he was, plus fours, not overly tall, the essence of the country gentleman. "Come in, dear boy," greeted Walsingham, "Gather you have a little problem with the lady."

"Yes, Your Lordship," I replied. Explaining the situation and her needs I continued, "I gather you have a few properties redundant to the needs of the estate."

"Indeed I do," replied Walsingham, "Don't want to sell them and they are Victorian farms, no good for modern agriculture. Have to keep sending down the bailiffs to turf out squatters." He moved to a large filing cabinet, opened a draw and rummaged through buff coloured files. Picking out a few he queried, "How many horses has she got?".

"Eleven," I answered.

"Oh, this might do," he beamed. "Not very big, four bedrooms, three receptions, tithe barn, stables, pig buildings; only six acres. Any good?"

"Fantastic Sir, and the......." He cut me short.

"I'd only want a peppercorn rent for it dear boy. Would she give it a lick of paint?"

"Yes, of course, Sir."

"Would four pounds a month be too much?" He was serious.

"Are you sure, Sir?" I was stunned.

"Yes of course. Good to get someone in there."

I drove back down the driveway mentally kicking

myself. It was the early 80s. I had just done the deal of the century and of course I had done it for somebody else. But Jane needed it and I was more capable of paddling my own canoe.

They were there for a few years before my former mate (they were now married Jane and he) fell out with his Lordship and they had to leave. Not the smartest move I thought. However, I helped them buy another smallholding. They were down to one horse by now and had children. Several children.

They sold that eventually and bought a large house in which Jane used her teaching qualification to run a kindergarten. Ironic, as when Jane and I had been together she had said she didn't 'do' children; a wish I respected. Later she went on to open and run also another kindergarten for the royal staff at Sandringham Estate. Another one of my people working for the royals; but more of that later.

While at Swanton Morley I had briefly known one of Prince Charles' helicopter pilots/instructors—this was when he was learning to fly. He told me of many an occasion when Charles and he would swap uniforms prior to landing. The pilot would run head down to the waiting car, jump in and be whisked away, while Charles would slip off unnoticed and disappear for three days much to the anxiety and chagrin of his security people. No one ever got reprimanded for these indiscretions.

This was long before the days of getting Charles married off and being a royal must be a nightmare with all the public focus on one's every move. Later, I was to get to know quite a lot of people around the Royals and the associated discreet, but unspoken, stories that circulate in those realms. Like certain entertaining by Prince Phillip. He was young then and handsome, still is in a way, and as the Queen said, when asked the success of their relationship, she answered, "Tolerance." Say no more.

Moving on. Michael Cole at BBC East was offered promotion, either Foreign Correspondent or Royal Correspondent. As he said to me, "The foreign job is bullets going past your ear." So he elected to take the royal job. Not many a moon later, it was coming up to the Queen's Christmas message when privileged correspondents get given a written early, embargoed, copy of what Her Majesty was going to say, some days prior to the broadcasts. This is so they can formulate their informed comments on the Monarch's thoughts on the day of transmission.

Michael found himself down at the Press Club and a little merry and worse for wear. He unwittingly leaked the speech to his mates present. It made the Sunday Papers prior to transmission and Michael was immediately fired from the Beeb. Not a man to be kept down, he walked down to Harrods and was taken on as their media director by Mohammed Al-Fayed at considerably better pay than at the Beeb. This would be deeply significant, as later he would be the man in front of the cameras, the spokesperson, in 1997 and beyond for that tragic time of the death of Princess Diana and Al Fayed's son, Dodi. More of that later too.

After Jane and I parted, I took up with a new lady, Sandra, who was a school teacher and came with a ready-made family, a boy and a girl aged two and three. We lived in her cottage for a while and then decided to buy a live-aboard boat on the Norfolk Broads, as we weren't sure where we would end up and the boat idea looked flexible.

We purchased a 45ft traditional wooden craft, which afforded the basic comforts of life and kitted it out for family living. It even had a bathroom with a hip bath, central heating, room in the wheelhouse for an electric piano keyboard that Sandra played and a washing machine which ran from an on-board generator. The engine room housed a huge four cylinder Lister diesel engine and the boat was fully operational for river and estuary purposes, but not really man enough for the open sea.

I knew the Chapman family; Colin Chapman the famous founder of Lotus Cars in 1952 which went on to much acclaim in the Formula One racing world. I was an Alternative medicine therapist to the family but I had no connection with the car side of things.

My only connection to motor racing had been back in France when for a couple of weeks, I had assisted the Graham Hill team at Monaco prior to the race. Later while with Jane in Nice in November 1975, Jane had awoken early that morning with the statement, "I've had one of my dreams!" These occurred occasionally in full colour 3D and were always prophetic. She recounted that in the dream she was looking at a light aircraft, coloured red and white, with a GB registration, which was flying in fog and crashing near a golf course.

We were flying back to the UK that day via Nice and Air France so it was decided the dream did not apply to us and we noted it, but could take no action. Upon arriving at Nice airport we were told our flight was delayed, still grounded at Heathrow due to fog and after waiting all day we were offered either to return in the morning or Air France would fly us to Paris and take care of us onward bound.

We jumped at the latter option and upon landing, the rest of the passengers stampeded off the aircraft to try to get included in the remaining available ferry tickets for the channel crossing. The somewhat harassed Air France staff apologised to us as we strolled down to their desk, as all the ferry tickets had gone and they would have to accommodate us at their five-star Meridian Hotel in Paris. We were delighted and having been served a five course dinner and slept in a rather delightful suite next day, we were bussed out to Charles de Gaulle airport where we again waited for fog to clear. We were then put on a cross-channel flight and upon entering the aircraft and taking our seats, Air France had provided copies of the daily papers; in French of course. We both read French.

There on the front page of La Monde, was the headline of the tragic death of Graham Hill who had been killed in an air crash the day before, at a time later than Jane's dream. He had died in a light aircraft, a corporate Piper Aztec, registration N6645Y (GB registration) which had crashed in fog near Arkley Golf course, North London. I was both saddened and stunned by the accuracy of Jane's 'dream'. Such prophecies had happened before and they were to happen again, as time would tell.

Meanwhile to return to the Chapman episode, as one of his business ventures, Colin had moved sideways for a while into designing and building fast motor cruisers called Moonrakers. He had sold these from a marina near Norwich owned by his wife but after the closure of the Moonraker business due to financial problems, the marina fell empty. It had a large steel and concrete overhanging hanger like structure to protect craft and resided in a lovely little offshoot off the River Yare, overseen and protected by a retired

SAS Sergeant, who lived in a waterside cottage on site. Colin was pretty together on security generally.

So we moored our wooden cruiser in the hanger down one end and Colin's two boats, a bright yellow Marauder and a Tango class fast cruiser were down the far end. On fine days we would moor out on the quay nearer the main river to catch the sunlight and enjoy the passing vessels. Near the inlet at that time was a quaint, but then mostly empty, timber-framed period building, which had at one time been a yacht club.

One dark night at about 2am while we were moored on the quay, a white transit van arrived outside the old building and I observed a few young men get out and started breaking into the former club house. What they expected to find I have no idea, perhaps they were looking to squat there. They had already forced their way through the perimeter fence and main gate, which lay out of sight off the main road.

I was by myself this night as Sandra and the family were off visiting friends, so what to do? A light breeze was blowing off the quay so I quietly extended the fore and aft mooring lines of the cruiser and she drifted off some 12 feet from the quay. Muffling the rowlocks of my little rowing boat, I silently rowed over to the warden's cottage on the other side of the dyke and knocked on the sergeant's door. He appeared in his nightshirt. Explaining the situation, we went into military mode, synchronised watches and he asked me if the cruiser had a searchlight.

I rowed back to the cruiser, set the unlit searchlight on the motley crew working on the heavy wooden door of the old clubhouse and waited for the appointed moment. On went the beam. There were the burglars, all lit up, and there was the sergeant some fifteen feet away having crept up on them undetected. He was holding his shotgun, cocked and ready. Don't mess with ex-SAS soldiers is a sound piece of advice.

The leader of the motley crew lunged at the warden, who let off a warning shot into the air. Game over. The police arrived and the night's adventures were concluded.

Chapman was involved back then with the engineering design of the DeLorean sports saloon, which was produced in Northern Ireland. Colin was a canny kind of chap and pretty sharp about business. Being moored in his private marina, I was aware of everything that went on around that location.

Every month or so, one of his executives, a smartly dressed chap, would arrive and board the Tango, moored at the other end of the hanger. Off she went single-handed for what was designated, 'sea trials'. Out through Great Yarmouth where she would have been clocked out by the coastguard station and off into the North Sea and maybe further south. She was registered in Jersey, Channel Islands.

Three days later she would return, moor and off would go the chap with the briefcase. Now, when you live next to boats you get to know them pretty well, every minor scratch, every very minor identification mark. Tango had on her stern, 'Jersey'. The boat that returned also said, 'Tango, Jersey', but it was not the same boat. She was a twin, a clone for sure. No one else would know the switch had occurred and likewise, when she went out a month later the other one would return. There was no explanation of this switching, although the boat was rumoured to be capable of 48 knots, a fair turn of speed in a calm sea. The smart chap was obviously a capable mariner but not dressed for the part— you don't usually go to sea in a suit.

One tragic morning Colin woke up dead. That may sound flippant, but those who knew him would understand my phraseology; he may have been a genius, but he wasn't the easiest of characters. Natural causes; it seems he had a heart attack in his sleep. His wife was, naturally, devastated. He was not that old, only 54, but had been very worried about the ongoing troubles with the DeLorean development. In the ensuing months, it appeared £2-million from those funds were missing. No one knew where it was, not even his wife. It was never found.

I recalled the mysterious trips of the Tangos. Can you get half way to Jersey, rendezvous and return with the other boat? What was going on? I didn't ask. Some things you just don't want to know. Lotus was taken on by new management and did well.

I had borrowed one or two on occasion, they are lovely cars and go round corners just like on rail tracks, although the early ones were small. You did not get in a Lotus; you put it on and drove it virtually lying down. There was no room for luggage. The standing joke was you could not get laid in a Lotus but you would get laid as soon as you stepped out of it. I think the term is 'a chick magnet'.

Sandra enjoyed entertaining and we hosted occasional dinner parties on our little ship. The tidal rise and fall can be quite considerable on certain phases of the Moon and sometimes we would be well down from the quay heading we were moored stern on. We had a gangplank with a smooth surface and side rails. On such occasions, the procedure was for the ladies with their long evening wear to gird up their loins and slide down the steeply-angled gangplank, just like we did at the fair as children. Everyone loved it. Great fun. We thought it should become an Olympic event. By the time the evening was over, the tide would have risen and folk could walk off the boat in a more sedate fashion. All they then had to do was drive home. Happy days.

Life on the river was colourful and often had its moments of drama. We wintered through the low times of the year and had to get down river every two weeks to obtain diesel, petrol for the genny and pump out the sewage from the holding tanks. One cold February morning, the basin and main river were frozen over with ice about a centimetre thick. We still had to get down river but could not just drive through the ice sheet, as it would have sawn off the bottom of the boat. So a cunning plan ensued. Sandra was positioned at the prow of the boat to swing the mud weight ahead of us. This is a large lump of lead, which acts as an anchor on the quiet-running Broads rivers. This would smash the ice sheet. Her son, now old enough to be useful, was positioned with the long boat hook to slide the shattered sheets of ice away from the boat and we made slow but steady progress to the Brundall Marina, our depot for fuel supplies.

On one previous expedition, we had hit the corner of the quay in a strong gust of wind and knocked out a neat square of planking, well above the water line inside the hull. With bilge pumps full on just in case, we had run hard back to our berth ready to beach if necessary to effect repairs but this had not been necessary. The damage was only cosmetic and quickly repaired the same day. Life afloat was never without incident. Sandra learned to iron shirts very quickly before the generator ran out of petrol as it was absolutely forbidden by me to refuel the genny while hot. Many boaters have incinerated themselves with a spill of petrol on a hot genny.

On another winter's morning I awoke to discover the river authority had opened slush gates upstream without telling anyone and with the tidal surge, the river had risen dramatically. The quay was underwater. The car park beyond was well flooded and all that could be seen of my Mercedes 220 was the roof with a sea gull sitting on it. To compound matters, in a temporary moment of panic, I dropped my big bunch of keys over the stern. However, cool thinking prevailed. Keeping my eye firmly on the exact spot where the keys had entered the murky waters, I cut a sighting mark on the top of the starboard sternpost and another to port. Thus I had a fix. Going below I found a large magnet, always useful for recovering tools from obscure places into which they can fall in the bilge of a boat, made up a fishing rod from a bamboo cane, string and the said magnet and went aft.

Sighting carefully from the two fix points I slowly lowered the magnet to the muddy bottom, paused and slowly pulled up the line on the end of the rod. Lo and behold there were the keys stuck firm on the magnet. There is a God, thought I.

When the tide went down the car was still full of water and it poured out of the door when opened. It was of course a complete write-off. Due to lack of funds, the Merc was replaced with an old yellow Ford van. Such is life.

Norwich was not working out financially so the boat

was sold and we moved, as a family, to Kent, Sandra's home territory. We purchased a contemporary house in New Ash Green, a model village designed by the famous architect Eric Lyons. It was totally pedestrian with traffic kept to the outside of its central, greened interior, which also boasted wooded areas.

The house was up for internal modification and was over a year turned into a Japanese-themed home, complete with paper screens and tatami mats. I had always had an attraction to things Japanese from the days of being with Chris and his collection of oriental swords and armour, to say nothing of the philosophy. For a while I became a Buddhist, but felt I was not a very good disciple of the discipline so reverted back to my Christian roots. Spiritual beliefs have always been close to my soul and I still believe in a deep purpose in life and reincarnation.

While at BBC TV in Norwich, I had helped to produce a number of documentaries on such variant matters in which we had interviewed many a witness of the paranormal and unknown. All genuine, ordinary people, who had nothing to gain from their bizarre stories of real-life experiences. Folk, mostly women, while under hypnosis, recalled many details from former lives, obscure items of information they could not have known or researched at a library—the internet did not exist back then.

One lady recalled being a farmer's wife on the Somerset Levels and living in a simple croft-like hut which only had an earthen floor. We worked out that it was around 1646 and even at that time, Glastonbury Abbey was derelict having been sacked by Henry VIII, I believe. The lady recalled, with some shame, having gone with horse and cart to the Abbey at night and stolen paving stones to cover the floor of their simple home, a feature they considered quite a luxury at that time. In the long evenings she was fascinated by the many bizarre cracks and marks on the surfaces of the paving stones and under hypnosis she had drawn these patterns.

We took the good lady back to the Somerset Levels and after much searching about and working from old landmarks, we actually found the hut, now just a chicken house. The owner, a local farmer living in his 1930s farmhouse nearby, insisted it had always been a chicken house, even with his father before him. The floor was deep in compressed chicken litter. We paid him £200 to dig it out. He thought we were mad, but he liked the colour of the money. After a couple of hours his spade made a 'ching' on something hard and sometime later there was the now exposed and cleaned up paving stones. The amazing thing was the cracks and marks on the stones matched exactly what the lady had drawn from her recall under hypnosis of staring at them over 300 years ago!

There was a pattern I noticed in the recall of the witnesses. Those who had calm and natural lives seemed to remember lives a considerable time back, while those with memories of an untimely end appeared to return for another lifetime very quickly.

This was the case with one girl, who recalled being a Polish Jew taken in the Holocaust. First her Father had been picked up by the goon squads, then her brothers and then her. She never saw her father again in that life, but on her death, which she recalled vividly and with much emotion, she was greeted by her father on the 'other side' to which she responded in tears, "Father where did you go?"

Another lady even recalled her name, address, education and occupation in Edinburgh, where she remembered being a man and a doctor. She drew pictures of the Edinburgh Medical School as she recalled it, but interestingly left out the later top floor additions, which were not present in the 19th century. She also drew a floor plan, which was not as it is today. When we consulted the School's archivists, it was discovered that indeed the building was as she had drawn it way back then. These old plans had been in the cellar for years gathering dust. No one had been down there for decades to look at them, so more real evidence that I felt made a good case for the spirit's return. We even found her grave from that time - a very moving experience.

These people from former lives were not figures of distinction. There were no memories of being Cleopatra, Roman Caesars or Napoleon. They were just ordinary people.

I have had strange recall of knowledge myself, that I could not have known. One time I arrived with a friend outside the high walls of a former bastion of the Knights Templar, now bare and gutted other than the silent walls. While still outside, I told my friend that I knew this place and proceeded to describe the interior, the location of the extensive underground stables, the dining hall and the Chapel. I had never been there before in this life. We entered and explored. The layout was exactly as I had said. The place was rambling and ruined. It would not have been possible to predict its layout from some expected standard format.

The New Ash Green house was built on chalk and this material was very easily cut and held its shape so I decided to build a nuclear fallout shelter. Obtaining the services of two Irish navvies who needed work, I set them cutting and excavating a deep square hole in the back garden near a tree. Skip loads of chalk were removed plus a growing mound of useful soil debris piled up in the corner.

New Ash Green is a kind of architectural cultural heritage and strictly governed by dos and don'ts internal planning regulations. The chairman of the local committee appeared at my back gate clutching his planning rulebook. I had already read the book from cover to cover. Thumbing through this small tomb he could find no regulation I was breaching. It was the allotted distance from the neighbour's fence. He thought it was going to be a swimming pool.

Two weeks later it was complete, built to a standard Russian published design, which simply digs a hole or deep trench, covers it with some suitable support and reinstates a metre of soil back over the top. It has no surface wind resistance and soil, especially chalk, is an excellent absorber of radiation. This one was suitably equipped with a steel hatch, a vent system, dry lined and waterproofed and hidden under a new wooden Swiss chalet through which it was entered via a hatch in the floor. 'Hidden in plain sight', as they say. The chairman reappeared at the back gate. His expression was curious, almost complimentary.

"How did you know?" he quizzed. It was late April 1986. Chernobyl nuclear accident had recently happened and a cloud of nuclear fallout was heading towards the UK. My children were playing in the bunker. I wondered too, 'how did I know?' The chairman gave me considerably more respect after that 'coincidence'. Jane, my ex, was not the only one who had informative dreams.

While at New Ash Green I practiced alternative medicine. I was qualified in acupuncture, laser techniques and general neurological muscular therapies, mostly a mixture of physiotherapy and ad hoc osteopathy, which I had picked up from various eminent practitioners over the years. You didn't need to be a member of any of the colleges in those days. I learnt from the people who had taught the college lecturers themselves or brought the techniques back from China.

Only later did the industry load itself down with paperwork and exclusion clauses to do with gaining insurance cover. In those days there were few laws preventing you from getting people well by whatever natural methods seemed appropriate, including diet. I became familiar with various techniques to treat serious terminal illnesses, usually only the domain of orthodox clinicians and pharmaceutical companies who make fortunes out of your maladies.

Sandra produced a daughter, my second now, the first having been by my previous wife. Family life proceeded alongside my Intelligence life, which was low profile and in the background. The work I did for HMG during this time remains sensitive and classified so I cannot divulge those details at this time.

While at New Ash Green, some 'kind souls' burnt down the local school. I was washing in the bathroom upstairs when through the frosted glass I perceived flames some several hundred yards away over the village green. A hurried but precise 999 call to the local fire service sent, I jumped in my car and tore over to the school with lights blazing and hazards on. I don't take prisoners when duty calls.

A police panda car was already there and had couple of teenagers inside who had apparently entered the school to try to 'put out' the fire, so they said. There was little to be done. The school built of beautiful pitch pine surrounding a central pyramid burnt with a vengeance. The whole village assembled to watch in stunned silence. I started an investigation immediately and began to collect whatever forensic evidence was available. I had a stand up row with the local police inspector who turned up and seemed pretty ineffectual, about as useless as a pogo stick in a swamp, and I made a real nuisance of myself with visits to the local CID over the next three weeks as the case developed with me and my 'mates' gathering more evidence as it came to light.

Finally, the local CID sergeant ordered us off the case. "Look Peter, we've got murders and rapes to solve. There is just no time to deal with your arson case just because it was your school, mate!"

They used the British secret weapon: the filing cabinet. Give it a crime number, put it in the draw and forget about it. I was furious! I started a restoration fund and raised over £10,000 for books and so on. The building was of course insured by the county, but it was never the same again. We decided to leave the village and looked for a new project.

After much searching, the new project turned out to be The Manor. Built in 1491 as a Tudor, three-bay, hall house it had two wings, several outbuildings and a commanding view. I brought together a small group of supporters and restoration commenced to turn it into everything we believed in for natural health and co-operative living.

It also had other purposes, as it would be a low-profile retreat for various theatrical and political figures. They would arrive often with their 'secretaries' or personal assistants for a very discreet weekend indeed. We were known to be 'on side' so everyone was secure. It took a lot to run and keep it together, but we eventually ran out of working capital in the late 80s, when it had to close down. We were all devastated.

I had tried to keep it together until the very last moment, but it was a hopeless case. The UK was going through one of those periodic economic downturns and the banks were hauling in their money, running scared. Fair-weather friends, banks, I find.

The Manor had quite a heritage, having been built in 1491 as a house with royal associations. It had been besieged by General Fairfax in the English Civil War and we came across musket shot and two cannon balls in the old roof space in the course of the restoration. It was Royalist and had been defended by 150 men against a besieging army of over 3000. It eventually fell, but retained a definite feeling of not wanting to go outside its fortified perimeter walls. The women of the house all felt this and some said it was haunted in the oldest timber-framed rooms.

The financial stresses at the end of the 80s took a toll on my relationship with Sandra and sadly, in we split up. I found a house for her nearby and we remained firm friends, even to this day. I'm proud to say that all of my children both genetic and by marriage get on very well, something that makes me extremely happy.

The liquidation and accompanying administration of the Manor took its toll on my health but eventually it was sold, which was a huge relief. Recovery took some time but this was made easier by a new relationship.

Annie was a fellow alternative practitioner, a very supportive woman and we soon fell in love. She was from an old military family with Norman and French ancestry, the second blue-blood I married. Jane, my second wife, was related to Lord Lister of medical fame. Annie can trace her ancestry back to the aide-de-camp of William the Conqueror at the Battle of Hastings and although we described ourselves as the nouveau-pauvre, the French side of the family had extensive holdings in Normandy.

The English decedents had come to England during the French Revolution, saved by their servants whom they had treated very well and that side of the family has remained firmly English and Royalist to this day. Annie and I could never enter a rational discussion on the English Civil War or Oliver Cromwell, whom she—maybe correctly—saw as barbaric in his governance of England and the Irish, which rumbled on for centuries into recent times of 'The Troubles' in Northern Ireland.

The Troubles caused the premature death of her brother, Simon, a sergeant in the Royal Fusiliers, who had been involved with Signals, a coded term, I am sure you all know. He was murdered on active duty by the IRA, which devastated the family. His memory is fondly remembered and Annie and her family remain connected to and respected by the Regiment, attending various annual commemorations at the invitation of their senior command. The family was awarded The Queen Elizabeth Medal for their loss and a signed scroll from Her Majesty was added to the military history of the family.

Annie's father had been an RAF Squadron Leader in World War II, until an ear infection had grounded him. Having lost all of his school chums in the Battle of Britain, John had joined Bomb Disposal and was known to have taken consignments of weeping jelly in the pannier bags of his RAF motorcycle over land to be disposed of on desolate Norfolk beaches. Despite all of his apparent hell-raising and dangerous endeavours he survived the war, otherwise Annie would not be here. For those not familiar, 'weeping jelly' is an eroded very volatile explosive, which can easily be set off by shock or vibration.

Although you can never replace a loved one, I think in some respects, I had stepped into Simon's shoes as I was now Annie's support, her 'rock,' and we even almost shared a birthday by year and month but for a few days. Although I have never actually been a member of the British Army, I have had several friends and mates in that fine service. My endeavours to secure the peace remained more in the shadows, as only time would tell. For the record, I only went to Dublin once and that was nothing to do with the IRA but a technical assignment. I like the Southern Irish; very real people and with a fine sense of humour.

The first time I got really ill was in 1988 while living at The Manor. I woke up one morning with the whole world spinning and my vision was badly affected. It was very frightening with tunnel vision and nearly blind in my left eye. I could hardly crawl from my bed to the en-suite bathroom. I was in this state for some weeks. I consulted private physicians but no one had any bright ideas. Some said part of my brain was inflamed but they were guessing. Medical science was not so advanced in those days. It wasn't until a full eight years later that I was eventually diagnosed with a form of Multiple Sclerosis, which has continued to flare up every so often depending on stress, exertion and particularly air temperature. I didn't mention it to HMG, that goes without saying.

It was just another nail in the coffin of closing down the Manor. It was all getting too much for me to cope with and although I slowly became stable and my vision returned, I was very shaken by it. So I was more than ready when an opportunity to travel a bit more and get away from the grey English weather beckoned.

That same weather had just recently killed my father who caught pneumonia while fixing a broken fence in his back garden. He was 86. One of my anchors had gone. My mother went into a home as she could not cope alone, even with private care nursing. I never saw her again.

5. Undercover Endeavours

OVER THE DITCH

1989 was my first overseas assignment for HMG to the United States. I had previously had some contact with US intelligence through Hans and at that time had made a significant contribution to PsyOps technology, for which I had been awarded an Honorary Ph.D. from the New York Inst. Of Technology where Hans was an Associate Professor of Technology. My work was classified and still remains so, however it had forged a level of Transatlantic trust.

So I headed to southern States of the USA and took with me Annie, who hadn't been to the States before and her youngest son, the older ones now having flown the nest.

Florida was the point of focus and the concern was the progressive takeover of the drugs trade by the Russians, who were taking full advantage of their newfound ability for global travel to bring to bear their dubious skills in various regions. In this case it was the one formerly dominated by Haitian drug dealers. They say, and it was true, that if a Haitian dealer wanted to take over the neighbouring territory, his gang might make a visit to his compatriot with the message, "You give me your patch or I kill you!"

The Russian technique was a little more convincing. The conversation would go, I'm told, "You give us your patch or we let you live but we kill your mother, wife and children!" This tended to get business done and the Russian mafia progressively took over Miami and worked their way north up the Atlantic coast, through Fort Lauderdale and Pompano Beach.

I bought a lovely five-bedroomed ranch house and moved in with my very British antique furniture. Next day there was a knock at the door. I opened it and looked around, then looked down. There stood Shana. Blonde, newly arrived from California in a little red dress and all pure woman but only four years old. She had parked her bright red, electric, model Porsche on the drive out front.

"Do you have kids?" she demanded.

"Yes," I responded, "My youngest son is six-years-old!"

Shana walked under my arm without invitation and looked, gobsmacked, around the house.

"You have very weird stuff!" she declared.

I spent a few tours working that coastline and ended up in Palm Springs. There was not a lot of opportunity to learn much. The Russians used mostly Romanian 'foot soldiers' to do their field work and stayed out of range in their villas around the swimming pool drinking vodka so if anyone got busted, more poor dudes could be drafted into the front line while the bosses remained protected behind their 'firewall'. Any leaks would be eliminated, as was standard Russian protocol.

I only got as far as the front line and then was prudently backed off, otherwise I, too, may have been given concrete boots and asked to feed the sharks. I was very alarmed at how common the use of cocaine was in Florida, even by normal business people you came across. They didn't seem to be able to get though their high pressure days without it.

I did put some downward pressure on a low-level dealer, who ran a hair dressing salon as part of a front for trading, but was then leaned on by US agents. Apparently they had an interest in this dealer too and I was getting too close for comfort. That darned Limey was sticking his nose in where it was not welcomed!

As formerly with the home-grown mafia, it appeared the Russians were getting more and more involved with legitimate businesses and putting down roots. This had been the case with quite a few 'hoods' over many decades in the Sunshine State.

We resided for a while in my pleasant ranch house in an upmarket precinct. One day, while moving a piece of furniture, I inadvertently set off one of the panic buttons, which are little hair-trigger switches concealed under dado rails and such like, for you to call assistance. All hell broke loose. Security lights blazed on, deafening alarms sounded and I could hear the telephone automatically dialling the local swat squad. In near panic, I stared at the array of flashing lights on the security panel, not knowing the correct code sequence to shut it down.

There was a knock at the door. There stood a diminutive sun-bronzed fellow in his late sixties, white hair, smiling, no shirt and in sandals and shorts. "Hi," said the little man, "I'm Jo. I know what you have done. I installed this system." So in came Jo and switched off the alarms, called the cops to say false alarm and peace returned.

The next day, I recounted the story to my near neighbour on the other side of the house. "Oh! Jo. Yes, he's retired. Used to be a big mafia boss in Chicago. Ran the meat trade up there. He does all the security around here."

Apparently Florida had a policy that, if you keep your nose clean in the retirement state, they really don't want to know where you came from. Jo was a perfect example of this. "They say he's killed over 30 people," volunteered my neighbour. "No hoods will break into anywhere down this street, not with Jo being here. They wouldn't live long. Jo's friends would pay them a visit!"

The Sunshine State was full of old people, many of them from New York. Large, not so young, Lincoln cars would crawl down the street with little old ladies peering over the steering wheel. At the supermarket they would emerge and totter into the air-conditioned interiors, which were often too cold for comfort after the heat outside. I was sure their white stick was on the rear seat of the limo. Women tend to outlive their husbands down there and there was a healthy market for fresh husbands, as the ratio of women far outweighed the men. I was several times chatted up seriously by good-looking well-turned out 70-somethings.

"Go on go for it" said my mates, "She's on the hunt and she's loaded!" I never did. I was not that desperate!

One night a mate of mine invited me over. I arrived on foot. He was an ex-NYPD homicide cop and now had a job working for a funeral director, driving a hearse. "My car's at work," explained my friend, "I only have the meat-wagon outside. I have to drive it upstate first thing in the morning."

"Is it loaded?" I enquired.

"Oh yes. Don't worry, I never have any trouble with the stiffs", exclaimed my friend. So off we went for a drink, driving this luxurious garnet coloured Cadillac hearse complete with silent company in the back. Every car gave way to us; even cops stopped and beckoned us through. Respect, I thought.

We pulled into a quiet 24-hour gas station for some fuel. The gas station attendant from Puerto Rico turned white and started crossing himself. "Oh! This is so unlucky," he bemoaned, virtually hiding behind the counter. We gassed up, paid and left. He was still shaking as we pulled away. I resolved that I would either buy an ambulance or a hearse if I needed to get through traffic.

While in Florida, we did the usual compulsory things like going to Disney World and discovered it was a very bad idea on a summer's day as the heat and humidity were unbearable. You certainly knew you were in a tropical part of the world, which sometimes became apparent in humorous ways. One day outside in the middle of the street where we had taken a house for a short time, there was a huge 10-feet long alligator, just lying there sunning himself. The local law was informed and lo and behold, along came the regular croc catching crew, complete with poles with loops to catch and secure the croc's snout and a big cage to put him in. It took four strong men to lift the croc onto the back of the truck in his cage. He would be transported back to the Everglades from where he had just emerged.

The other real pain in that neck of the woods were the mosquitos. Venomous little buggers who flew around in squadrons looking for human blood, especially at night. You learnt quickly to use protective nets on the windows and doors and not to venture near any swamps at dusk, their favourite hunting time and place to lay their eggs in shallow water. One also had to avoid the stinging jelly-fish in quiet lagoons.

One day, I was standing on the beach just a foot deep in the soft surf, up to below my knees; the little colourful fish nibbling at my toes when a great shoal of their kin rushed towards me some of them jumping out of the water. The reason for this soon became apparent. Right behind came two triangular blue-grey fins. I froze instinctively. I was too far in to run and predators usually go for moving objects, so I just thought 'rock'; I am just a rock. The two three-feet long reef sharks shot past me in their pursuit of their lunch and as soon as they were a good few feet away I legged it back onto the safety of dry land.

Walking back up the beach, I mentioned it to the bronzed lifeguard sitting under his umbrella in his little observation perch. "Oh, yeah," he exclaimed, "People get chunks taken out of them all the time!" I bet they don't put that in the travel brochures, I thought. Neither do they mention the red ants, which can infest the grass and are highly defensive of their territory to say the least. You don't mess with them either. Florida was fun, great on a mid-winter's day to wander down the beach in British summer temperatures, but a nightmare in the summer – just don't go there.

Money was getting tight again, so we sold the ranch house. A short time later, a major, grade-four hurricane went through there and pretty much totalled the place. Angels on my shoulders again. I missed having the swimming pool, but not the expense to maintain it.

So back in the UK again, pretty much broke on funds and with two boys to bring up, step children and another on the way, to be our only child together. I had lent another agent my company credit card in the States and he had racked up over $7,000 having a good time in Texas, which didn't help. I sold some antiques, couple of family pictures and soldiered on supporting the family any which way.

I got ill again and that was not helpful either, but it brought me back into my interest in alternative medicine as I researched ways of getting better in the course of which, and unrelated to my own MS condition, diagnosed finally in 1996, I came across some amazing new cancer treatments from Sweden.

These had been tried and tested for several years, had no contraindications, no side effects and were totally safe, unless you had a heart pacemaker as they used TENS electric techniques. The breast cancer treatments were particularly successful and involved a Teflon coated acupuncture needle with just the handle and tip exposed to be inserted into the tumour, which of course one had to have located accurately beforehand. Then a ring of bare cathode needles are inserted around the tumour at some short distance, a centimetre or two. This was all wired up to three 12-

volt car batteries in series, giving just 30 six-volts, moderated by a rheostat and connected to the needles. Anode into the tumour, cathode earths around the outside. The voltage would be slowly brought up to 36 volts, kept stable for 20 minutes, while a little gas bubbled out from the needle entry points. End of story. Three treatments and the tumours would be dead, calcified and not spread to other body parts.

Thrilled with this breakthrough, I made a couple of simple explanatory videos and tried to bring it to the UK. The police raided my house some months later. My wife was in the bath, my new child, just a toddler, was crawling around naked and I was 30 miles away in Tunbridge Wells. Without me there, a WPC the two CID officers interviewed my wet and bewildered wife, clad only in a towel on the lounge sofa. She phoned me and I spoke to the officers and made an appointment to see them at the local nick the following morning.

My church curate, who lived next door, had witnessed the 'raid' and volunteered to come down with me. Always helps to present yourself at the local police station backed up by the clergy. Amusingly, he knew the police sergeant and ticked him off about the events of yesterday. In the meantime, my wife's father, ex-squadron leader RAF, had phoned the chief constable and complained of Gestapo-like procedures of his officers. They were on their back foot when I arrived in the morning.

Moving into the interview room and switching on two tape recorders, they started in with their questions, but were just a little surprised when I read them their rights and informed them that the interview would be conducted within the protocol of 'General Orders', the working procedures of the Police.

It took all day to go through their issues, which mainly centred around that I didn't have a formal medical degree and cancer must only be treated by 'medical professionals'. I quickly detected that this lucrative trade in potentially terminal illness was the sole territory of the pharmaceutical big boys. I was obviously threatening their accounting bottom line and the simple process of healing folk at low cost and time-effectively, was not their objective at all. Oh, no! Much too much money to be made with dependent long-term patients in tow. If thousands died in the process no matter, the important thing was making money both in sales and 'research' for which many lab rabbits had paid the price too.

At the end of the day at the police station, it was obvious I had broken no laws and the two CID chaps looked at each other, turned off the tape recorders and apologised for the intrusion on my family and privacy.

"Look", said the senior of the two, "We want you to know it was not our initiative to visit you. The word came down that we had to raid you. You've made some powerful enemies and they'll be after you unless you give it up."

It was not the first time I was to realise the corporate powers that be, the serious money, has a lot of influence on the authorities and can call the shots when they feel threatened financially. I had to give up the research, as have others who also found other simple treatments for the big 'C'. In Switzerland and France let alone the UK, the business of the dying continued unaffected and profits continued to rise without interruption. About £90,000 per annum for big 'C' patients.

It also caught the attention of a consumer TV programme, which misrepresented the facts in a major way. I offered to appear on the programme live in studio, but strangely this was never taken up. Can't let the facts stand in the way of a good story!

So back to a focus on the Intelligence world, spying and checking out targets tasked by Special Branch who I had worked with for some time. This did not just confine itself to national security, but also masqueraded as keeping the peace.

In fact, I felt that at times, it followed the same protection of corporate interests that I had detected was the motive for shutting down my off-message cancer research. Targets included animal rights activists, anti-nuclear protesters, union members and many others including some MPs. I tried to take an ethical stance on this work, declining politely any unethical missions, but still being very onside to investigations where foreign agencies might have planted sleepers in otherwise environmentally conscious group working with good intentions. This had often been done before as the record showed and these sleepers would remain under cover unknown to their fellow activists.

Big Brother's need to know was always insatiable. The Special Branch boys themselves never knew where their data ended up; they were just tasked to find out all the details as tasked from on high. They themselves were not sure where 'on high' was.

The system was compartmentalised so orders would come down, operations would be planned and set in train. Handlers would elicit informers and people like me would be set up to infiltrate the target groups. This involved taking on pseudo-identities with acceptable backgrounds to the target group or individual. One dressed, spoke, acted in mirror image of the style of the group in question, and this could last for months as good data takes time to collect. It cannot be rushed, as the urgency to pry would flag up that something was amiss.

I was an excellent candidate for this intrusive undercover work. I had long hair, dressed a bit unconventionally and I was already the author of two very successful fringe books on the paranormal and UFOs. So I was readily accepted in circles where I already had connections and knowledge. I never wrote up anything other than the simple facts; I had been schooled in that by my publishers at Granada who had a doctrine of, "The facts, the facts and nothing but the facts".

When I could, I wrote well of people, moderating the insinuations that were being thrown at them behind their backs. It seemed to me on occasions, that when certain of the 'powers that be' wanted someone or some group taken down, they would go looking for dirt, misdemeanours or anything that could be used in a suitable character assassination or negative PR to isolate them and alienate the general public from their views.

The media would also get involved and be used for a 'set them up and shoot them down' documentary. These were more in the days prior to the Internet, when if it was on TV, then it had to be true. The public had a kind of blind faith in television reporting back then. The goggle box was 'all powerful'.

I remember in the course of trying to promote one group's objectives, I was invited to attend a meeting with a sympathetic Peer of the realm at the House of

Lords, which is the unelected part of the Houses of Parliament where members are appointed or, in those days, could still inherit a seat from an aristocratic relative (this changed in 1999).

Having been given the tour of the House and sat through some very boring dissertation from one of the aged clergy members, our small party was invited into the inner sanctum of the Lord's tea rooms. The scene was a little surreal.

Venerable members sat discussing the business of the day and reading The Times. But amongst them, several members were accompanied by attractive 'ladies' who – and I could, of course be mistaken - were just a little too made up, revealingly dressed and brash to be their wives. The venerable fellows obviously took their work and pleasures seriously on their trips to town. After all, as Lord Manchester had said when challenged in the House by Oliver Cromwell, "If one cannot take advantage of being in Parliament, what is the point of being here?" Nothing changes much.

I have met many influential people over the years including one of the NASA astronauts, Edgar Mitchell, who landed on our Moon. We had worked together for a short while and I had access to an office next to his. They did indeed go to the Moon, contrary to the conspiracy theory that they did not. All his teeth had been broken off and filed down to the roots so that none of the astronauts had any possibility of dental problems on the journey. His teeth were giving him trouble some years later due to that and he would sit for hours at his VDU playing solitaire. He has made a bit of a comeback since those days when he was very much out in the cold having come out publically against 'Star Wars' defence systems, which was definitely off message to the establishment at that time.

Conspiracy theorists have also picked up on lighting anomalies on the Moon photographs but that was easily explained. Most of those shots were done in studio on the Earth before they went up. NASA knew that the background radiation in space would fog the film and one of the main objectives of their Moon expeditions was US PR to be seen to keep ahead of the Russians. Good clear photos would be essential to wow the world so a complete look-alike dossier of snaps was put on file to be released at the appropriate moment as alleged to have been shot in live footage from the Moon. The Hollywood boys did too good a job in their perfect framing and infill lighting, so that many years later they were detected as fakes. Never let the truth stand in the way of a good story.

Ed, said many of the astronauts had cracked up on their return. As he said, "We were only test pilots, we were not ready for what happened out there!"

He related how, while asleep, astronauts would find they had out-of-body experiences visiting unseen, their families back on Earth. In later conversations with their wives they realised that their experiences were not just dreams, but real time fly-on-the-wall observations. Some had come back with enhanced psychic powers, which were never spoken of, as it would get them grounded. Some of them had either 'got God' or become alcoholics or had mental problems. God was hard to take when you came face to face with him, so to speak, in the majesty of being out in space.

I summed it up on the final page of my 1980's book *UFO-UK* when I quoted Archibald McNeish, writing in The New York Times on the occasion of man's first landing on the Moon on 20 July 1969: -

"For the first time in all of time,
Men have seen the Earth.
Seen it not as continents or oceans,
From the little distance of a hundred miles or two or three.
But seen it from the depths of space.
The medieval notion of the Earth, Put man at the centre of everything.
The nuclear notion of the Earth put him nowhere.
Beyond the range of reason and lost in absurdity and war.
This latest notion may have other consequences,
It may re-make our image of mankind,
No longer that victim off at the margins of reality
And no longer that preposterous figure at the centre.
To see the Earth as it truly is,
Is to see ourselves as riders on the Earth together.
Brothers who know now the truth of this!"

Ed Mitchell died at the age of 85 on the 4 February 2016. Now that he has passed, I can reveal that he did confirm to me that they were accompanied on their journey and observed on the lunar surface by UFO craft on the other side of the crater. Two, in fact, quite large craft, but they could not say exactly the dimensions as it is quite difficult to gauge land distances on the Moon in that unfamiliar environment and stark terrain.

Around this time, I was contacted by a media guy called Gary. He wanted me to write a 'factional' (a mix of fact and fiction) account-come-film-script based on the true stories contained in my *The Welsh Triangle* book. So over a few months a script with a working title of *Abduction* was created.

Gary tried getting it funded but with little success. Another script by Clive Harold, a Fleet Street hack, had already been written and he was trying to get it filmed at Pinewood Studios. It was based on Clive's book *The Uninvited*, which was indeed faction—more towards fiction. In his book, I appeared as a character under the name of "Paul Palmer". I had never actually used this pseudonym in the field, but it was obvious to anyone who read the story that it referred to "Peter Paget" which was indeed my 'avatar' for field operations in West Wales and the UFO scene.

I never heard of Clive again but rumour had it that he had got on the wrong side of the security forces and had sort of disappeared. I had to stop the Pinewood film dead in its tracks as it impacted directly on my copyright of *The Welsh Triangle* and any film that might emerge from those stories. *The Uninvited* was plagiarism and they knew it. The proposed film did not proceed. Neither did the *Abduction* script, but that was not the full story, which could not be told at that time. Perhaps now or later that may be remedied.

Out of the hiatus of the failure to bring the breast cancer cure to the UK, we were all getting a bit fed up with the media circus and moved to Devon where I had childhood roots.

The house I rented was a Victorian converted stone barn set atop the high cliffs of Bigbury Bay overlooking the picturesque Burgh Island. This was a magical place and with much literary history as Agatha Christie had written *Evil Under The Sun* there, based on the mysterious island that's only connected to the mainland at low tide by a sand causeway.

Later during our few years there they filmed a television version of Evil *Under The Sun,* with the indomitable David Suchet playing Hercule Poirot. It was claimed that he never came out of character while on the set, even when eating his lunch; a true professional. I never met him, but we enjoyed seeing the filming from the cliff tops and the little sailing dingy with the red sails. Agatha Christie lived in Devon during her writing years in a lovely house overlooking the River Dart. I knew it as a child.

From my Intelligence connections, I was recruited into the Customs & Excise 'Coastwatch' scheme. This was a plan to cover every single inch of coastline of the United Kingdom with volunteer observers, who would report suspicious maritime activity to the Customs and Excise Intelligence Unit. This was heralded by the Government of the day as being a central plank in their defence of the UK borders from smuggling.

They did not mention that at the same time, they had cut the budget allocation, which meant there was in fact, only one Intelligence officer working out of Bristol to cover the whole of the South West. There were their four customs cutters based in Plymouth, but these had to cover the whole of the seas surrounding the British coastline and at any one time, perhaps two of them would be in for maintenance.

Hence, the only really successful operations they actually undertook were when overseas field intel had already briefed them that a particular yacht laden with a drugs haul had just set sail from North Africa for the UK. All they had to do would be intercept it as it approached the English coastline laden with drugs and claim they had picked up the intruder while on patrol.

The standard method of getting lots of drugs ashore was by a Spanish fishing vessel dropping off a load, suitably waterproofed. It would be weighted to be submerged underwater by some fifteen feet, atop of which was a fishing buoy equipped with a low-powered radio homing beacon. Thus, the fishing boat never had to stop, which might have been picked up on local coastal shipping radar. Later a British boat would go out knowing the general drop area, listen for the homing signal, and pick up the haul while again still on the move. This was a known technique to Customs and Excise and us observers were front line in detecting suspicious activity.

These plans went awry if there was a storm during the gap between the drop off and pick up, when likely the load would break loose and get washed up on a deserted beach. Quite a few such loads got discovered this way.

Annie and I used to walk the beaches on a regular basis collecting sea-eroded driftwood, which my wife crafted into picture frames and mirrors. I have never done drugs or even smoked, so I assure you there was no gain in anything found. But we did enjoy collecting all kinds of sea shells and treasures of the sea which works its own art into anything that has been adrift for some time, even the odd coconut nut, maybe from some Caribbean island. We never found any messages in bottles though, we did occasionally find dead dolphins that had sadly been caught in fishing nets, drowned and then chucked overboard by fishermen.

Back in the 60s, the US Navy in California used to train dolphins to take magnetic mines and stick them on the side of enemy subs. How they knew who the enemy was is a bit of a mystery, even if their brains are bigger than ours. But their loyalty was ensured to return to their trainers as they were regularly injected with heroin so they had to come back for their fix. I am glad to say the practice stopped some years ago; antisubmarine warfare moved more into the electronic era and dolphins were no longer needed.

There were often pods of Dolphins in Bigbury Bay, South Devon, during the spring, always led by a dominant female. They are a matriarchal society, as it's believed were human prehistoric societies, but now we are patriarchal. You can debate for better or for worse. I know what I think, but then again I often feel I am not living in my natural comfort time period. Politicians might argue the modern day rights of men and women are, and maybe should be equal in our modern times. In their dreams, the body politic often subscribes to popular myths. Gets votes. Why should women settle for equality when they know they are superior beings – bloody obvious I would think!

It was the mid 90s and my intelligence work was becoming more demanding. Since the first Gulf War in 1990/91, our enemies had been far more active. The hostilities had created dissident groups all over the place and we now had far more to worry about than before.

Home-grown terrorists were popping up all over, from the hardened professionals to the rank amateurs who were far more dangerous, as they were mainly off-radar to the security agencies.

I was handling a number of agents in the orbit of the London mosques. These agents would mingle and merge in the prayer meetings and, being undercover and in a suitable mode to be one of the younger band of followers, they along with the congregation in general would be plied with very inflammatory leaflets encouraging uprisings and forming cells in effect to undertake the causes of Allah. Regretfully the 'average' Muslim, who is peace loving and obedient to the Koran, was being made to feel that they were not true believers if they did not subscribe to the extremist elements who were, and still are, very active.

These extreme elements have the desire to expand the coverage of the faith to as many countries as possible and to strengthen the its representation in any country where they already have a foothold. This is not multi-nationalism, this is an intent to completely take over, even to the extent of some thinking they can turn the UK into a Muslim State under Sharia Law.

I have the greatest respect for all religious beliefs, but when anyone thinks they are right over all others, trouble usually follows. One has to say Christianity is just as guilty of this as history shows, but it is an out of date concept now and is just another kind of colonialism, same meat and veg, different gravy.

Sadly, many of the hostilities worldwide where we have become involved, sometimes unwisely, have fostered quite a strong anti-Muslim feeling in certain areas of the military. This is not politically correct to mention, however it is a fact, now and over the past 24 years. I will tell you some of the reasons why later, but I am only reporting the facts, unfortunate as they may be.

It has also served politicians to foster this, using the well- known 'sheep dog' effect. It used to be the Reds, the USSR, the yellow peril, Libya, North Korea, and now the Russians again or such general groups like, Wall Street, the Establishment, the Bilderbergers or the Illuminati. While people can be encouraged to use these clichés, they can be diverted from seeking the real facts or trying to understand them.

The function of Special Branch was to keep an eye on any elements that might become a threat to the Government or the people of the United Kingdom. It used to be called the Irish Special Branch and emerged out of the early days of Troubles in Northern Ireland. Then its work became more general and focused more on anti-establishment personalities, such as Arthur Scargill, who led the miners' strike, and others of his ilk. Arthur had a Special Branch informant alongside him much of the time during the strikes and in the Maggie Thatcher days.

Maggie herself was not averse to the odd masterstroke in political strategy using the events of the day. In the Falklands War for example, the captain of the nuclear-hunter killer submarine HMS Conqueror, was tracking the General Belgrano, (formerly the USS Phoenix sold to Argentina by the USA in 1951). The British Navy captain wired for instructions to the Admiralty as the Argentine ship sailed away from the combat zone, as she was getting low on fuel. The matter was referred to Maggie who gave the order to sink it. Such flag-waving exercises are helpful in rallying the nation and winning elections.

When I was working, 'tasked', as they say, by Special Branch, they were always quite interested in any dirt that could be found on target subjects. This included marital problems, affairs, sexual peculiarities, political connections and who people knew and hung out with.

This was no different to the KGB in Russia who had buildings full of files on citizens who might be described as 'persons of interest'. That all came out after the old USSR became more liberal and devolved into the many independent states that exist now. It's a state of affairs that is far more complicated than before, as in the days of the USSR, there was one central command and you knew who the enemy was. Now there are many different regimes with their on individual policies.

For example, Ukraine selling four of its old Soviet nuclear warheads to Iran – they never did have their own production capacity and are unlikely to get one. In an internal, tactical coup-de-grâce, the CIA managed to buy them back and they are now 'neutralised'. Iran needed the money more than the hardware and we are talking serious money.

The CIA has a general policy that everyone has their price and they have been buying the 'loyalty' of many states and warlords in various parts of the world for decades. They are probably right.

6. Things get serious

WAR AND RUMOURS OF WAR

Apart from working for Special Branch, I was also working directly for GCHQ although that came via Special Branch, however I was sending data, reports and material directly into the director's office and speaking via telephone with his personal assistants.

This had started as, in the course of my infiltrations, I had picked up that 'Q' as GCHQ is known, was a prime target for a whole bunch of people. This included activists, various 'enemies' and also the just plain curious. If you make something 'secret' it has a magnetic attraction to many folk wishing to get in there and read that rare and mysterious stuff. Much of Q's work is mundane, bordering on boring and often sub-contracted from the National Security Agency (NSA), which makes a considerable contribution to the budget of the establishment.

Unlike MI6, which is almost a law unto itself and

often sees no reason to be solely on side to the British people, Q was kind of more administrative in its approach to its work. Said by one to be a remarkable establishment staffed by unremarkable people. Well you don't expect much imagination from computer super-geeks do you? I studied for a Degree in Computer Science, but when at Birmingham (red brick) University, I found Ph.Ds. in that department knew a great deal about very little. No common sense but they were Maths whizz-kids when it came to that abstract stuff. However, the real world was often a mystery to them that existed on a galaxy far, far away.

One of the problems at Q was, because their work was 'secret' and highly compartmentalised, it never let the left hand know what the right hand is doing so staff got bored and sometimes liked to tell people, wink, wink, nudge, nudge, what they were doing. There was also quite a bit of internal discontent with certain chaps leaking stuff almost bordering on treason. It was difficult to analyse why. Were they anti-establishment? Gone over to the other side (whatever side that was)? Or were they just plain making their personal bit of knowledge public to show how clever they were and their super-secret status?

I was tasked to mingle socially and at union meetings, get to know people and report back. Much of it was of no matter. There was some talk of the "number stations", an old system that transmitted streams of numbers worldwide, which they claimed contained somewhere in their data streams messages for agents in foreign parts. It sounded as about exciting as invisible ink. This was before the current Internet world of the hacker and super, supergeek. Remember, my Birmingham KDF 9 computer was only about third generation after Bletchley, while Q in its old buildings, a jumble of concrete and temporary accommodation, was only approximately fifth generation depending on how you calculate it.

But sometimes there was more interesting stuff. Some members of staff had been 'bumped', a term for 'deliberately run into' by inquisitors, who would strike up a 'friendly' relationship and see what came across.

One supervisor had allegedly leaked nuclear launch codes. I have to say this could have been misinformation or part of a sting that I did not have access to in my compartment. However, the enemy in question, Iraqi Intelligence, bought into it and was rather excited about their inside track.

This data had come to me second hand via a curious little fellow who made a career of trying to know what was going on at Q, even to the extent of automatically monitoring all their UHF gate security comms. Even when he was at work, his RF system would be beavering away recording all this stuff which yielded names, places and such like. As they say, you have to kiss a lot of toads, but there is gold in them there hills.

Through another of their sub-contracting agents, Iraqi Intelligence had hatched a plan. This other chap was working on a mass activists' incursion into the underground nuclear command centre underneath Salisbury Plain. I won't actually say where it is for protocol reasons. Obviously the Russians knew all along, but they don't like too much attention and with all the subterfuge around entrances disguised as farmhouses etc., it would be a shame to blow their gaff.

However, this chap had gained access on a number of occasions and also claimed to have identified the location of the facility's own private nuclear power plant, which was, so he said, the same as on a nuclear sub. The plan was to get together about 200 dedicated peace activists and storm the place by *force majeure*. This was ideal for the Iraqis, they hoped, to place their people within this activist group and gain access to the control room.

Armed with the data of the launch codes from the 'leaked' information from the Q staff member, they had this 'wild and evil' plan to try to re- programme the target instructions, send out a false DEFCON One, as the Yanks would call it, and flight the birds away to wreak havoc on unsuspecting victims in the NATO States which they blamed totally for the Gulf War.

Over some months, I managed to destabilise the internal equilibrium within the UK and French elements of the group and sow mistrust and discontent. The rumour now, was that it was all a sting and the chap getting the activists together for the incursion was in fact a double-agent. Maybe he was. No matter. It didn't come together and it did not happen, which was the only thing that mattered. A non-result was a success in our tasks as far as we were concerned.

However, the devils did not go away and a second plan was hatched. This involved leaked information, also from Q, that British nuclear ordinance was routinely transported overland in a low-profile convoy from the Navy bases at Plymouth & Scotland. It was bound for the service facility near Aldermaston in Berkshire for upgrading and checking, as the nuclear fuse material 'goes off the boil', so to speak, over time and has to be replaced.

The plan was to intercept one of these movements and, armed with conventional explosives, to blow up as many of the items of hardware as possible and create a dirty bomb blast. It would not have been possible to get the nukes to go 'pop' as the fuses are transported separately for safety reasons, but it would have been a major nuclear 'accident' if the plan had succeeded. This, needless to say, was serious.

Something had to be done and I was not the person to do it. I'm not Grade 7 Executive Branch. Ian Fleming, the creator of James Bond, did know a thing or two having worked in intelligence. I am intelligence – field data gathering and analysis in these latter years, not the executive branch. I had managed to ID the movements of the two principle Iraqi agents and their English sub- contractor. Orders apparently went out. They never went home.

These were times of both open and covert war. You cannot get much joy in court and to ID the way the evidence had been obtained and assembled, would have outed the undercover personnel involved, including myself. I had suggested that Special Branch raid the location of the conspirators. They would have none of it. I would have been identified and that is not the way with intelligence. You keep your people in place and out of sight, unidentified at all costs; otherwise your intel source has dried up.

Some of my old chums retired along the way after these events. The senior sergeant was a dry old salt. One of his expressions was, "Intelligence is like the constipated elephant. It just keeps consuming but it rarely shits". Make of that what you will. We used to have the odd meal in the police canteen. Special Branch never mingle much with uniformed branch. Their cars were scruffy things, bashed, often untaxed. You had to merge into the wallpaper, be as the people you were tasked to look at. They often got stopped by traffic division but never identified themselves; it was not allowed. The traffic tickets would be taken out of the system later, but no one would know.

The whole process was 'off base'', left of field, out of sight. 'Meets' as they were termed when we met up would be obscure or in plain sight. Motorway service stations were favoured, or the cafes in department stores surrounded by ladies who lunch. Little did they know matters of state security were being discussed at the next table.

One of my mates would always have his mouth half-covered in case anyone in the room could lip read. It was bizarre really. Drops of funds were always cash and passed out of sight. Pay was modest to say the least. The state got very good value for its few shekels that it shelled out. However, lives were saved, that was for sure, and the people involved were not there for the money. It was a lot more meaningful than that. These were the days when the word 'vocation' meant something.

If I have not identified the exact time-line on these events, it is for good reason. Some of these on-side chaps are still alive and in service and I do not want to give any indication of who they are by anyone working out where, for example, 'Fred' was on June 4th in Plymouth. Oh, my God he did lunch that day – bingo! There are too many variables worked in here for that to be possible. I don't want to cause anyone a problem here. Not the regular chaps/gals in service or the military; they just do as they are told. *"Ours is to only do and die, ours but to do and die"* Always sad, but too often true, as you will see later in this dialogue. In fact, there has been too much dying in the ranks and they are getting pretty pissed off with it, especially if from so-called, 'friendly fire'.

During the building of GCHQ's new base, 'the doughnut', as the high tech structure was nicknamed, various unfriendly elements tried to place their undercover operatives or sub-contractors on site in the construction process.

These might be actual paid agents, in effect, or just loud-mouthed geezers they had 'bumped' down the pub. One 'well-meaning' (I am being charitable), young fellow, who had an insatiable curiosity about Q and 'the doughnut', was not only trying to place enemy agents on site, although he only thought they were 'peace freaks', but also get himself employed there as a driver. I was, as they say, all over this, and it did not happen. You can't, well not in those days, prosecute someone for trying. Now it seems you probably can for even thinking about such a stunt; the law has changed much since then.

The object was to install some on-site listening devices and wire them into the electric power source so they would work forever – good theory. That didn't happen either. The Yanks had tried similar ploys in Moscow, even giving Russian officials various 'gifts', which had mics and transmitters built into them. It was likely in some instances, that the Russians picked up on that and used the feed to pass back duff information. That is all part of the game. If you detect someone is working for the other side, you don't necessarily bust them, but feed them a sandwich of fact and fiction to lead the enemy astray.

Nowadays, the geeks prefer to just earwig using all kinds of sophisticated software which can tap into any laptop, cell phone or the like and use it as an on-site listening device or camera. In the good old days, only hard-wired telephones were used, but in these 'wireless' days of computers, direct connection isn't needed. People can even be listened to from satellites, let alone tapping into the in-traffic comms, either via the airwaves or the fibre-optic cables, particularly at the relay stations or where they come/go offshore. All this is common knowledge, I'm not breaking any firewalls by telling you this, and all sides have done it for years.

America listens to itself via the Menwith Hill facility in the UK to get around laws that restrict the practice in the US itself. The UK, meanwhile, uses their big Cyprus facility to earwig the UK and just about everyone, as well as using GCHQ that operates both for the UK and the Yanks (sorry 'our American Friends').

In truth, the UK is really only seen as the permanent 'aircraft carrier' moored off-shore from Europe. The 'special relationship' amounts, in most part, (being just a little cynical as well as factual), as the Americans paying for the services of the SAS to do an op if it's really difficult, as we do them far better than they do. US Navy Seal Team 6 is mostly for PR purposes for internal consumption to the US public— the Americans won the Second World War, as of course only they know.

They also use Q for the information gathering that's illegal Stateside without Congressional approval, as well as stealing any of the British technology that they might find useful. 85% of the CIA's work is industrial espionage, everyone is very clear about that, and ensuring US economic and geopolitical interests predominate in any particular overseas territory.

You might think I am anti-American. I am not. I have many American friends and I was actively very pro-American when I was younger. I just happen to observe that America has been hijacked by corporate interests over the past decades. It does a great job working against itself by thinking that everyone in the world thinks like them and can be bought into their domain. It controls its politicians by blackmail, bribes and premature deaths (spelled suicides) by a very few super-rich and fanatical psychopaths who are totally amoral. I believe in democracy for which, at one time long ago, America flew the flag high, but not now, sadly.

"*The Truth Will Set You Free,*" says the mosaic on the entrance hall of the main public CIA building, but it is often very uncomfortable and it will occasionally get you killed or at least character assassinated. The powers-that-be like really dumb people – perhaps Homer Simpson is their perfect model - a fat consumer with an average family life and an irrational love of pizza. Don't you just hate that advert, 'Don't cook, just eat'. Poor Jamie Oliver must be furious, with his campaign to get us all to cook wholesome meals at home. Sadly 85% of Americans get take-away and much of it is eaten on the move as I know from personal experience there in the USA. Have you ever found an American car that doesn't have cup holders? I rest my case....

But your diet and diabetes are not my problem, your mental awareness is, because if you don't have enough real information you won't make good, legal, political and economic life decisions and you will ruin the world in an ignorant malaise of illusions based on pure monetary profit, while forgetting to survive or preserve the futures of your grandchildren.

Many things that are put about are sadly far from the actual truth. They are carefully stage-managed both by the tame media and incessant mind-boggling, truth-bending advertising. Everything from photoshopping the leg length of models to telling outright lies. It's been going on for years.

For example, the ill-fated, '*Titanic*' was actually the RMS *'Olympic'*. She had been in collision with a British warship the year before and was never going to pass another full safety inspection. She had to be sunk, run deliberately along a suitable big iceberg and sent to the bottom of the sea. The sad thing, is the cargo ship that White Star line had sent ahead to anchor and wait for the 'disaster' got its position wrong, it was just too far over the horizon to see the distress rockets from '*Titanic*' and the result, in a calm but freezing sea, was that many people died of hypothermia. When they sent down the remote controlled submarines to view the wreck, the riveted letters Titanic, which had been overlaid on the prow of the ship in Belfast were rusting off. Clearly visible underneath was etched '*Olympic*'. White Star got the insurance money in five days. Mission complete! Did lives matter? Not when serious money is involved. Nothing changes.

Another example is that of the archaeologist, Howard Carter, who was inside the tomb of Tutankhamen years before he 'officially' discovered it, allegedly breaking off bits of the booty and selling it to collectors. Only when that was mostly exhausted and the bigger pieces would cause too much of a stir could the tomb actually be 'found'.

His deception was quite sophisticated, as he had come in originally from the back of the tomb underground, led there by the guile of local tomb raiders. Carter was a skilled artist and he not only had to wall up his original entrance, but paint a whole new fresco to obscure the deception. His wall painting has grown mould since it was painted on damp, new plasterwork. The size and style of the newer work is also very obviously fake to the experienced eye. I have some knowledge of Egypt in those days, but that is another story, as is the story of the pyramids themselves.

The purpose of the Egyptian pyramids was based on the resonance functions of their internal chambers, like an organ pipe. Granite has piezoelectric properties if vibrated, like on the pickup of an old phonographic record player. You can get a lot of electricity out of a granite slab if you vibrate it well. By the same token, if you stimulate a crystal with an electromagnetic field you can get it to 'sing', glow and even disintegrate as when a wine glass meets the opera singer hitting the right note. I had researched this for over 20 years.

While lecturing in London in the late 90's on such matters, I was approached by a couple from near Seattle. They had been sent to Europe from a sect in the State of Washington run by a lady called J C Knight, entitled *Ramtha's School of Enlightenment*. She had sent them out to look for further intellectual input to the group and apparently I fitted the specification. I agreed to go to their community and lecture to about 2000 spiritual folk.

I worked it into a round-trip to catch up with some of my American Intelligence friends. They wanted me to take in a further trip to Nevada and the UFO conferences being held there. So off I went. The videos made of all that are still available, '*Secret Science Revealed*' and the gig up near Seattle for J C Knight's School of Enlightenment.

While there, I teamed up with some local CIA who had been briefed that I was coming. They wanted me to keep an eye on the UFO folk and their inquisitive activities, which also revolved around a fascination with 'Area 51', part of the Nellis gunnery weapons testing range up in the hills where the US military has thousands of square miles of land, all off-limits to the general public.

This is where the US used to test and keep a lot of its secret aircraft, the U-2 flew from there as it has a very long runway for such craft. It was also rumoured that anti-gravimetric back-engineered flying saucers were being tested and flown out of Area 51 and the more secret S-4 facility, which is mostly underground.

I had done some development of electrostatic drive mechanisms myself and built 'lifters', simple toys, using EHT from old cathode-ray power drives that can float in mid-air. I do not recommend you fool around with this stuff, as the high voltage electricity can easily kill you. The mechanism is used on the B-2 bomber, which is slow in its normal aerodynamic mode, but can get a wiggle on when it powers up its electromagnetic shell. It shoves electrons from the front of the wings to the rear, assisting thrust, obscuring it from most radars and giving it a fair turn of speed. Ironically you can detect them when they fly over in 'black' mode as they cause a glitch in the cell net microwave transmitter stations, so a traveling glitch reveals where the aircraft is, even though radar can't 'see' it. No secret; the Russians, Brits and Yankees all know this.

My work on that stuff was all classified, but it's years ago now. The Stealth fighter flew 22 years before it was officially rolled out as the new kid on the block. If you are told about something officially, it is because it is already out of date and things have moved on. They don't tell you that after a mission of ten hours a B-2 has to be grounded, repainted and not be available for about a month. Hardly a sound tactical weapon.

It's also like the PR that is put out about the American B-52 nuke-carrying bombers. They are dinosaurs. Only 10 in service now, most of which depend on cannibalised parts from grounded wrecks out in the aircraft graveyards, so at any one time only two are operational. Impressive but quaint. Strictly for the press and Joe Public, like the Russian Tu-95 Bear equivalents that sometimes fly over the North Sea and up the English Channel. It is all yesterday's technology and totally expendable dating from the 1950s.

When the B-52s were used in Afghanistan, dropping tons of 'dumb bombs' on the mountain passes, photographed by the press some miles below on safe ground, the reporters were told it was a big operation to take out insurgents and their cave bases. Bullshit. There was no one up there; the B-52s killed a few goats and the main purpose was to blast some rock out to improve ground communications. Of course the press were on safe ground!

It reminds me of when the US Navy launched over two hundred Mk 1 cruise missiles to destroy terrorist bases up in the mountains. The operation had been deliberately leaked to French Intelligence three days before. They tipped off the terrorists, to whom they were selling arms, who moved off their training bases in short order and the missiles killed three shepherds and more goats. Lo and behold the US Navy went running to Congress via the Pentagon, cap in hand, to say they were now very short of cruise missiles and could not adequately defend the free world. A replacement huge order was procured of the Mk 2 missiles, which had just become available. Remarkable coincidence; just business as usual!

How do I know? Friends in high placement in the US military. The only reason you put a project into the Pentagon is to make money. If you need a reason, you invent an enemy or create one for the purpose. The USA always needs enemies. It used to be the USSR, then China, Vietnam, North Korea, Libya, Iraq, Iran etc. etc. As I said before, the sheep dog effect. Create a problem; offer a solution. When old hat, create another problem. It keeps people busy and employed, even though it also kills people. The film 'Iron Man' touched on that, but obscured the reality at the same time. That's known as a 'snow job'. Give the public a titbit, dress it up as a fiction and it keeps the idea in a safe zone, hiding in plain sight.

I have been shown around a variety of government facilities and ex- facilities that were up for disposal. These were mostly nuke shelters and bunkers that would be far too difficult and costly to remove or demolish. One of them is at Bolt Head, near Salcombe, Devon in the UK. It has its own little airstrip atop the cliffs, tricky getting in as the updraft from the cliff is a little problematical if you are flying an old Auster, as they tend to float even at very slow speed, but landed a Piper Arrow there without running off over the other end and back into the drink. The bunker itself started as a WWII radar station but then graduated to a regional government fallout and blast shelter. Partly above ground, the walls are nine-feet thick and contain a radiation protection sandwich, which is classified even to this day. A mate and I wanted to buy it some years back when it came onto the market and convert it into a timeshare survival pad, but it sold for £80,000, which was beyond our budget. Cheap really, seeing as it had cost the taxpayer about £13 Million to upgrade over the years.

Apart from the former US Navy listening station at Brawdy on St. Brides Bay, which was mostly on the surface, I have also taken a look at the now privately-owned former HMG bunker north of London and the Burlington complex which is very extensive underground near Box Hill by Salisbury Plain.

The problem with these establishments is they tend to fill with high levels of radon, a natural, but highly radioactive gas that comes up mostly from the deterioration of granite rocks. So, while trying to shelter from radioactivity on the outside, you are slowly being fried by the radon on the inside. You cannot really keep it out and it means the bunkers have to be air-purified and 'flushed' on such a regular basis the cost of doing this would be prohibitive for such large facilities. They can be encouraged to remain clean by air convection, but that defeats their sealed-off function in the event of an attack or nuclear accident.

The other 'live' one under Salisbury Plain that's still in use, had problems from leaking tritium from the small nuclear reactor plant used to make electricity. They have the same problems on nuclear subs as their bilges get contaminated with daughter by-products. The muds in Plymouth Sound are full of the stuff, just don't go fishing for bottom-feeding flat fish around
156

there, your fish dinner may glow in the dark.

If you do get irradiated by some accident or fallout blowing in the wind, drink plenty of fresh water, load up with natural iodine from tablets and seaweeds; eat lots of natural foods including freshwater green algae and plenty of baked beans which carry heavy metals out of the body. Make a will and don't expect to see many after-effects for at least 15 years.

A good friend of mine was on the official international survey party to Chernobyl shortly after it blew its top. As they approached, their Geiger counters went off the scale. My mate wasn't too concerned, as he was approaching 70 years old, but he worried for the younger men in the party as the RNA/DNA changes take 15-20 years to kick in. That's unless the counts are so high that bone-marrow is being taken out in radical quantities like at Fukushima currently, where it's rumoured over 800 workers may have already died. When you are only allowed on site for three days before you reach your annual exposure limit, you are, by definition, in trouble.

The Japanese don't see covering up the truth about nuclear fallout as lying, so much as 'saving face'. But be warned: do not eat any sea products, fish or shellfish from the North Pacific, as far east as the US coast including Alaska. Of course, there were going to be economic consequences from that, so Hillary Clinton made an agreement with the Japanese not to test their incoming foods to the US and on the California and Oregon mainland to switch off the air pollution fall out monitors. What you don't know won't worry you.

Little girls under the age of six are most vulnerable,

clinical stats have shown. They're not sure why, but it is probably because their cells are multiplying faster. As you get older, it all slows down and you are a lot safer. Cockroaches are virtually immune, so in a thousand years from now, California might be only populated by huge mutated cockroaches (if that is not already the case in Hollywood!) and it follows that large-leafed vegetables should be washed. Some bio products concentrate the isotopes so check out anything from the West coast with a Geiger Counter, although some radiation does not register on them due to the way they work.

As for Japan itself, I warned all my friends in Tokyo of the fact that the precincts all around were contaminated, but by some 'miracle' Tokyo itself was 'spared', a piece of physics that defies logic. Although I suppose it depends whose logic we're talking about – if Tokyo had been devastated I expect it could have affected the value of the Yen or the tourism industry there and we can't have that, can we?

The classic advice came from a Japanese government official. "Just smile and be happy and it won't affect you," he declared reassuringly. The fact remains that three of the devastated power plants did actually go critical and melt down within three days of the earthquake and tsunami. Over 40% of girls under the age of six now have malignant tumours on their thyroid glands and the expected premature death toll in Japan is over three million people. They are unlikely to get compensation, as every time they release radioactive material, currently 400 tons of water a day into the Pacific containing among other isotopes Caesium 137, they just raise the 'safety levels', which is a bit of a con unless you are really stupid.

The main flow of radioactive debris was calculated by scientific analysis of the ocean currents to arrive big time on the Pacific Coast of the US from August 2014, but it takes another seven years before it will filter into the Atlantic. Most of it in the Pacific will stay north of the Equator due to the natural division of both air flows and ocean currents in the respective hemispheres.

Later in the 90s I was put on the case of a national TV presenter, Jill Dando, who had been murdered on her doorstep in West London on 26th April 1999. She was killed in the middle of the day as she arrived home, assassination-style, by a single gunshot to the head. She was much-loved by the British public and her death sent shockwaves around the country. It was less than two years after another untimely death of a blonde, short-haired, "British national treasure", Princess Diana, and the public still hadn't got over that tragedy.

I was assigned to the case within hours of Jill Dando's murder. The purpose of my mission was to find what had 'gone wrong' because I was informed (by a US source) that the intention had only been to kidnap her as a publicity stunt to encourage the public to keep on side to counter the various aggressive 'Serbian foreign policy involvements'. Can't have the 'special relationship' damaged by something as inconvenient as the Brits seeking the moral high ground or using logic. No, scare them into thinking the 'enemy' is at their door and alive and well in Fulham, where she resided.

Using only solid, cross-referenced data and

eyewitness reports, plus some inside track from very well-informed insiders, the plot went like this: Having charted her expected movements, a van had been positioned opposite her house. This was to have been the abduction vehicle – no windows and pretty anonymous in London. A crew of field operatives was scheduled to come into the area and make the pickup, but here was where the 'planning' started to go tragically astray.

Firstly, the man chosen to do the job was not British by cultural tradition – I am being obtuse – I am not saying it was a British op, neither do I think it could have gone ahead without a certain agency being aware and looking the other way. I was working for the Yanks at the time, so I will allow you to draw your own conclusions on that. However, this single man was on the street to abduct her in the first instance.

The script was supposed to go that Jill Dando is a young female, you will threaten her with your gun, she will be afraid and you will put her in the van where another will drug her, keep her quiet while a driver takes her off to be detained in an anonymous safe house. Meanwhile, the PR boys cook up an already prepared overseas involvement story. This, I have to say, is very American thinking, as they all assume everyone is shit-scared of guns, just like they are.

But Ms Dando was a Brit, had guts and did not respond as expected – she screamed the place down! The operative panicked, pushed her against the door, swiftly put his handgun against her head and blew her brains out. The exit wound was much larger than the entrance wound, that is how I know that, and I did have access to all the reportage on the case.

Now in the course of all this fiasco and due to her buying some fish on the way home, the black Range Rover back-up car was on the other side of the block when all this was going on. So the operative now trots, I won't say runs, down the middle of the street looking for his escape vehicle and completely misses them. He has blood all over his hands and he still has the weapon, which in standard protocol had been fitted with a 'clean' replaceable barrel that of course would be disposed of and never used again. Operatives like to use the same butt and weapon, they get used to it and it is often hand crafted to fit them perfectly.

One failing that showed up in forensics; he had used custom hand-made ammunition. This has a special specification for the job expectation, with just enough explosive loading, otherwise it makes too big a bang and is more difficult to be accurate. Unlike Dirty Harry, no one uses Magnums and it was before 2003 anyway. The ammo has the specialist armourer's dot punch markings on it, so everyone in the business knew it was a professional job. Inappropriate ego and pride crept in and gave the game all away.

All this was passed off later as the work of one man, Barry George, who was described at his trial as having an IQ of 75, in the lowest 5% of the population. And yet he somehow managed to convert a replica gun into a live firearm, or to make one himself, a specialist skill as otherwise the barrel will split and blow your fingers off.

Returning to the now unscripted part of the f**k up. The operative goes down to the River Thames, finds access to the river and washes his blood soaked hands, dismantles and hides the gun- only amateurs throw guns in rivers as it is the first place plod will go looking. He boards a bus, sweating profusely, and gets off at a nearby Tube station, where he disappears into the underworld of trains and tunnels. While on the bus, he made several frantic mobile calls as his 'handlers' were all calling for their brown trousers.

He was picked up, cleaned up, sent to the airport and was out of the country by midnight. To be on the safe side, and to avoid 'blow-back' as the PR story has now all been scrapped and buried, within three weeks he met an untimely end, as is policy on assassins who get it that wrong.

But Jill Dando is dead and someone must be held responsible. The Metropolitan Police started closing in on the case. They were being monitored, so the investigating officer was replaced and poor Barry George was arrested and charged. Despite the evidence showing severe mental impairment and epilepsy, he was convicted of the killing and imprisoned in 2001. Seven years later, after two appeals, he was finally acquitted and released. But his trial and incarceration had served the necessary distraction exercise. A 'snow job'.

Cover-ups always take far more effort than actual operations because ops are imbued with eternal optimism, theoretically perfect scenarios, concepts of precise timing, unemotional operators who do not make mistakes and rarely bring into play those unknown variables like buying a piece of fish. The random factors! As it's said, no plan stands up 100% when confronted with reality. But those who believe in karma may find that those who live by the sword might one day find they are falling on it.

I made a few documentaries for the BBC on reincarnation. Proven case as far as I am concerned, but more of that later. The Buddhists say you might come back as some lower creature if you did not do well this time around. So don't step on that beetle, it might be evil Uncle George who passed on a year or two ago – I jest? By the time this gets published one expects a few more souls might have passed on, they are all getting on a bit and many have gone already, which is why this can be written. You cannot slander or liable the deceased. It might be in bad taste though so we will try to be kind and show the logic and 'justifications' but laced with a little satire and black humour here and there.

7. Matters More Domestic

CALMER WATERS

The mid 90s was a happy time for me. We had moved into a bigger rented property right next door to my previous house and this was a converted stone barn dating from about 1860. It was an upside down house with the living rooms upstairs and the bedrooms and bathrooms on the ground floor. This suited my MS condition better.

The house had lots of wooden bannisters and a flying gallery over the atrium entrance hall, which gave the whole place a sense of medieval grandeur. The place was owned by a North Sea diver, who spent very long periods off in the North Sea underwater, sometimes pressurised for days in special chambers so that time-wasting decompressions were not needed. He told me that as they pressured up the chambers to get them ready for their descent any unopened Coca-Cola cans would just be crushed. This gave you a very good idea of the forces these guys worked under on a regular basis.

I set about making the house 'my own', so to speak. I was very sensitive about my security as I was doing pretty dangerous work and was by now on at least one hit list from the enemy – the Iraqi forces we had really pissed off by taking out a few of their key people and foiling their plans to kill several thousand Brits on their home turf, using their own ordinance.

So the house got well-equipped with video cams, microphones and other gadgets so I could keep tabs on what was going on both within and without the house when in my comms ops room. This was the most secure room in the house, had no external windows and was kitted out with numerous signals decoders, monitor screens and all the usual toys. Outside, an array of satellite dishes locked onto a number of communications satellites and although low-profile, any close inspection might have given the indication that this was no ordinary seaside house looking out over Bigbury Bay, where the Royal Navy exercised on a regular basis.

They would come out of Plymouth, roar around in tight manoeuvres practicing anti-submarine warfare, I'm sure there was a sub or two down there. They'd then go back in to port for the late afternoon for the mess dinner on shore. Not a bad life. I knew a few fellows at Plymouth, good lads. It's known as the senior service and they are probably right.

I turned the property into a full-blown survival station. The walls were two feet thick, there was a self-contained electric generator installed at the foot of the garden in a Faraday cage and two wooden chalets were put in; one a workshop and the other for additional accommodation. An old chum of mine from American Intelligence moved into the second hut and we were all set up. Close contact was kept with Special Branch, GCHQ and other agencies.

We did some good work for several different constabularies and for London's Metropolitan police. One task was on the run up to the year 2000 when the Met was concerned that due to much gloom and doom talk, various sects and groups might commit mass suicide. We were tasked to identify and infiltrate these groups. We did a great job.

Ironically, some of them were Jewish in origin and some were 'Christian' if somewhat out on the fringes of those religions. Any rate, I had a very stabilising influence on them, as I do, and no great mass killing occurred.

Unfortunately, there have been the odd family murders where husbands had been convinced that their families were going to die horribly at the turn of the century. So, apparently out of 'mercy' to their supposed impending doom, the man of the family had taken out the children, mostly very young, and their wives before committing suicide themselves. But these were not part of any organised group and were totally unpredictable, so one had no way to intercede. This kind of event wasn't confined to Y2K, of course. It still happens for many reasons, mainly mental illness-related, and it is always a horrific tragedy.

I got brownie points from Met. Special Branch on my research, and was told by my handler that I was considered rather exceptional. Nice! I had completed the main task in just seven weeks, which had involved some long hours, but there was an urgency to it at that time.

During the course of that work I was lucky enough to

see a large bolide, which is a big meteorite come in and break up over Dartmoor. It was a very bright object and split into three parts. There was a sonic boom and so I was aware that some of these fears of cosmic retribution were not entirely unfounded. I have kept a close watch on the Sun, Solar flares and NEOs (Near Earth Objects) ever since. I also understand the apparent connections of solar weather, that's the solar wind etc. on earthquake triggering, although saying when and where is a very unpredictable science. All one can do is follow the patterns, watch the shifts and stresses in the tectonic plates and flip a coin.

On that basis, the only very predictable analysis, which I would put money on, is that Istanbul will get a big shaker within a few years and due to the poor building standards there, thousands will die. When I was given an office for three weeks in California in 1990, the whole building, which was only three stories high, was set on huge concrete rollers and huge shock absorbers so it could withstand a force 8.6 on the Richter scale. That kind of engineering costs a lot of money and only in Japan and the US West Coast do they seem to take the threat seriously.

Fracking causes thousands of minor earthquakes, it is designed to, and can destabilise major faults if it goes on for some years. The New Madrid fault line is at risk from that in the eastern central section of the USA. Fracking also causes methane to be released into aquifers and some folks in the States have been burnt by their showers turning into mini flame-throwers. Don't smoke in the shower!

Of more pragmatic threat to myself, was my quacks again gave me only three months to live. I can always tell when the prognosis is going to be poor, they call in the nurse and ask me to sit down. I laugh at them and tell them I hope it's nothing minor and could they put that in writing please, as the State might chuck in a bit of support for old buggers like me who won't lie down.

My mother put herself in a wheelchair for the last 25 years of her life and my father was a dedicated hypochondriac. But not me. The Japanese have found that if you fight back, work through the pain and immobility, the body rallies and survives much better. My uncle remarried aged 96 to his nurse who was just 29. He died at 98, but with a smile on his face. She got all the family money then, which I guess is a good two years' pay.

I have very good longevity DNA that seems to govern these things. Comes down more on the mother's side they say. However never say die, you only live twice - or in the case of cats nine times it seems according to popular myth. My cat is 19 going on 20, so he must pick it up from me. I love cats, very smart animals.

I had more work around sects, having to check out some overseas survivalists. One really dedicated group was in Italy, where they had dug a huge underground city by hand, yes by hand. They then got picked up by the local Mayor, who fancied turning it into a local tourist attraction, as the sect members had worked in a lot of wonderful art and they had a big legal battle to retain control. I found myself on their side and pulled a few strings in the Latin Quarter. They retained their control, but became more open in their interface with the world.

Underground facilities have always fascinated me; you can still to this day buy the odd decommissioned nuclear missile silo in the States, if you're really worried about your beloved leaders taking you down that road. The US President and the 'great and the good' over there have a huge complex under Denver Airport that can fit over 2,700 people down there for six months at any one time. When the President heads for Denver, it's time to worry!

In the course of interacting with the Italian sect, I found myself brought to the attention of a Dutch group of dedicated lesbians and their male counterparts. So I went to Holland a couple of times, damn cold in late winter – did not suit me at all, but they also thought the world was going to end sometime soon. It was murder driving in Amsterdam, what with dodging trams, bikes, boats and the like; narrow roads too.

One always walks the red light district; well you can hardly miss it. "Hello stranger; I give you good hard fuck", said the leather clad 'lady' outside her pink doorway. I did not feel inclined to take up the offer.

However, I was a little concerned that apart from being Star Trek fans, the lesbian group also seemed to be into Satanism. I could not see the connection. Perhaps they were just into the edgy symbolism. One girl who had been a professional prostitute said she had given up the trade after she was stalked by one of her clients. He had his 'member' in a small manacle secured on an iron chain girded around his waist. Weird, but I suppose it kept him amused during the long Dutch cold nights!

During the course of these bizarre contacts, I was invited to the lesbian group's pad in Portugal, to meet a guy trying to set up a community in a derelict Portuguese village. Most of the houses there were for sale for ten cents on the dollar. He turned out to be a complete nut. Was pretty much completely anti to everything. Maybe even including himself, who knows? He accused me of being fascist on the basis that I was English and we had ruled the world a century ago.

I quite hark back to the days when a lot of the map was pink, the colour used on maps to designate the British Empire. A friend of mine used to be an African correspondent and had seen the changes and takeovers first-hand, the wind of change. He referred to the new breed of African bureaucrats as the 'Wa Benzie', the tribe of the white Mercedes.

Of course, colonialism is out of date and bad, so why does the USA remain stuck in that old pattern? Except now we call it peace-keeping or give it cosy names like 'The Arab Spring'. Have you noticed there is a kind of swing from evolution to devolution better known as civil war?

I thought of inventing an exciting new board game like *Cluedo* for compulsory distribution to all staff at MI6, except it would be called 'Spot the terrorists'. The players would have to guess who, on any one move, was actually the enemy. Unlike *Cluedo* however, you would be allowed, in the game, to sell them weapons when they would likely be 'on side,' (that means allowing you to take over the country's resources), but you could also bomb them into the Stone Age when they crossed a neighbouring border and attacked another country of little or no importance. You would get bonus points for armaments sales, which you would describe as supporting an emerging democracy. Then, with a twist of *Monopoly*, you could use a 'get out of jail free' card after happily killing large numbers of relatives, grandparents and children of identified 'insurgents', by calling that, 'unfortunate collateral damage'.

These decisions could also be blamed on mis-firing software programs on board 'drones', that would use artificial intelligence to identify an enemy with their aerial spy cameras whenever they saw an indigenous person wearing cloth head-coverings. These 'enemies' would be designated as 'rag heads' who may likely be carrying a concealed weapon, so would be targeted by hi-tec attack helicopters. If the 'enemy' turns out to be a dangerous team of journalists, then the incident could be passed off as 'friendly fire'.

If you were in any real danger of losing your reputation for being gung-ho and had to be removed from the game, then as a consolation prize you would be given a military medal and entered on some role of honour or, even better, Hollywood would completely rewrite that piece of history and ensure you were seen as a hero, role model and generally brave fellow.

If your mission had in the game had been a complete, unmitigated failure, then a special make-over would be awarded, termed 'saving-face'. Thus all would be well and life would continue seamlessly with business as usual. You would watch the ball game, drink beer and eat pizza. As the Aussie joke goes, 'American beer is like making love in a canoe; fucking close to water'.

Another overseas caper that I was asked to attend to was taking a look at the Tuscan villa near Lucca, where our beloved leader at the time, Tony Blair, was going to take a well needed and deserved holiday. When I say villa, imagine a palatial mansion.

The security team was to go in a week before and

make the place as tight as a duck's arse so no unwanted itinerants could wander in and take a pop at the dear boy or even worse, photojournalists equipped with 600mm lenses perhaps snap his manly chest. The villa and grounds were, of course, walled and gated. Its location was secret, but public enough to be advertised on the Internet should you wish to avail yourself of a quick Mediterranean break at £30,000 per week. Cheap at twice the price! If you can't have a decent duck house on your pond what's the point of getting elected? Even better, when you get deselected or simply voted out of office, go off and become a European Commissioner or perhaps even a special envoy, even better paid.

I can see now that when, as a youth, I had joined my first political party, the young conservatives, I should have stuck with it and made it to the House. There, I could have learned how to throw my order paper into the air, make loud animal noises, rule the country with complete detachment and pretend I knew most things better than my fellow man. I could claim control over economic situations – spelled 'crisis' – and award myself pay raises much in excess of the rates of inflation because I would know my real worth. All I would need to ensure this would be to have attended the correct school and know how to suck up to the people who were there first.

Bizarrely, soon after this, I was invited to help organise a Star Trek convention at Wembley Stadium. A mate of mine was commissioned to handle the video production and he enlisted my help. All went well until 24 hours before the grand event at which over 2000 dedicated Trekkies were expected to attend. Unbeknown to us the organiser was in serious financial difficulties and things were not going well. The Stars of the show had not been sent any air ticket money and more importantly Wembley Stadium had not been paid either. Our dear organiser was planning a little overseas holiday, and with no extradition from Venezuela, it's a good life on the beach with other people's money. So muggings here, gets a 'phone call from the chap who is already at Heathrow, could I go down to Wembley and tell all the fans just to write in for a refund. Like could I just volunteer to be lynched by Klingons. The scene was bizarre. These dudes had come from all over the UK fully uniformed and made up in character to their selected avatar role models. The girls were sexy, some were really way out; I think there must have been a large Goth contingent in disguise and the hairy bikers had taken on other worldly roles, only their Harley Davidsons gave away their true origins. I elected to 'get involved' and instantly took over a large nearby restaurant who saw this as good business as the Wembley staff would not allow anyone entrance there, so they all piled into the make shift venue. It was like being on another planet. The Star Wars hang out bar scene had nothing on this. I've never had an attraction to green dripping flesh but I can see it has some useful points. Mating and dating was obviously going on, in the crush of the venue it reminded me of salmon in a frenzy to reach their spawning grounds before they expired.

I got chatted up my several nubile maidens but as I did not speak the speak; I think they sussed pretty quickly that I was actually an undercover Earthling and I did not have a three-foot-long studded penis in my pants or a hidden tail let alone mottled skin. Like Spock I elected to remain emotionally aloof and refused to get drawn into irrational mating games. I knew in the morning they would emerge as blood sucking robots only concerned to consume my bodily fluids. I have watched 'Red Dwarf' so like 'Cat' my whiskers were twitching. Bad vibes!

We spent Christmas in the Ardèche region of France that year, winding roads, steep low mountains and fast running streams bounded by chestnut orchards with an occasional wild boar, both animal and human. Our French host was a writer and photographer with a spiritual bent and she had arranged for us to stay with her neighbour who was building his own small DIY castle on the mountainside out of local rock. He was an expert mason and the place looked really authentic. Although it was December, our host was very hardy and invited us down into the nearby canyon where a fast running and beautiful river was only interrupted now and then by still deep ponds.

Stripping off completely, our host dived into the pool dived. "Come on in", she beckoned. My wife, in some trepidation, stripped off and tiptoed over the boulders towards the pool's edge. Paddling into the ice cold mountain waters she attempted to gracefully enter putting on a brave face. Disaster struck when she slipped on a boulder and she fell completely into the deep icy pool. Her screams echoed around the mountain canyons like the cry of a demented Yeti. Fortunately unhurt, she braved to swim up and down a bit until the slightly blue colour of her lips indicated imminent hypothermia was setting in. I remained on shore giving only mental encouragement and helping to rub her down with towels and words of facile encouragement like, "You did well". She was shaking a lot, however no signs of a cardiac arrest. I gather some folk do this on a regular basis in Finland; however Polar bears have the wisdom to keep their fur coats on when taking the plunge.

We had taken as Christmas presents 'Furbies', a pair of them, and having fired them up with their batteries, read the instructions and 'fed' them (you tickle their beaks) we were amazed that their bright little cyber-brains were speaking a few French words and phrases after a few days. This is why they were banned from being brought into GCHQ, as they can listen and remember things. They then proceeded to talk to each other in their own Furbie language. One would speak, then the other, and after a short pause, the first would respond. Furby toys have more computing power in them than NASA took to the moon on the first Lunar landing missions and I can believe it.

While there, our mason host taught us how to kill a sheep while lovingly holding it, which I thought at the time a very philosophical, if rather disturbing act. We also went outside and made large banging noises with pots and pans to try to drive away the wild boars that were tearing up his vegetable patch. We were above them on an elevated terrace and were warned these bastards can kill you, so don't get near them especially any mothers with young.

The boars ignored us, they knew we were just humans, but they did run off when some red-hatted hunters arrived armed with guns. The red caps were to prevent them accidentally shooting each other in the forest, mistaking the noises of movement behind them for boars in the undergrowth. This tends to happen after lunch, which always lasts three hours and requires the substantial consumption of alcohol. If the hunting hasn't gone well, they trot off to the local butcher who always has a few un-skinned rabbits on hand for them to take home to their wives justifying their long day out hunting for the pot.

Lunch, what lunch? Oh! And my breath, well in the cold it is needed to steady my aim. This is why competition shooters are not allowed to drink, it really does steady their aim, so if ever you get confronted by an inebriated hoody packing a side arm, don't think he can't shoot. However, dive to your right and down on the deck as his weapon will climb to your left and high, especially on the second shot, which is the one that might kill you. If he is holding the weapon on its side or with both hands, one holding his wrist, you are in trouble. He's probably a professional. Just give him your wallet, that's the spare wallet you keep with a few out-of-date credit cards and ten bucks that will buy him his drug fix, which is why he is a hood in the first place. Tattoos are a bad sign in France too, usually means they have been in prison.

Another good mate of mine in earlier days was formerly the most senior pilot in the Royal Dutch Air Force. A skilled fighter pilot, he was a key man in their equivalent of the Red Arrows display team and had many an anecdote to tell. Like many a maverick he had lightning-quick reactions. When flying once out at Nellis air base, Nevada, he was near the back of the diamond formation as they barrel-rolled out of a loop only about 500 feet off the desert floor. You get a lot of heat turbulence out there off the rocks and his wingman hit a bubble and sliced into the side of my mate's jet. Both wings on those collision sides sheared off.

The planes swiftly rolled over being now totally unbalanced. The wingman instinctively pulled his ejector seat release and piled himself tragically straight down into the deck. Instant death. My mate waited as the aircraft continue to roll. He fired his ejector headed skyward and survived unscathed. That's being cool. That kind of experience and training shines through in moments of severe danger.

Another acquaintance of those days was flying his nearly-new helicopter over the waters around the Channel Isles on a filming job, when something radical happened in the gearbox. Without power or lift, the helicopter plunged earthward. With an icy calm, he put her into autogyro rotate and fortunately the rotors span faster and faster as the force of the descent drove the wind through the freewheeling blades. Shouting to the life-jacketed film crew to jump on his command, he dragged the controls into collect, that's lift, just a hundred feet from the sea surface. There was a terrible groan as the blades bent up, taking the strain of the air pressure, powered only by their rotational momentum. The aircraft stopped. "Jump", yelled the pilot and out they tumbled. He got out under water as he was trained to do being an ex-Royal Navy chopper pilot and they were picked by the lifeboat crew shortly thereafter. I heard it on the news that evening and put in a call to the company base in Liskeard where they still operate to this day. "Good God man, that was truly professional flying", was my comment, "I thought you would have been a gonner!" Well that's the Navy for you. Makes you proud and I mean it.

I've only flown model helicopters with video cams on board and that is tricky enough even when they have on-board gyros to keep them stable, but the modern toys are a lot more sophisticated and you can have a lot of fun with them. They are also very useful for surveillance and there are companies who will get great footage for you without the unnecessary expense of about £450 an hour for a real machine. I don't really trust helicopters, I prefer fixed wing, you can glide if need be. I was once, however, given a go in a dual-seat glider by a professional lady instructor over Cornwall. Terrified me, I just wanted to keep getting the nose down to avoid stalling. They fly so slow it seemed quite unnatural, my old plane did everything at 70 knots, gliders can go down to about 40 knots, which seems like almost standing still. It's difficult to stall a glider, they just drop their nose and keep going.

8. Osama bin Liner

THE OFFICIAL STORY IS FULL OF TRASH

I'm running the chronology a bit out of order here, but no book on intelligence would be complete without mentioning Osama Bin Laden. You probably know that he was a member of the influential, Saudi Bin Laden family who have a massive market share in engineering and construction. Supporters of the Wahhabi Muslim belief, they are dedicated to the physical removal of all infidels from Saudi Arabia, the homeland of Islam and the imposition of Islamic, Sharia laws and traditions on the whole world. They are an expansionist movement in keeping with the exponential recruitment of nation upon nation to the Islamic faith. Having said that, Osama was in fact very westernised and was the CIA station chief in Afghanistan during the Russian invasion and occupation of that much-troubled country.

At that time, he was given at least $13 million by the CIA to fight the Russians, buy arms, equip caves and bases and recruit warlords to being 'on side' to American interests. Hence, he was well-known to the Americans. Several of his senior family members lived in the United States and were personally known to the Bush family.

Before he grew his Islamic-style beard, he was known as Tim Osman and spent time in America where he commanded some considerable respect for his power to inspire people. However, in his mid-life years he was not a well man and he was visited by the CIA Saudi Arabian Station chief six weeks before 9/11 while in hospital in Dubai on a dialysis machine. He was dying slowly. Not a question of if, only when. Tim did a deal with the CIA. He probably did not realise at the time what he was getting into and it is unlikely that he knew about the planned 9/11 attacks as these had been in the making for over three years. Such complicated events take lots of planning and are unlikely to be mapped out in some cave in the Asian foothills. They need lots of known reliable logistics in place to even begin to work.

Tim, Osama Bin Laden, was to be the new bad guy, the man you love to hate. America was running out of identifiable enemies so a plan had been hatched to create an invisible enemy, one that had no known country or definite location – an enemy that was abstract, just an idea – hence 'al-Qaeda' was born. The name actually came from the Afghanistan anti-Russian campaign and had been used by the CIA to describe the rag tag collection of arms dealers, mules and warlords who had been co-opted to fight the Russians with an internal guerrilla war. This they did for money rather than belief. The term in local dialect actually means 'The Toilet' as in the lavatory, and gives an indication of what the CIA thought of them.

I had a mate who would go over the Himalayas via Nepal for months, into Tibet and the borders of the People's Republic of China and was a brilliant single operator. He spoke five local dialects, looked swarthy and could double as Mujahedeen. He identified several Chinese underground nuclear weapons plants up there, never got caught, had no radio and would disappear for months at a time. The kind of man I like.

But back to Tim. The CIA guy probably offered his extensive family, he had several wives and children, continued support if he would work with some other known CIA dudes and be seen to head up this newly-founded cult. This all suited the master plan to have an ongoing bogie man under the bed of every American who couldn't sleep at night. It elicited lots of budgetary requirements for campaigns and gave an excellent reason to invade Afghanistan, where the local rulers at the time found themselves in a strategic situation for some proposed gas pipelines, being near to the old USSR and China via their territorial corridor to the East. The area also grew opium, which was restricted in production at that time. This is all widely reported.

The CIA and Mafia had – and still have – an alliance dating from the end of WWII making them the main dealers in hard drugs into America. The Golden Triangle opium-producing area, which was the main cause of the Vietnam War, was somewhat unstable and a second production country was urgently needed to maintain supplies to the Western world due to political instabilities in the region and losing control of the region according to my American Intelligence chums.

They used to fly cargos in from South America, but

folks down there were discovering revolution and democracy, albeit of a Latin flavour, which sometimes meant a more benevolent dictator than the last one you had just thrown out. The CIA had supported quite a few of its pet leaders down there, not in the name of freedom but economic controls in the American sphere of influence. They were much more on the side of Argentina in the Falklands war than with the UK. So much for the 'special relationship?'

Looking at it as a strategic operation, the 9/11 plot was absolutely brilliant. As black ops go and in its execution, it was just about as good as it gets. Unfortunately, some folks like Joe Public to know just how clever they are and to indicate, 'we can do anything,' so just shut up and be afraid. Ego gets involved and the need to establish that the Inner Keep is above the law and can treat the general public with contempt.

Did you know some 30 witnesses were killed over the two years after the Kennedy assassination just to tidy up the history book? JFK was taken out in a turkey shoot in Dallas, Texas by an operation signed off by Lyndon B. Johnson, that involved two shooters lying down on the top of the rail cars that JFK's limo was approaching. Clean frontal shots from sniper rifles. Lying in between the two snipers was their supervisor, to make sure all went well (self-confessed on his death bed – St. Peter was not impressed). There was another shooter on the famous 'grassy knoll' and then the final head shot from the Secret Service chauffeur actually driving Kennedy's open top limo, as captured on the 8mm film of the assassination before it was scratched out. The chauffeur even slowed down to give his mates a better slow moving target. Why do you think Jackie Kennedy tried to climb out over the back boot of the limo? Because she saw all this. Then on Air Force One, she was told we have your kids, co-operate or accidents can happen.

The man arrested for the assassination, Lee Harvey Oswald, had been equipped with the same calibre rifle as the professional assassins, but he was a rotten shot and very slow with that hand-loaded antique, if he was even directly involved at all. As he said, "I am the patsy" or fall-guy. The un-doctored Zapruder film, which I have seen, also shows all this and the various bullets hitting the car from several directions, not just behind. The driver's handgun was scratched out on the negative, a crude job. However, if you control the media and have total control of all the lies you can get away with most things. Like the BBC announcing the fall of World Trade Centre building 7 before it had actually happened. They are obviously psychic or just reading their script a bit prematurely.

If this sounds like conspiracy theory, it's because it *is* a conspiracy. Explain how the 'dancing Israelis' were in the car park opposite the Twin Towers well in time to set up their camera and film the whole show. They have since gone on Israeli TV and openly admitted they were briefed and there ready and waiting. They were all Mossad agents. Other Mossad agents had been caught driving around in a removal van loaded down with high explosives ready to blow up one of the major bridges, but that was also all hushed up.

As for the Twin Towers events themselves, that had started by the actual aircraft alleged to have been involved being electronically highjacked at the radar cross over points early on their westward journeys, changed out with modified automatically controlled older aircraft which were expertly flown on exact pre-destined timed routes to impact the towers as everyone would witness. One of the aircraft had an under slung extra military design fuel tank, not known on the civilian aircraft that went missing and their final approach to impact was obviously not from on board control, as one of the turns pulled eight Gs, pretty heavy for a human to stand without a G-suit.

One of the engines from the impact fell on a parked taxi cab two blocks away. It was not an engine from the aircraft it was supposed to be from and that original aircraft has been seen in service by a flight engineer since the disaster. As for the passengers, one plane was seen off-loading them into a remote hanger on the same day as the event. God knows what happened to them, I figure you can guess! One of the 'hijacker's' passports was miraculously 'picked up' in the street below the Towers, almost unburnt, while the fuel was alleged to have melted steel beams. Of course, while undoubtedly hot enough to burn a passport, airplane fuel at its normal burning temperature in open air it will not melt steel, otherwise how would the engines remain intact in normal operation? This is established knowledge.

The towers were actually demolished by the later ignition of two W-54 modified nuclear warheads, which are tactical nuclear shells modified to become suitcase bombs by the Israelis at the Dimona Negev desert site. This was all outed by an Israeli nuclear engineer who went 'over the wall' and who was later killed for his troubles. These mini nukes have a very low yield, can be directed weapons, upwards, and are kept at all Israeli embassies worldwide, including New York, to this day; detected by anti-terrorist's oversight surveys that overfly and detect the tell-tale signatures. They had been installed over a recent 'maintenance' period on the Twin Towers, disguised as fire extinguishers strapped to the key central steel upright girders to bring down the Towers in virtual free fall. All this was revealed in 2015 complete with video recordings taken by the operatives involved, such was their arrogance.

Much of the Towers, several hundred tons, was vaporised in the multiple blasts, which were also assisted by shaped Nano-thermite charges, as shown by the forensic photographs of the structural steel girders remaining. The jet fuel just caused high-level fires in the office furniture and cooked off very quickly. Most of the key government staff had been told not to come in that day, including the Secret Service, which was why only a third of the normal contingent of staff were killed or injured, as verified by the hospital records; they expected many more casualties than they treated that day. Some key directors of companies who had been warned off without saying why, watched the whole thing nervously from a coffee shop opposite while their office staff fried aloft or jumped. I wonder if they sleep at night?

In Building Seven, which had not been hit by anything, a more conventional demolition occurred, as stated by the Mayor of New York in a later interview. He did not explain how these demolition charges got there as rigging a building for a controlled drop takes at least three days and WTC7 went down within hours of the other two. All this is common knowledge, but as Goebbels said, back when managing the Nazi propaganda machine, "*If you tell a lie big enough and keep repeating it, people will eventually come to believe it.*" Never a truer word spoken. Perhaps Machiavelli had it right when he said in effect, "The business of Princes is War. Any Prince who does not know this will not be a Prince for very long." (my translation).

There were multiple gains from the 9/11 events. On the minor side, a large quantity of gold was stolen from under WTC 7. The final truck, only half-laden, never got out and was buried under the falling building. No crooks buried there, they knew the timing and just could not carry it all out in time. Gold is very heavy. All of this is in the public record of what was found under the rubble.

The Twin Towers buildings contained a lot of critical financial docs, which were going to have to meet a very heavy call the next day. A financial call that never came. This is multiply documented. It is surprising that the MSM (main stream media) choose to ignore it. 9/11 was one of the greatest thefts on record apart from covering up multiple fraud and losing millions into the invisible world of black projects. It is said over three trillion dollars are not accounted for.

The buildings had been reinsured by the new owners only weeks before with a special, very high cost premium to include payment should they befall acts of terrorism and war. Not a normal policy inclusion and these same buildings insurance cover gave massive pay-outs to the owners upon their destruction. They had already started to consult with architects on the redevelopment of the site and the normal demolition of the Towers would have been very expensive. These were just beneficial side effects. 9/11 allowed the whole redefinition of the 'war on terror' against an enemy who at that time hardly existed but would serve as a prodding stick to move America and Americans into a whole New World Order of control, loss of fundamental rights, surveillance and suppression which would not have been possible without a new 'Pearl Harbour', as it had already been speculated in the ideas of the 'New American Century' thesis published some time before.

In reality, Osama Bin Laden died weeks after 9/11. He used to use 49 mobile telephones. Do you not think the NSA always knew exactly where he was? You can track those phones to within one metre from a satellite by their GPS signal 24/7/365 days a year. The only way to stop that is put your phone in a tin box and close the lid. It is then in a faraday cage and no signal gets in or out, or you can take out both the SIM card and the battery as that has its own reporting chip which transmits its position every thirty seconds or so. Did you not notice in one of the Bourne movies, the female operative takes out the SIM and battery, stamps on them and runs off? She is then under the radar so to speak. I have done it myself several times when necessary.

Usually though, I like everyone to know where I am. I am also RFID chipped, as are most spies and military these days. Much more effective than the old dog tags. It is a bit like in the 'Men In Black' films where all the aliens are tracked in the central control room to make sure none of them are going 'over the wall'. It will come to you all eventually. It's already being offered in Australia and they are trialling it in India right now. No chip, no ID, no money. It is for the good of your health you see, so if you have an accident all your medical records are right there on your chip including your blood group.

They do not tell you they also can receive wireless

messages and give you inculcated hormone releases and brain pattern influence. Does the 'lone assassin' come to mind? You have to be pretty experienced and smart to control these little gadgets. They are very small physically, no more than a few millimetres long and easy to disguise and insert. I expect your cat or dog has one. There is also one built into your UK passport now. They always know where you are. It's all logged on super-computers but that's not the problem; it's who runs the bloody computers, not the machines themselves.

You can even buy civilian software now to track your partner's phone minute by minute and if you are really smart you can turn on its camera and mic. High schools in America are doing it right now to spy on their students and Michele Obama wants them to report any non-politically correct thoughts they observe in their parents. "1984" is alive and well in the US of A, as reported in the American press.

Worry not Brits, "Minority Report" is also with us too as some electronic billboard posters by bus stops in London can now ID the gender, approximate age and clothes style of the people waiting for their bus and change the screened adverts to suit their social group. Google has "unintentionally" collected your unprotected wireless computer data while photographing your street and Amazon has the largest consumer database in the world and probably can predict your Christmas purchasing habits before you have even thought about what those little ones would like.

This manuscript is being read in Utah before it even gets published and between them, GCHQ and the NSA have all your phone calls, e-mails and texts on file forever, suitably filed and categorised by the super-computers that have also photographed you naked, making love or jacking off from your lap top or iPhone camera (The good stuff gets passed around from desk to desk rather like in 'The Truman Show') Meanwhile, HAARP can modify your weather and give you a storm or a hurricane given a few hours' prior notice or a favourable weather front.

Geeks rule OK! Well, actually they only do as they are told and they are not told very much. The real power brokers are not very smart, but they can employ smart young people to do their thinking for them while indulging in their own fantasies and dreams – like ruling the world. They also gamble, but not in casinos, they do it on the derivatives markets, futures and hedge funds and they pay their bankers handsomely for their efforts. Good God man, if you don't get over £6 million a year how can you get by? They actually use a measure, which is a multiple of the UK Prime Minister's annual pay. So you might get twenty PM or fifty PM. It lets the politicians know who is really in charge. Tony Blair makes millions a year now and pays approximately 5% income tax overall. Not bad for a second-rate lawyer-made-good. I say good luck to him, a true socialist through and through! He knew all that Oxford University education would pay off one day! And he didn't even have student loans to pay back.

Pissing off Bush Cartel politicians can be a dangerous game. The journalist from the Florida Sun who exposed Bush Junior's daughters over some minor irregularity was one of the first to get Anthrax spores in the post. Wow!

But back to Bin Liner. The bogie man had to be out there being an online evil-doer, making videos and threatening the world like Fu Manchu (and his evil daughter Fu-Ming ...always fuming). It reminded me of a tabloid newspaper cartoon of Bin Laden sipping a rum and coke by a Stateside private pool, while in the background a film set is waiting complete with polystyrene boulders, sand and a camel. The director looking through his framing viewer, calls over to Bin Laden, "Tim. We are ready for you now!"

The videos that were released were played by actors. The biometrics of their faces were not those of Osama Bin Laden and they made some really classic errors. In one famous fake item, 'bin Liner' is seen to be writing with his right hand, which has upon it a huge gold ring and what looks like a Rolex watch. Everyone knows in Intelligence that Tim was left-handed and further, decorative ornament on men is absolutely forbidden by the Koran. Hollywood got it wrong again. Dare I say, "Wag the Dog!"

When Obama needed a morale boost at home, it was decided to kill off Osama Bin Laden in a Hollywood-style raid, reminiscent of the remake of "Black Hawk Down" that rewrote another major fuck-up as an act of heroes. Allegedly, he had been 'discovered' in a compound near a major Pakistani military establishment and who would do the noble deed? Well of course the famous Seal Team 6, perhaps better known as 'Team America'. So at night in they went with two helicopters, fought their way past house servants and allegedly destroying all possible intelligence gains, popped off Osama who was hiding behind his wife unarmed. In fact, the guy they blew away was a distant relative of Osama, who had, of course, died naturally some thirteen years previously. Making their escape (why was that necessary?), the team then took off, crashing the smaller chopper in the compound and taking the cadaver of the evil-doer with them. This had to be disposed of quickly at sea we are told, to prevent a martyrs' shrine being created, but in reality, it was because the relative did not look very much like Bin Laden at all. Then pre-prepared photos of the dead Bin Laden were posted online to cement the story. These did not fit the real Bin Laden biometrics either, but were suitably dramatic.

 Americans celebrated, drank beer and waved the Stars and Stripes. All was well until leaks needed Seal Team 6 to be blown up in an old Chinook, so old it was a write-off before the 'tragic crash', again all those 'brave men' were killed to ensure the dodgy story continued to hold water. 'Ours is not to question why? Ours is only to do and die'. Do you think there could be just a few cracks appearing in the guaranteed loyalty of certain Special Forces when they are used and abused in this manner?

Barack Obama is not even American in his original birth, he was not born in Hawaii and his birth certificate there was faked to get him into the US education system. The Birth Certificate does not stand up to scrutiny. It is not even his original real name. The CIA just call him Alan. In the UK positive vetting goes back as far as great-grandparents; one doubts whether Obama would get through that process with a clean bill of health.

The first Iraq war, or as it was known The Gulf War, was a key turning point in the involvement of American boots on the ground in its Middle-East foreign policy. Saddam Hussein had been a CIA Station chief up until the moment he was assisted in completely taking over Iraq, which is of the record. The historical facts you can look up, but he was well 'on-side' to America until such time as he started to become bigger than his boots, owed a lot of money to Kuwait and there were disputes about lateral drilling for oil under borders by Iraq. This means you are getting access to oilfields, which are actually underneath somebody else's territory by drilling down and then sideways. He made a back door petition to the USA to invade Kuwait and was in effect given a green light.

This was a set-up, as the principle problem as seen by the US was he was prepared to sell oil in currencies other than the petro-dollar (the US Dollar), which would start to undermine the value of the US Dollar as the reserve worldwide currency. Hence, he was encouraging a US Dollar devaluation, which was the main reason why he suddenly found himself not on the US Christmas card list. The rest is history.

Some say it was not Hussein who was hanged but a doppelganger, of which he had three. When he would leave his palace residence in Iraq, three identical convoys would emerge and go separate ways so no one knew in which convoy he actually was. The other two were occupied by doubles so similar it was difficult to tell the difference.

Hitler had played the same game and it was neither he nor Eva Braun whose bodies were found burnt and charred in his Berlin bunker by the Russians at the end of WWII. Hitler had months to prepare for defeat in Europe; it was no surprise. Witnesses saw him fly away in a light aircraft and he then travelled by stealth submarine to South America, where preparations had already been made for his secluded retreat from front line warfare.

The Russians willingly conspired with the other Allies to give credence to the story that he was dead.

This ensured a sense of true victory when in fact, the objectives of the Nazi regime had always entertained the possibility that they might lose the European war. They had constructed large hi-tech cargo submarines to cover this option and when they sailed a circuitous route down the mid-Atlantic Trench towards Argentina, the Allies had frantically sent a flotilla of naval vessels in pursuit but they did not locate them or make contact.

Hitler was recognised staying at one of his favourite retreat hotels by staff who had seen him before. He had shaved off his distinctive little moustache and reports showed he died naturally many years later. The influence of the Nazis after the end of WWII should not be underestimated. Project Paperclip took many of the top Nazi brains to America, where they became the core of the US space programme at NASA.

Back in the UK, I came across a low-grade smuggling operation to supply soft drugs into the British Army. This had been going on far longer in the US Army, ever since at least Vietnam, but had not really become part of the scene for squaddies over here. I managed to shut down this particular incursion at the time. No one was charged and the Army wanted it covered up as it was a little embarrassing, so that's what happened. The matter was forgotten and lost forever, never to be mentioned again in polite circles.

I suspect it may have recommenced later down another route, but I was not asked to look into it as no one wanted to know and what you don't officially know you can ignore. As the Navy would say, 'If you find anything unfortunate, just hide it and if you can't do that then destroy it.'

Cover ups take up over 20% of all intelligence work worldwide. Everyone makes mistakes and then they have to be obscured by issuing 'snow jobs'. As I've said before, where do you hide a tree? - In a forest.

9. Times they are a changin'

R & R FOR SPOOKS

The 21st Century had arrived, the millennium bug had not ended the Western civilised world and only a few odd people had committed suicide expecting imminent doom.

My children were growing up, my finances were not looking bright and expenses were getting out of hand. Maintaining the previous structures was not looking good and my health was suffering. I was now in my mid 50s, the Multiple Sclerosis was a problem and HMG still needed me on side.

I had survived the Blair weeding out some of the best men in the agencies. Blair never wanted the truth, he only wanted what fitted the script and although I had been complimented for 'intelligence excellence' like many others, including several of my mates, I was moved sideways, totally now only a sub-contractor, affording HMG complete deniable responsibility.

I was asked to help take care of other special forces and intelligence staff in similar circumstances, assisting with the setting up of safe situations for them, keeping them out of sight and ensuring nothing unfortunate made it into the press, as rumour had it that memoirs were being written.

Stella Rimington had written her memoir, "Open Secret", which said very little and HMG was still nervous of another "Spy Catcher". As a former senior scientific officer for MI5, Peter Wright knew a great deal. The government had tried to ban the book but that just made it the most sought after thing since sliced bread. They had been smuggled in by folk in their holiday luggage; you could buy it abroad and they sold on the black market for a nice profit thank you, so HMG had learnt that suppressing something like they had tried too before only made it more desirable.

It was 2002 and it was time to go back on the road, do some more intelligence infiltration work but only use the safe houses and locations that were available to me and keep moving around. That cut down my overheads and also made me less of a vulnerable target. Since I had been instrumental in supplying intelligence on Iraqi operatives resulting in their neutralisation, my persona was now on two priority hit lists. I understand 'kill on sight' may still be written under my name.

I was using different names and using legends also in use by others. Some of these I had created myself as handler so I knew their scripts quite well and could rattle off their differing passwords and histories pretty much from memory without needing to brush up on the provenance too much. All legends have to be capable of checking out by the enemy digging into

196

past friends, whatever files might be available and seeing if the avatar looks like a real person, hence they need to be maintained by their creators and operatives over years, not just a few days or weeks.

When Ian Fleming first created his mythical but based-on-fact character, he saw the 'Bond' legend as one that would be used by different agents and hence in the films by different actors. This directly paralleled the way he knew it actually worked, where similar aged and looking agents would take on the role for a particular period of time or task and then fade away back into other legends or even their real name. However, their real names are never used in the agency, neither are their family home addresses as obviously that would make all connected to them very vulnerable and possibly to blackmail or threat of retaliation.

My brother-in-law had been murdered by the IRA while on active service with 'Signals' in Northern Ireland and the family was warned to be 'on watch' by the Army as grudges are held for a long time. Only recently the family was awarded The Queen Elizabeth Medal with a scroll signed by Her Majesty for the loss of their beloved son. His memory is fondly remembered with great respect by his unit The Royal Regiment of Fusiliers, a long standing and noble band of men with close community connections with all who have served with them. Invites to their headquarters at The Tower of London and to the National Memorial Arboretum, where dedicated trees mark the memory of individual soldiers, have been an annual event for the family for some years. They are emotional times when tears are shed for the fallen, no matter where that may have been. They live still in the hearts of their loved ones. I could not match the bravery and dedication of these men.

However, I can help the living and those who find themselves marginalised by having worked in grey zones where their work and services can rarely be acknowledged. This is especially so if they have had to be distanced from the main frame of the armed services, because their work and tasks were sensitive or even outright illegal in the countries they had operated in. To name or identify these chaps and gals would be to put them very much in harm's way as we have all made enemies, powerful enemies. Many of them are still out there and have powers to reach out and strike in unexpected ways, as you will see as this dialogue continues.

Please excuse my careful sanitation and editing of personal details from the accounts herein contained, but I am sure you understand the responsibility someone like me must maintain in order that no one is put at undue risk. The brutal murder of Corporal Lee Rigby in Woolwich reflects and concentrates our need to be aware of the unseen enemy who may not be a million miles away. Lee Rigby, a drummer musician and medic, was a member of the same regiment as my brother-in-law and both of their unnecessary deaths hurts and saddens us all.

I cannot help but reflect that a similar fate may have awaited someone in my own unit had it not been stood down in the early years of the 21st Century. Then, we had live agents in field and we were told to stop sending up data because we were making, "Too much work for Special Branch to check out". However, to be fair, the culprits were already on the radar of MI5 and it is very difficult to predict when a radicalised belief may flow over into radical action. The human mind can be an unknown territory, especially if in oneself it is impossible to entertain the thinking that may be going on in these men's minds and emotions. They must be mentally sick.

Back to my own story, for the road a number of vehicles were obtained and donated. The flagship accommodation was a Winnebago motorhome of some cosy vintage, but equipped with a flushing loo and on-board sanitary system, shower, kitchen and comfortable captain's chairs that swung round when not in the driving position. Central heating and air conditioning came as standard and it was all based on a manual, if underpowered, Renault Traffic diesel unit. Solar panels were added on the roof and a number of communications gadgets and toys and navigational aids. She was known as 'Winne' and she suitably had low millage as is often the case with true RVs. She had been supplied via our American chums in Suffolk, say no more, and had been built in the United States but modified to UK requirements. As the ops we were focusing on were Anglo/Atlantic under the umbrella of NAIG, North Atlantic Intelligence Group, we also worked in cooperation and liaison with an American chum. This meant we also had another Renault RV, a couple of saloon cars and another baggage van, all UK registered. I can mention these now because they have all outlived their purpose and were officially scrapped some time ago, so don't go looking for them.

We would often focus on the same tasks, although in theatre we would not necessarily 'know' each other. The general rule is you try to have back up if it is available without looking bloody obvious. Where did this happy band hang out? You won't be far wrong whatever you guess as we were all over the place, including gatherings of various factions and beliefs,

Stonehenge comes to mind, others I hesitate to say. Thousands go to these events, to ID the above would be like looking for a needle in a haystack even if you knew where the haystacks were.

Sometimes vehicles would go into Europe and in the welfare and care department it was deemed prudent to set up some more safe houses in Europe for staff, special forces and operatives needing to bail out from the Middle East and Africa as they could just merge into the remote countryside of some of these countries without being noticed unduly – just tourists. We set up a fake tourists' web site and a couple of locations to facilitate this where chaps could live under canvas or in rather primitive accommodations, which was not dissimilar to some of the places they had been 'working' in. Sometimes the culture shock of going from one cultural zone and style can be unhelpful to spies; staying 'in character' for when they return to their duties. At one base we had built a crude compound similar to those in Iraq.

Real names were not used. I would supply a cover, means of support, basic services would be there waiting, water, sanitation, and medical kits etc. and they would basically look after themselves. These folk are often very independent and don't like being ordered about or set in fixed routines. Their own vehicles when they arrived were the usual ram shackled heaps that go unnoticed both in the UK and Europe and they too, often had fake ID's so they could not be traced back to any of their true origins. Sometimes they were armed. We had a few ranges set up safely so no one down the line of fire would get hurt. I assure you these people knew what they were doing in that department and I think the kit came in via official routes, but it was never discussed. They did talk a bit about their work and history and that I will have to carefully edit here so if you detect holes they are there deliberately so.

They were all agency or sub-contractors or SAS or former SAS now working on set tasks only, so they were no longer on the official Army payroll. Many of them were living in a legend on the tasks they had been commissioned to undertake, but all people need some R&R and you don't want to be recognised by anyone from the theatre of operations so they stayed pretty much out of sight and under radar. We did not entertain much, although there were a few ex-intel people locally who hung out in these regions for similar reasons. There were several nationalities involved; I won't mention them but you can guess the likely sources. The whole thing was undercover. Again I can only mention it at all now because it no longer exists in the places I am referring. Everything has been cleaned out, tidied up, burnt and sanitised, even the transport; we are very thorough at that.

Of the local dudes who came along later into the area and set up their own facilities, birds of a feather stick together. There was one chap from Menwith Hill and another who had been technical crew on Air Force One. These were pretty high-powered guys who had high clearances. He told one story of being called in urgently to RAF Lakenheath, it's actually a totally US Air Force frontline fighter station in Suffolk. The President's plane, Air Force One had landed with its buddy coms aircraft that always travels with it and had a technical problem in his field of knowledge. So off he drives to the base main gate, where security is pretty tight. Arriving at the gate he does not have a base entry pass and the MPs are all twitchy, they never go a bundle on guys with English accents, so they make the call up the line and down comes the base Commander accompanied by a US Air Force four-star general. The guards snap to attention like pieces of finely carved granite.

"Come on in son," declares the general.   "I'll sign him in sir!" snaps the Corporal.   "No", says the general. "This is off the record." They move off to his staff car.

"He's a spook", whispers the corporal to his other guards. The staff car drives out onto the apron where an exclusion zone has been set up around both aircraft. Armed guards have the right to use lethal force against anyone found inside these zones who does not have the right clearances. Again guards snap to attention and look to the Englishman for the necessary paperwork. The general waves them away; they just salute.

Having fixed the technical problem overnight, The President arrives with the First Lady. The general says to our chap, "We don't want that glitch happening again, you had better fly with us on Air Force One," which he does chatting now and then with the President who was the essence of good manners, he said, and very user friendly to the helpful technical Brit on board. It is nice to know our technical expertise both in the comms department and on special missions is highly respected by our American friends and correctly so. Credit where credit due. We like to help when we can, hands across the sea so to speak. While chatting, our chap did bring up the subject of UFOs. The President was interested, but not dismissive at all. 'More things in Heaven and Earth', was the phrase used.

Air Force One is quite an impressive aircraft as is told

by my mates who have been on it; not just another Boeing 747 but with a fancy décor. It has much bigger engines, so powerful that when she took off they tore off part of the runway surface at the 'rotation' point – that's lift off. She has a rate of climb far in excess of normal commercial aircraft and is full of comms toys as we call them. A flying office suite in the sky. The buddy aircraft carries also all the necessary comms kit for strategic command and can send out all the signals to launch birds (missiles) should the occasion arise. All personnel have to have top grade clearances – Q clearances in effect – that is one covering nuclear capability and may include launch code knowledge. I have a lot of respect for senior military; they carry a lot of responsibility, which they seek to deliver with caution. It's the politicians that worry me.

In the course of fixing up some of the safe houses and camping sites, now and then we employed a few Romanians. These were economic refugees, initially not very legal, although they did have passports, but they all became legalised later when Romania became a member of the EU. They were good workers and some spoke quite good English, which had been taught in their schools. Most young Romanian men realise that if they are to get anywhere in life they have to leave their home country and move abroad. The EU afforded a good opportunity to them to do this.

One of these chaps was ex-Romanian secret police, which does not mean a great deal, but he was quite enthusiastic to work for us and practice his language skills. He spoke of trying to ride on the axles of lorries or trains to get into the UK, which they all saw as the best place to be. They knew the streets were paved with gold and of course the UK had the best social security welfare systems to support them and their families. I dissuaded him from his plan and over time managed to get him and his hardworking chums proper legal documentation in Europe. They ended up working for the local authorities on public building works, which was a good stabilisation of their lives; they all married and had children some years later.

Their fellow countrymen of whom they spoke did make it into the UK, one way or another, where they mostly ended up on building sites or in agriculture. Somehow the system allowed for them to claim benefits for their families and children in Romania. I never quite understood this but it appeared that legally they could. As the Brit ex- pats overseas in Europe were being prejudiced by the British social security system, it seemed a little off-balance that the UK was persecuting its own people while supporting others who were very new to the whole United European thing.

One thing the Eastern Europeans had to be educated on was safety. They were quite prepared to take undue risks, which I guess was just due to the way they had been brought up. Unfortunately, the unemployed young men of that ilk (there were very few women), would go out in small groups of four people and steal anything they could get their hands on.

A favourite trick was to be very active when there was a fiesta and families would be going into town to celebrate. The Romanian thieves would meet up in remote parking areas in a couple of cars; one would be needed on the 'job' and a defensive look out to flag their mates by mobile phone if anyone was seen coming home. I would drive to where I would know they would be congregated, stop my vehicle to block the entrance, emerge and take pictures of them from a little distance. I kept the engine running, but they were not used to this pro-active approach and it did stop a lot of crime in the area but they probably just went off a few miles to a safer location. To cut down living expenses they would rent a town house suitable to house four people, move in twelve or so, even the living room had three sleeping in there, share the costs as a group and send the spare money home to Romania. These places did not have gardens so they would all pile out at night into the squares where a hundred or so would gather, smoking and chatting mostly about possible work opportunities that they had heard of, or football about which they were all keen and the allure of getting into Britain. Plans would be hatched, stories told of successful efforts by others and intel exchanged.

Later some of the men would bring in 'wives'; these were almost immediately deployed as prostitutes to bolster the family funds. I am not being judgmental of this; they were all born survivors. I gather that in the local brothels, which are legal in most European counties, Romanian girls make up the largest contingent of ladies of the night.

I used and employed a few Bulgarian workmen. These were generally tougher characters. In the days of the Warsaw Pact when Bulgaria was solidly a part of the USSR network the Bulgarian Secret Service were a force to be reckoned with, second only to the East German Stasi. Bulgarians were considered very effective assassins and had been contracted to do some more tricky jobs for the Russians. The Ruskies, although very effective themselves are quite keen to farm out work to others, thereby keeping them out of the firing line.

The Yanks do the same and it's nothing new; so did the ancient Romans who would always send in the captured men of previous enemies who were told, fight for Rome or be killed. It was an easy choice to make.

Today, Muslim extremists don't mind dying on missions in their warped understanding of the noble religion. Suicidal missions however, give them a definite advantage as our chaps always had to have exit plans and the need to be extracted from theatre. If you are up against men who are going to be martyrs and have no need to go home, then their operations can take on a whole new dimension. That includes suicide bombers of course and increasingly, there are women who are prepared to blow themselves up as well.

Roadside bombs are unfortunately relatively easy to produce. I am not going to tell you how but it is kitchen sink technology. I regard them as very cowardly and car bombs aimed at markets, women and children. Can you really blame our chaps being somewhat unkind to the enemy and then being court-martialled? Civilisation may be alive and well in the UK but certainly not worldwide – it can be savage out there; Africa in particular has a poor reputation.

One of the very senior men told a harrowing tale of an extremist enemy field unit taking one of their own women, a young girl, and staking her out near the British forces, cutting her open and laying out part of a lung. Of course she was screaming the place down. They backed off and waited for the Brits to investigate – the perfect ambush. She was beyond help, as would be obvious from blood loss alone. What the hell are they supposed to do, consult the Geneva Convention? Of course we have high standards and we should maintain them but many others do not!

These are extremes however and should not be regarded as the general rule, but you will find the SAS/SBS are set against the most vile and severe enemies. They have a lot to cope with and I have been the agony aunt to several men who just needed to talk about what they had been through. These men, both British and American, sometimes find it very difficult to assimilate back into normal society when they come out of service. That was particularly true starting with Vietnam. Many men were so insular in their psychology they needed to relocate to remote places like Alaska where they did not have to deal with regular society. The American dream had long gone for them and they saw through the plastic superficial world, which makes up 90% of Western culture these days.

 Ghandi, when asked what he thought of Western civilisation, said he thought it would be, 'a very good idea'. True words and never more true than today. The world is now run by very selfish and counter-productive forces. They seem to have no regard whatsoever for the lives of their grandchildren, if they have any. The accounting bottom line is the only thing that counts and it must be a mental disease when multi-billionaires are prepared to levy misery on millions just to manipulate the markets and make a few more millions. I am not making this up, research it yourself.

They say 4% of people are psychologically amoral, that means they have no problem with being as cruel as is needed to be to obtain their objectives that day. These objectives are not based on need. No, they are based on abstract figures, gaining further advantage, like ruining the Greek economy so they will have to sell off everything they have including their newly discovered oil and gas reserves. Or stealing the same black gold under the Eastern Med (I was fly on the wall at a bankers' closed shop meeting). No names need be mentioned; I am 25% Jewish myself so don't say I am anti-Semitic please. Then again it's claimed Hitler had some Jewish blood in him too, but killing off a few million people is standard practice in ways and means of psychopaths getting what they want. It is in the DNA of primates. The Alpha male has to keep down the pretenders to his throne. Perhaps Machiavelli was right; he certainly seems to be often read in the halls of power that I am familiar with on both sides of the Atlantic, in fact most places!

One of the places we set up was not far from the last stand of the Spanish Republican Army. They had made a gallant counter attack on Franco's Nationalists but this had stalled in a hill village where they were partially besieged. Franco called up his mate Hitler, and arranged to borrow 300 front line aircraft of the emerging Luftwaffe. They needed to test out the concept of aerial Blitzkrieg, so the German planes were quickly re-designated as Spanish and undertook three weeks' saturation bombing on the besieged Republicans who retreated to the mountains where deep caves and narrow passes allowed them to survive.

Forced after weeks of hunger and being surrounded by the main Nationalist forces, four young officers decided to advance down the single narrow exit canyon armed only with revolvers. The encircling guards below thought they were an advance scouting party for a mass break-out and spontaneously fell back, expecting imminent attack. This allowed large numbers of the Republicans to escape and vanish into the vast wild countryside with its forests and scattered fincas. Here they lived off the land and were branded outlaws when Franco won the civil war and imposed his dictatorship upon all the Spanish regions.

When once I was in a supermarket near Barcelona, an old lady was coming towards the door and being British, I opened it for her and held it as she entered. Looking suspiciously at me, the old soul turned to the checkout guy and said, "The Bandito opened the door for me!" My Spanish was not good but I could understand that. Anyone who lived outside of the village had to be an outlaw. In fact, Franco had made living in the countryside illegal in order to try to control the rebel forces still out there. So farmers had to live only in the villages and travel to their fields every day then back again in the evening. Only at harvest times were they allowed to remain sleeping at their fincas for a few days. Even to this day it is difficult to find farms out there where full time occupation is allowed and documented. Every ten years they hold an amnesty when buildings that have grown like mushrooms in the night are made official. This allows for taxes to be collected on them, which are the only reason they tolerate the illegal buildings going up in the first place. In recent years, many Brits have been conned into buying properties that do not, on paper, legally exist and can be demolished by the local authorities, should they wish.

I attended an International Brigade Memorial inauguration up at the mountain retreat attended by the military attaché from the British Embassy in

Madrid and his charming Basque wife. He was a Brigadier and we made first physical contact there. Distinguished sort of chap; came in useful later making that personal contact, but let's not be premature. The British contingent had fought bravely alongside their socialist companions way back then. George Orwell had been there; it had a strong influence on his later writings.

I was told by a local character, the son of one of the original fighters, that in the cellars of all the local villages, rifles, ammo and the armaments of the Republican Army that escaped remained hidden and maintained just in case they were ever needed again. I am sure he was right; he could shoot well.

One of the chaps I had a limited therapeutic input to was Wolfy, a very skilled German pilot. His story was rather tragic. He had been driving his Mercedes in his home country containing his entire family, wife and three boys. It was late at night as he headed down a city one-way street, when another Mercedes pulls into the other end and starts quickly towards him running in the wrong direction to the correct traffic flow. Wolfy in determined, Teutonic style carries on at speed flashing his lights and determined that this idiot should get out of his way. He did not. The two cars collided at speed head on and Wolfy's entire family were killed outright. This left Wolfy in a very negative self-destructive state of mind. He undertook very dangerous missions and that's why I got to know him.

He sort of semi-retired, but carried on flying mostly twin-prop executive air taxis. I heard on the news he had flown into a Scottish hillside, killing himself and his two passengers. The accident report simply said pilot error, which translated to me as pilot pushing the parameters and not caring about it. Wolfy was not untypical of the men who were referred to me from various quarters of both the semi-retired or sub-contractual military forces. They had been recruited from various places including military and civilian prisons. In some respects, they were indeed the kind of 'on-side' mercenaries that are depicted in films as being very useful to governments and also very expendable.

They would, by their psychological makeup, be on for dangerous missions. Some of them were indeed psychopaths. How long they had been that way was not easy to tell. When someone is under orders it can give a lot of license, notwithstanding the findings of the Nuremburg Trials. As Peter Pace, the Military Commander in Chief of US Forces had said, if an order comes down to you officers that contradicts your ethical code, you are not obliged to obey it. However, it is very difficult to disobey orders.

 Often in Intelligence you have to go off on one's own, while families are left, supported but without you. I was now hanging out in an RV in the vicinity of Rochester Airport. There were a number of vehicles over time that had served my wandering purposes. Not only was there the Winni, but also the Renault, a Merc 209 Camper and a couple of Ford Transits. I was also given an ex-government armoured Jag, built like a tank. I was in having a coffee one day at a roadside café, when the bloke next to me says that someone had just hit my Jag. I laughed and wandered outside. A black Ford Mondeo was zooming off to get away. There was my Jag, not a mark on it. He had hit the corner of the front bumper; bits of his plastic spoiler and rear lights lay all over the road. Jag one, Ford zero.

I joined in an extra-mural observer role at the Jesuit Observatory near to one of the R&R locations. The skies were clear and the staff extremely liberal minded. The Pope had declared that there was likely life throughout the Universe and that aliens could be educated and brought into the church. The observatory had commenced in the early 20th century and had taken a great interest in sun spots and their possible relationship to the triggering of earthquakes. Although they could not figure it out then because they did not have the detailed satellite data we now have on the sun. We now know that the solar wind speed from coronal holes and CMEs, coronal mass ejections, do indeed tend to trigger earthquakes and can also effect weather patterns on Earth, so the Jesuit priests peering down their telescopes and solar display instruments were not too far wrong all those years ago. I became certificated as an assistant observer for the unit, which was an extra mural university department.

This was not the first time I had been involved in astronomy and space research as I had done some work in Surrey on Earth Sciences, which involved looking at the Earth from satellite imagery as if you were looking at an alien planet. This had thrown up some interesting, if alarming, results, one of which was that every year we were destroying one 200ths of the Earth's trees (that's 0.5%) and at an increasing rate. Therefore, oxygen was likely to get a little thinner over time. However, these things are not an exact science and much of the speculation on global warming is questionable as to what are the exact causes. Solar output is a key factor and it is possible we could be in for some more extremes, heat waves, drought and severe winters with more snow as heat evaporates more water from the oceans, both causing more hurricanes and snowfall around the poles if the jet stream brings it down to lower latitudes.

Once, I came out of one of the safe locations in the Iberian Peninsula to find six feet of snow had fallen overnight. The previous day it had been warm and sunny. Most weird! There was also a rolling freezing fog, which would roll down off the mountains dropping the temperature instantly as it arrived and in the morning the trees had grown the most elaborate ice crystals on their windward side. Beautiful but scary; weather scares me much more than human conflict. I was brought up by the sea and learnt from an early age you never take for granted Mother Nature, she is a lot more powerful than you and can be fickle with it.

2008 was an interesting year in Europe. From 2006 the 'enemy', whoever they were, started to get more pro-active with us 'left of field' special forces. The ending of the Gulf War was not really an ending at all. All the same forces and groups were going strong, gaining power, re-grouping and changing sides according to what they thought were their best options.

A lot of these people are always there for their own benefit, survival and self-interests. Yes, there is the religious fervour, but like with the Irish Troubles much of the flag waving is just a bluff for straightforward criminal activity. Helps the conscious if dodgy folk think they have a just cause. As Tony Blair had said, "We must fight for peace!" Something of an oxymoron, perhaps the double meaning also applies.

That year, someone arranged for the car I was using

to catch fire; I obviously knew too much, so certain persons were getting nervous. Got in, locked the doors, standard procedure, turned the ignition key and there was a bang and the whole engine under the bonnet became a ranging inferno. Doors would not open and the undergrowth caught fire. One responds instinctively, seconds count. I kicked out the passenger door window and climbed out through the low flames from the grass fire, which was now catching well in the light wind. Rushing inside I shouted to everyone not to go near the car. I figured there could be more fireworks and indeed there were, the first pop had not been complete, which is why I had survived. Sure enough, shortly afterwards another bang ensued.

Jumping in another vehicle, I tore down to the local fire station, screeched to a halt blasting my horn and then ringing the alarm doorbell. After about thirty seconds a fireman appeared clutching a cup of coffee and smoking a cigarette. I explained the situation. He scratched his head and consulted with another colleague who had appeared to see what all the fuss was about. Then a committee meeting was held. The station manager came down and discussions were had on what equipment might be needed. Gear was off loaded and on loaded to the fire tenders and telephone calls were made while I slowly pulled my hair out trying not to get too frustrated. Apparently because the incident was out of town, the rural forestry commission would have to supervise the fire. They were on their way.

Some ten minutes later they arrived and a convoy was formed, me in front to show the way, then the forestry people's two jeeps, then two fire tenders behind and another fire managers jeep. We set off slowly. I had to stop now and then to let them catch up, I had been only doing forty miles per hour but these water laden fire trucks were not built for speed and looked a little post WWII in their vintage.

Smoke came in sight; the fire had spread now to a couple of acres. The wind had got busy with it. Trees were on fire. The crews now actually showed they did know what they were doing. They went ahead of the fire and started more fires, which they controlled to form firebreaks. Water was spayed around, more fire trucks and police and forestry people came along. This was a day out and they made the most of it. I told them to ignore the car, it would be a right off anyway and was still popping as bits of mechanism exploded and flacks of glass flew around. Four hours later the fire was out however they watered the whole area until it was soaked, the trees would really appreciate that, I thought, as it had been a severe drought for weeks. The incident was written off as an unfortunate accident and everyone went home happy. No point in causing trouble or starting a pointless investigation, the culprits would be long gone and over the hills far away by now; these were professionals, one could tell. A replacement car arrived soon and was a later model. All's well that ends well!

Not long after, a depressed spy arrived for care and overseen R & R from Saudi Arabia. He had been in field far too long and had become very down with his role. He'd been shifted off to Dubai where medication and hospitalisation had not really done very much. Apparently the loneliness of the job had got to him. He had been working alone for some time with no break and in a socially very isolated situation. Not by location but by cultural separation. From experience,

I know that no infidel is really accepted inside Saudi, although they can be very polite when overseas from their Kingdom. The families are large and the chain of succession extensive and complicated, with that many wives. It was apparently standard procedure to take their R&R in Dubai, which is a bit like the equivalent of the Las Vegas of the Middle East.

Well, this chap did quite well for a while on the 'farm' as it was known but was then whisked away back to conventional treatments in Dubai. He committed suicide some weeks later I was sad to hear. What can you do? When conventional medicine works it is claimed as a success; when it fails the illness killed them. Doctors, licensed to kill it sometimes seems to me. They had tried to get me to have a major brain op some years previously on the basis that I would lose some faculties and then be in a wheelchair for life. I declined the op, which only had a fifty percent chance of success anyway. I am still here by the grace of God.

10. A Very Serious Character

PROFESSIONAL KILLERS

I knew he was trouble as soon as I clapped eyes on him. It was not that he was not white, I have no colour prejudices, but he was a man with a face that had seen and delivered pain. His gait was a giveaway, always aware of what was happening on the street, this fellow had been shot at and also fired at others. I recognised his kind and they are trained killers. He had been sent to me to try to keep him out of trouble. I was told to go and meet him personally and tell no one. This was a very serious and troubled dude.

I led him to the safe house. He brushed me aside and examined the place in detail. He always expected someone out there would be in the process of trying to take him out. He neither trusted me at this stage or indeed any living soul on the planet including his own mother who he said thought he was 'a little shit'. He was scary and I don't scare easily.

So where to begin? I made tea, so damned English, and he started to calm down. "What do you want done?" demanded my newfound friend. No, not friend, patient maybe, bodyguard it seemed too, but general helper. He needed to be kept busy. "Well," I explained, "There's a lot of work to do on the farm and I have MS and I'm not as young as I was, so if you could help out I would really appreciate it."

"Yes, of course," was the curt reply. "I need to work to keep me sane." This was such a true statement as I learnt over time. I got him doing farm work and some building tasks, which he really focused on. While he was busy he was normal, I think. The evenings would be the difficult times. He would sit in his room and just stare at the wall. Others who had come would stare at the mountains or the exotic birds or the sunsets, but not him. There was a lot going on in his head. After a while, I carefully asked him, "What do you do?"

"I kill things," was his impersonal reply. The phrase 'things' bothered me; it was as if this was a mechanism of distancing him from the real implications of what he had been tasked to do.

"Things?" I enquired, "You mean people?"

"Yes."

"More than one?" I kind of knew the answer would be plural.

"Over seventy. It got easier as time went on."

It was a simple factual statement. There was no drama in it. It was not a boast. The comment about 'as time went on' rang true. I had heard that said before from such men. This man was a professional assassin.

"I told my daughter what I did", he opened up a little. "She totally rejected me. Never spoke to me again. Now I only talk to military. They are the only people who understand".

He was beginning to trust me now and I'd mentioned some of my own capers. I don't kill people, never have done, but I had been around these guys before and I spoke their language. I knew the mind-set.

It was enough for that evening. He was beginning to get stressed out, I knew the signs.

He had first occupied a single room in the farmhouse and shared the kitchen, but I felt he needed more headspace and I was nervous that one of the other guests might say something inappropriate and the situation would get out of hand. There was an ex-military command vehicle on site. A seven-tonner that I was in the process of turning into a useful RV. This work was now accelerated.

A small kitchen was installed as he liked to cook, and the usual creature comforts you would expect in field quarters such as an outside loo and some entertainment media. It had its own genny power supply and was settled down in a terrace out of sight and partially sunken into the ground, just as it would be in a war zone. He felt more secure there. He would sit outside holding his own rifle, loaded and ready for any attack. Inside he kept a variety of specialist knives. He told me he preferred to use knives; they killed silently without noise. He explained how he would creep up behind people, cover their mouths and slit their throats.

He had a really uncanny ability of moving absolutely silently. Often just for a prank or practice he would suddenly just be there, behind me, without sign or sound. No one had ever been able to creep up on me like that before. I had to be careful of this fellow, he was fucking lethal. He said he always slept armed and if I came in unannounced he would kill me. It had become a kind of instinctive habit. Who was after him? He related a few stories, all sounded authentic.

He had been in the SAS, recruited young. In the practice parachute jump, which is done on a wire line machine indoors he had jumped high and early, been noticed by the sergeant and recruited as good material for the regiment. But things had gone wrong. On a brief R&R in Germany, there had been a bar brawl. He had hit a guy too hard and probably instinctively using his SAS training, in a lethal place. The guy did not get up. He was on a serious fizzer, a standard military term for Court Marshall and had been sent to military prison for 12 years.

While inside, he had been taken under the wing of another inmate, a hardened man we will call Sergeant O and when Sergeant O got out, he had been re-recruited into the 'other capabilities', as it had been referred to by the head of MI6, before the parliamentary committee.

In other words, mercenaries who have no official recognition, but do the dirty work for the government when and as required. On the recommendation of Sergeant O, X as we will designate him, had been released four years early on the understanding that he worked for the incremental force, but if he went AWOL then he would be straight back in the slammer. Military prison is a hard and unforgiving place, not like civilian prison and men will do anything not to go back there.

I realised I had met Sergeant O some years earlier

when he had needed a little R&R himself. Any rate Sergeant O was now, in effect, his immediate commanding officer. These chaps work in small groups and are usually kept together so they know each other's methods and personalities. They can get pretty close as they are sent on very dangerous missions and the bonding that produces is very marked.

Sergeant O had related some confidential anecdotes when I had previously spent time with him. Like others, they need to offload to someone they can trust. The alarming thing that had done it in for X, was O had been killed on a mission they had been on during an extraction.

X had Sergeant O's cremated remains with him in a metal urn. This he would sit under the little shrine tree where we scattered the remains of such men in an unofficial war grave area. Flowers and a cross were there. Undisclosed grief and nostalgia is not an unknown emotion with military men. X took to sitting at night by that tree and talking to his lost friend. After a while, we scattered his ashes there with a correct Christian burial and the Union Jack. The flag became somewhat weather worn over time and looked, for all the world, like seasoned battle colours.

X had undergone serious re-training upon his release after eight years inside. He had kept himself fit and his body battle-ready. He was pretty bitter about how the Army had treated him before, but now he was back with mates and part of the unit. The trainings went on and on, Egypt, Norway, Alaska, until he was up to speed and honed in the required skills. Then missions began. I have to edit this here for security reasons and find a path between what is correct or inappropriate to mention. I will start by using some of a book X was writing of his life. This was a memoir that he felt would help him deal with what he had been tasked to do and his 'other activities' that he related to me as his confidant and unofficial 'therapist.'

As part of my job, I had been keeping an eye on these fellows, reporting to GCHQ and the military attaché in Madrid. The writings of these men who had entrusted the editing (and sanitisation) of their works to me as a professional writer. Little did they know HMG was keeping a strict eye on what they were putting down.

More than once one of the chaps would come in very upset, "Who's nicked my fucking laptop!" was the usual phrase. It had gone walk about because HMG did not want that story published or even in print anywhere. Its author and I were probably the only people who were fully aware of the implications. I was trying to be responsible, piggy in the middle, trusted by both sides one hoped, but still a very difficult and heart-searching situation to be in.

X related that his early missions had been protecting UN International troops in Africa. Although armed, the UN peacekeepers were generally not allowed to shoot at anyone, so themselves had to have unofficial guards who could shoot to kill and not be held accountable. In one field operation, a strong insurgent force was heading towards a UN position. Overnight, the small unit of which X was second in command, had infiltrated enemy territory. Unfortunately, they found they'd been cut off by advancing units of the insurgents, who had camped in a small canyon blocking off their retreat. The enemy did not know they were there and X elected to take out the picket position that was in their way.

Three enemy soldiers were sat around a small fire in the jungle. X crept up on them with his favourite knife, he called it his 'old friend'. He grabbed the nearest man and slit his throat ear to ear. He said this was the first time he had done this for real and it was a disturbing, but exhilarating, sensation. The second enemy soldier had gone for his rifle and X had managed to wound him in the arm enough to immobilise him. The third enemy now came at him with a machete. X ran, feeling his position was now untenable.

They ran hard through the jungle with the enemy gaining and delivering a glancing wound to X. A shot rang out. One of his unit had taken out the enemy assailant, but this gave away their position and they all had to flee for their lives as enemy reinforcements moved in the direction of their incursion. They were lucky to escape using only the cover afforded by the thick jungle at night. X still had the war wounds from this early encounter with potential death in a foreign field.

X said when they were hiding in the villages, were undercover, not in uniform. The enemy insurgents could later be seen driving by in trucks with blue UN helmets on their heads. These were shown off as trophies to indicate that they had killed some of the peacekeeping force and wanted everyone to know. This was not a game. This was real life and death stuff.

People do not expect to live to an old age in these regions. Life is cheap. When X eventually got back to base camp, they were very welcomed, as the back-up unit had felt very vulnerable without them. One of the medic nurses had rather needed his emotional support that night. They screwed each other's brains out. Such things happen when death seems near.

So X had tasted first blood and it changed his life, his attitudes and probably his brain patterns forever. He was both concerned and confused by the feelings it had stirred in him. Was he a real man at last or some kind of deranged animal? Any which way, he was now a more experienced member of the unit and given more responsibility.

This involved getting more into the darker side of operations and the inner keep who were trusted with them. Unfortunately, this did not always involve a clearly defined overseas 'enemy' as in Africa, when he had been dealing with dedicated bloodthirsty killers. This now was being around blokes who were on missions that could be said to be more political rather than military.

X was never directly involved with these in field but in the mess, talk is shared among blokes who need to exchange their feelings about what they have been tasked to do and sometimes not too happy with it. Let's cut to the chase. X claimed that two of these chaps said they had been involved with the Paris assassination of Princess Diana and Dodi Fayed.

The story went like this: The word had come down from on high at the last moment. They were only told late in the day although they had heard it had been green-lighted within only ten days of the scheduled op. Top brass had flown to Paris to oversee the events and the French Secret Service were co-opted into the operation. That is not difficult, the French Secret Service are the whores of the business in Europe and will get into bed with anyone, especially if the money is right officially or even unofficially. The French President was on side they said, but that was unconfirmed.

The first preparation was using the already in place assets of both the French and MI6 and a Merc from the fleet that services the Paris Ritz had been borrowed, it was reported stolen, and re-rigged on the cruise control, the second throttle control with a radio-controlled override. A similar technical modification had been applied to the braking control system and the front tyres were drained of the air/nitrogen in them and filled with a five point six per cent propane to oxygen/air mixture and fitted with a small self-destructing remote controlled ignition device. I was also briefed later on this by another incremental member who knew all about it too, so this aspect of the story was in fact confirmed. It meant the tyres could be blown out at will by the press of a button from a nearby operative.

Henri Paul, the driver on the fatal night was on side too and had been briefed that afternoon of the 'accident' as to which route he would use to 'avoid' the paparazzi. He was paid cash for this at the time. Reports later say the money was still on him when he died in the 'accident'. It was influenced by Paul that a repeat subterfuge would be used on exit of the Ritz to travel to Dodi's Paris apartment. A dummy car would be placed out front and the real transport would come to the rear entrance of the Ritz, from which Dodi and Diana would leave. This was the rigged Merc that had gone missing earlier and had been 'found' undamaged on a Paris street shortly afterwards, except it was now fitted with its remote control mechanisms.

Paul drove off at speed and quickly distanced himself from the paparazzi in various transports behind.

At the entrance to the Alma tunnel a number of 'reception' vehicles were in position. These included a dark saloon and the famous 'white Fiat', which was being driven by another British Agent, James Andanson.

The Ritz Merc approached the tunnel at speed and the reception vehicles were waiting. The Fiat took off and placed itself moving in the offside lane position ahead of the Ritz Merc. The role of the dark saloon was unclear, but probably just back up and control. The remote functions of the Merc were activated, causing the throttle to open up; the car physically took off over the sleeping policeman at the entrance to the tunnel and landed with the rear wheels rotating at high speed. Henri Paul successfully regained temporary control of the car at which point he was overtaken by a high speed motor cycle with a rear facing pillion rider who popped off a military grade strobe flash gun, temporarily blinding Paul. At that exact moment, the left front tyre was blown out by the implanted device and a minor collision also occurred with the rear light of the white Fiat. The Ritz Merc ploughed into the unguarded concrete pillars of the central reservation exactly as planned. Similar RTAs had happened there before.

Now the real plan got under way. The rear seat belts had been disabled in the previous modifications to the Merc so the passengers took the full force of the impact. Dodi was killed outright as planned. Diana somehow escaped relatively unharmed, except for a cut on her thigh. The rear passenger compartment of the Merc was pretty much intact as Mercs are designed and built to protect their occupants, but Henri Paul was dead from the impact. The bodyguard, Trevor Rees Jones who was also onside but had no knowledge of the plot was injured, but escaped death.

A motorcycle rider had stopped, looked into the car and indicated to the intelligence vehicles now ahead of the crashed Merc that Dodi was dead. It was he who was actually the number one target of the mission, not Diana. Apparently, if he had not been dead, his neck was to have been broken with one quick movement by the motor cycle operative, another skilled assassin, grade seven as they are designated.

A French doctor travelling on the other side of the carriageway stopped to help but medical 'assistance' was taken over by a French ambulance that appeared almost instantly on the scene.

The Paris Air Ambulance was never deployed and the CCTV cameras were out of action that night, some say just turned towards the wall. This mysteriously quick ambulance assisted Diana inside to its rear patient bay. The rear doors of the Merc opened OK and the reports that it took the Fire and Rescue service, arriving a short while later, 45 minutes to get into the Merc, only applied to the front doors which were deformed from the impact.

This is where my tasked investigation of the 'accident' kicks in. I was on service in London that fateful night and got a telephone call very early in the morning that the 'accident' had happened and Diana was injured. I was on the case straight away and accessed immediately all that was on the airwaves and online. There, in front of me was a picture taken by a member of the public of Diana, sitting up, not prone, in the back of the ambulance where it had pulled over near a bridge. She looked OK, was not unconscious and showed no signs of low blood pressure, as claimed from the internal heart injury, which would have had her by definition lying down on the bed/stretcher, maybe hooked up to life support. None of that was attached to her in the photo, which had come online so quickly that it could not have been faked or photoshopped. That photo disappeared within hours from the web, as did certain paparazzi photos from a news agency that had been about to market them after was raided and sanitised.

Inside speak later told me the procedure was now to sedate Diana and give her an unsolicited internal abortion of the foetus she was carrying. She had recently been photographed on Dodi's yacht in the Med looking quite pregnant. This was another reason that certain folk in the 'establishment' had panicked that the mother of the future King was pregnant by a Muslim Arab. It was believed that the very next day after the 'accident', the happy couple were going to announce their engagement, her being with child. Their plans, it was thought, were to move to Miami, taking the Royal Princes with them, as Dodi had bought a small mansion there.

The French medical agents in the ambulance were not experienced gynaecologists and could neither find the foetus, nor get it out. However, Diana was now bleeding internally. Drastic decisions ensued. Who or where they came from at that moment is not clear, may be they were taken in the field as the situation was very tight on time.

The reception vehicles had all departed at speed in close convoy back towards the British Embassy, the white Fiat had disappeared and weeks later, was found stripped down and scrapped. Andanson later disappeared and was found months later with two bullets in his head, locked in another burnt out car miles away from his home, the car had been covered in petrol with no ignition keys in sight. It was of course designated a suicide. A suicide by a very clever Houdini who succeeded in covering himself with whisky, covering his car in petrol, shooting himself twice in the head, setting fire to his car and disappearing the keys which had apparently locked the car from the outside. Quite a feat of magic, worthy of the magic circle, or perhaps just a clumsy murder relying on a pet insider French coroner. As I said, the French are anybody's as I know from working with them.

The ambulance departed the crash scene but did not go directly to A & E. It was necessary to allow Diana to bleed to death. It took over an hour parked outside the principle Paris morgue where the foetus was to have been disposed of. That was why the journey to the hospital was so protracted when it should have taken only six minutes even in rush hour traffic.

 The hospital surgeons tried to resuscitate here but when the unconscious, probably DOA Diana, got there, the X ray showed up the foetus but that got lost very quickly and the body was embalmed on the orders of the British Ambassador. That order came from London so no sign of the enforced sedative, abortion attempt or the pregnancy could show up on the later post mortem, which they tried to get around anyway but that had to happen under British Common Law.

Trevor Rees Jones was told to keep his mouth shut or he too would quickly meet an untimely end as he had witnessed most of the accidents' unreported events. The paparazzi who had showed up shortly after the crash served as a useful bunch of patsies who had 'caused the crash'.

It has been claimed that the murders were instigated by Prince Phillip or Prince Charles, but I know that not to be true. If the Duke of Edinburgh had any involvement, he was probably tricked into unwittingly giving a green light in the same manner as a previous monarch had uttered that time honoured phrase, "Who will rid me of this troublesome priest?" Prince Phillip can be relied upon to blurt out something unfortunate if he is led in the right direction. No, it was the lower ranks that panicked and set the whole thing in train.

The man who was the Spear of Destiny took charge, even if a bit of a Dick. Did it come from higher? Higher than the tenth floor gets into a grey zone where it is difficult to see through the fog. What is the tenth floor?' Stand outside Vauxhall Bridge MI6 Building and count the levels. It is not too difficult to work out. Also note the marks in the stonework façade. I can tell you what level of alert they are on from the guards who are on duty outside, the serious boys or the old guard. I can see who's working from the lights on inside, although a lot of it is underground. The vehicles going in and out are also a bit of a giveaway. I just passed by there several times a day up to 2015 in the course of other duties. Mind you most serious folk use the Tube access. Only the geeks and the office staff troll in and out of the main entrance. They are front of house, do you really think spies would use the front door and arrive on bikes?

The problem with this particular 'serious character,' 'X', was one not entirely uncommon, coming from the policy of making such operatives completely sub-contractors, thereby giving the government and authorities of the day total deniable responsibility. It meant that they were, in effect, freelance mercenaries.

This happened to a variety of special forces and spies like myself when, under Tony Blair, many of us were moved sideways.

Blair did not want to have to listen to the real intelligence that was being sent up, preferring to make it up off-the-cuff himself to comply with his orders from overseas. Yes, dear Tony, I knew friends of his at his old school; he was known to be a little shy** then, he did not improve and was not working for the United Kingdom from about 18 months into his reign after 'New Labour' gained office.

Instead, he was indeed the 'pet spaniel' of the corporates and Bush junior better known as 'Shrub'. Shrub would in turn receive his daily commands from Daddy, Bush Senior, both a former President and head of the CIA. He would receive his remit from the vested interests that actually run the United States just like any other major corporation.

The interests of the 'staff', i.e., the population of that great country and indeed the peoples of the rest of the world, including the United Kingdom, come very much second place to the company bottom line and the annual profits to the Directors of said corporates.

My former charge, X, ex-SAS and then part of the incremental forces or as politically correctness calls them, 'other capabilities', was working off-base to anyone who would pay the money. The standard fee from the back door of HMG for an assassination was £20,000, paid discreetly into an overseas bank account, usually Switzerland, where it would be quietly lost and certainly never disclosed.

X was on the 'market' for the same fee to any private quarter. This he said he needed to do, as the work from HMG was sporadic and as these people have no regular income, their funds often run thin. To keep the coffers full, had accepted contracts from the Dutch mafia. Prior to knowing him, I didn't really know there was such a thing, but this work had resulted in him taking out two of their own kind who had been found to have their fingers in the till. This had been an easy job on both occasions as the men were already prisoners of the family organisation, had been 'found guilty' and it involved X just going to an underground cellar of the outfit in both cases and putting two bullets into the heads of the accused while they had a paper bag over their faces.

This was apparently done in front of other gang members and pictures were taken as a strong deterrent to the 'staff' not to copy these off-books transactions. This was very much to do with the drugs trade where sums of money involved are prodigious. Holland is full of serious drug dealers.

In another job when X was giving 'close protection' to someone and driving a limo, the vehicle had been followed at high speed outside of a European city and into the open countryside. X was rather proud of the result. He had broadsided the limo, blocking the road and as the following car screamed to a stop, had popped two bullets into the head of the driver. That was enough to stop the attack and X and his passengers escaped.

However, he was still on the market and apparently there was a coded Internet site where 'contracts' were offered up. The selected elite of his profession tendered their services for the work available. This was international and the jobs could be anywhere. There was no political or loyalty element to their services, it was simply a job.

The general routine was the job would never be in the country of residence of the asset or preferably not his nationality origin either. The asset would fly in, do the job and fly out in short order. By the time any police interest was getting going they would already be long gone. This had also been the procedure when foreign assets had often done jobs in the UK and UK agents had been commissioned to do US jobs both in Europe and particularly the Middle East, where the British have much more of a handle on the local domain than the Americans.

X, it seems, had found a taste for killing. At one point he told me if he did not kill someone over a period of more than eighteen months, he actually got withdrawal symptoms. After about a year of abstaining, he would begin to look for a suitable victim. He mentioned, quite causally, that he would probably kill me eventually. It was a disturbing thought.

He believed himself to be invulnerable, certainly, as far as I was concerned, he had 20 years on me and was sharp, hardened and always armed. I was no threat to him at all.

He was, however, a threat to himself. He had diabetes and had lost his blood analyser. He used to just guess how much insulin to inject, depending on how he felt and what he expected to be eating and doing over the next few hours. He was also a kleptomaniac, borne from a kind of arrogance that because he could kill anyone he wished and had done so for decades, he could simply take and use anything he wanted to, whether it was needed or not. He would pick things up and walk off with them, or would kick down doors to gain access, a technique I recognised as pure SAS training. You run at the door with full force, extend a boot and get yourself inside the building straight away. Works 95% of the time, as the door just gives way. The other five per cent it doesn't and can hurt a lot.

At the farmhouse, the snows came in. X was still in residence, but moved out to housesit a farm up in the hills. He said he expected to murder the owners when they returned and take over the place. He had done this before apparently and leopards don't change their spots. I was relieved that he had moved on, but other people in the area had started to notice him and were making moves against him. He said he had this in hand and planned to burn their houses down with them inside, thus annulling the problem. The fact that they had children was of no significance to X. The word 'immoral' is not psychologically correct here. He was amoral, he had no conscience to worry him. He had seen and caused too much death already and meant nothing to him.

I made every move possible to get him legally arrested and returned to the UK for proper containment and treatment but the UK Police did not want to know. This was not on their manor and they had too much to do with their own workload. It was military anyway, off base to the civilian remit and this guy was security services so an untouchable. I reported all of this to my British security contacts. They scratched their heads and sat on their hands. Only his book made a difference. He was writing his memoirs and notoriety called. He wanted people to know what he had done with his life. X actually wrote quite well I found as he had asked me to edit it. It was explicit, gory, even emotional at times.

Writing was how he was coping with what was in his head when he was staring at the wall. I erased as much of the worst of it as I could get away with believing it could encourage others with the bravado of it all. Not good stuff. It also named names, times and places. This was exactly what I was there for to keep this shit quiet and unpublished. He had nicked one of the laptops to write on so I had access when he was not around.

Whole sections started to get lost, but he was writing more and more. I briefed my people and said, "This is getting out of control!" I had probably just signed his death warrant, but I had done this before with other very dangerous people. The decision was never mine; I am not tenth floor. I just supply very accurate data and it is trusted that whatever I send up is 100% true. I have to be very responsible in that.

I never knew the exact cause of death. I actually think nature caught up with X before anything else did. It was very cold, freezing. I was suffering with the cold very much myself with my MS and feared I could die from the freezing temperatures too. You would not believe how cold it can get in the mountains. During a brief thaw, X appeared at my door. He wanted my medical opinion on his foot, which had turned completely white and bloodless. He told me he had kicked in a door in the intense cold, got back to where he was hiding out and had lost the feeling in the foot, which started losing colour. I knew that given his diabetes, this didn't look good. Gangrene and blood poisoning looked a very likely possibility. I recommended that he attend hospital immediately. He of course ignored this advice and left. The mid-winter weather closed down again. I never saw him again.

It wasn't the last I heard of him, though, as he had apparently been busy. A neighbour's car burned out and they were lucky their house didn't go with it. It did not help that the vehicle had been given by me to them some time ago and it had a diesel engine. Diesels don't catch fire by themselves and I knew he had been around the farm, even though he moved like a ghost.

I had many little toys that picked up and recorded movement. My security was obsessive; it was well known. The Spanish secret service told me that my life was in danger and I should disappear although they did not specify from where. It may have been from more than one source including X, who perhaps had decided my usefulness to him had expired. I made an appointment to see the British Consul to seek assistance. He was not available when I called but a hit team was.

Oops! It was obvious that I knew too much and in true tradition to the incremental code, matters needed to be cleaned up. I had heard that X had been found dead and his hangout ransacked, presumably looking for all of his records and writings of his evil deeds over the years. I had already flagged that these had to be recovered and destroyed. However, it seemed that some idiot on the tenth floor knew I also had access to this stuff and could not trust to my 50 years' loyalty to the Crown and HMG to be careful with it. I was on the bloody hit list!

Fortunately for me, the old fox that I am, I know their methods inside out, upside down and backwards. They were young men, no match for my experience. I had dodged the German Stasi, the Bulgarians before they were EU and fucking deadly and been tasked to infiltrate the Russians in Florida.

I first read the eyes of the receptionist as I filled out my name at the consulate front door. Having got around her and up a level or two, the next uniformed guard looked a bit alarmed. "How did you get up here?" he questioned.

I can get in most places if I need to, but I could get no further. I had tried to play it straight and honest and inform the Consul of the death of X and that we must retain his writings before all hell broke loose. This was before Cameron had been elected; a good man with a high security clearance even before he became PM. He had the time honoured security briefing within three days of coming to office. The briefing that tells a new PM the way it really is, not the public PR bullshit, which is shelled out by the media on a daily basis.

I noticed the first man lurking at the back of the office. The next two I picked up as I left and made my way to an adjoining department store where I played snakes and ladders with the stairs and lifts, drifting into the lingerie section where scruffy security types stand out rather like neon billboards. As I turned on my heel, the man behind me dropped to his knee to tie a shoelace, an old and very well recognized procedure. "I hate amateurs," I muttered audibly as I passed him.

I exited the underground car park ASAP and drove my car two blocks to another underground car park, swiftly walked out onto the street and lost myself in a crowded bar. I figured they would have bugged my car and I didn't have time to find the device. I had a glass of red and perused the local paper from behind which I could keep an eye on the door. Another fellow came in and took a drink at the bar. He jumped on his mobile to make a call a bit too quickly to look casual. I had been spotted.

Another man joined him, also standing at the bar and pretended they did not know one other. Were they British or Spanish or who? It was not clear. In the noise of the bar I couldn't overhear their language and they made a point of me not being able to see their lips, yet another giveaway. In a corner, a group of slightly merry students started to leave. I joined them and joked with them making myself part of the group. As I passed the first on-scene operative, I looked him straight in the eye and said, "Don't follow me!" He looked away. Undercover people are always thrown when they know they've been ID'd.

I circumnavigated the plaza and arrived back at the underground car park, bought my exit ticket and walked towards my car. There, four cars away was the same large black saloon I had seen before when this caper started a few days ago. I had noticed its forged number plate, much older than the car and obviously added to this recent Ford model. There was one man in the Ford. As I started my engine, he started his and pulled ahead of me towards the exit, up the ramp and stopped in the middle of the fortunately wide entrance. My smaller, nippier car could fit alongside his offside and I pulled up adjacent and eye-balled him.

He was an older man, but a little younger than me, wearing a pale yellow sweater. We smiled at each other. We knew the name of the game. The street was empty at this moment with four lanes of impatient local drivers waiting for a change of traffic lights to our right. The lights turned green, the cars surged forward. I paused, then gunned my little car right across the street in front of the advancing hordes. Horns blared, curses rang out! I shot down the outside taxi lane towards another set of traffic lights. They were red.

I stopped, no point in getting killed in a traffic accident. The black Ford saloon caught me up and roared down the same taxi lane behind me. If I'd had any doubt in my mind that the other driver was not part of the hit team, it was now clear this chap was intent on breaking any traffic laws to keep up with me. My doors were locked, but that was little comfort. Just as he arrived behind me, the lights turned green and I took off. Blue smoke came from my tyres, their fronts spinning a little as I revved and slipped the clutch for more acceleration.

His heavy saloon was no match and I quickly changed lanes and took a series of erratic and last minute turns into back streets, praying they were not dead ends. Luck was with me and after five minutes of evasive driving, he was no longer there. I had lost him.

I quickly took all the sim cards and batteries out of my mobile phones and again prayed that any tracking device attached to my car would be inhibited by the tall city buildings. I stayed in heavy traffic and kept changing direction while trying to keep a working idea of what my compass heading was at any one time. A local police car got on my tail as I negotiated a back street. Were they just cruising or after me? I decided to find out. I stopped, got out and casually walked back to the two uniformed men, asking for directions to the airport. They obliged. There was no problem, but I knew that local protocol was to follow, so that did not mean I was not on the airwaves. Intel staff at the level of the chap in the pale yellow sweater can sometimes call on the assistance of local law enforcement to be eyes and ears. I wanted them to think I was heading for the airport. I was not.

I was getting low on gas. Spotting a petrol station, I figured I'd better fill up as I was on a street heading away from where I intended to go. I figured they might trace the credit card transaction back to me, but that would take minutes and be yet another red herring. While I was there, I got the maximum amount of cash out of the ATM. This would be the last time I would use a credit card.

I wasted no time in leaving the gas station and when not in sight of any street CCTV cameras I could see, I turned through a series of lesser roads in the direction that would give me more security away from the overviewed streets of the city. I passed under major roads where occasionally I could see local police road blocks and check points in action. Was this just the usual procedures to monitor drunk drivers or was it more? There was no way of knowing but I assumed the worst and selected a major detour route back in the direction of my safe house bases, many miles away by now. Good job I had gassed up; I needed the fuel.

The sky grew dark but I felt much more secure in the remote countryside. As trained, I stayed in close contact behind any heavy transport trucks, so my car was shielded from observation from any oncoming vehicle. I detected nothing coming up behind. I stopped off-road and searched the undersides of the wheel arches with a torch. There it was, the little bugger. I carefully pulled it away as its magnetic grips tried to hang on. I walked, unseen, to the secondary road I had just left on the hill. Obligingly, along came a slow moving, open top truck and I lobbed the little device into its open rear bucket bay. Walking back to my car, I drove off in the opposite direction. I was safe now from the high-tech surveillance favoured by the modern intelligence community sat at their VDU screens drinking coffee.

I had some knowledge of the local terrain and so I headed for a very remote, dense, olive grove in a valley. I could hide the car, rest and sleep for a couple of days. It always confuses people when you just disappear and go to ground as they think you'll be running away or running around, when in actual fact the smart thing is to do nothing. It was cold and I only had a few emergency biscuits to eat. There was no way I was going to use any electronic coms and give away my position.

I knew that some chums of mine were engaged in a routine operation, heading out some time in the near future. Usefully, that was some days away and there was some security cleaning up that needed to be done.

Overnight I motored back to my number one base, the farm, came in from a back road and parked out of sight under the trees having arrived using only the light of the moon. I walked as silently as I could down the lane to the farm, opened the door, turned off the alarm, which squeaked at me annoyingly as I entered and busied myself with as much haste as possible. I did not know for sure who, or what I was up against, how many operatives might be involved, and from which outfit, foreign or home grown, but I was on the target list and I had to assume the worst.

Knowing their protocols, the locals would only be on observation, eyes and ears, however I was aware there were some serious dudes around out there in the region and they were not local at all. They were the real danger and being not in their home country they might get up to anything. It was a big country with many remote regions. If I got 'disappeared' out here no one would find me, but that was not my intention. 'Never say die'.

In haste, I got together some basic kit. There was too much for one little walk back to the car. I elected to take some clothes and such first. This proved a very wise choice, as it happened. I exited the farm back door and padded my way back to the car. The soft scrunch of the gravel of the lane sounded like an earthquake in the silence of the night but I dare not walk over the rough ground; you could easily break an ankle. I reached the car under the trees. It was pitch black. I had left it unlocked and as I reached the driver's door there was a fleeting shadow behind me. I turned and ducked but it was too late. Something, a man's fist, hit me very hard on the mouth.

I knew it was much later when I woke up, the moon had moved. The car was gone, my case, my coat, my hat. It was bloody cold but my God, I was alive. What the hell was going on? Obviously the farm had been staked out, someone had been watching and clocked me one. I figured they must have been alone in their op as I had not been there for days. Whatever was afoot, I had very little time to make my escape. I moved swiftly back to the farm. It appeared undisturbed. Into the computer room and grabbing the essential laptops I stuffed them into a case and made essential cover tactics to confuse my enemy. I closed the blinds, turned on the additional security cams, powered up the emergency low level lights and left all the systems running.

This was to give as much of an impression that the place was manned and I was there somewhere. Out to the back-up car praying it would start. In with the key. No! Fuck! Try again. She started! "There is a God", I thought. There was no time to be discreet now I roared out of the drive turned into the hinterland, motoring as swiftly as was possible under only moonlight while displaying no lights. The tracks I had chosen were twisting and rough. A couple of times I hit brush off to the side. As I wound around the mountain high above I could see lights of vehicles heading for the farm. I slowed to reduce the engine noise and thought, "Thank God I only just made it!"

I made my way carefully over miles of dirt tracks that litter this rural landscape until I found a tarmacked road. I knew where I was. The highway was empty at this late hour. I motored towards my objective location. Suddenly there, ahead, I spotted headlights heading in my direction. I swung off the road and killed my lights. The cars appeared, three of them and shot by. As soon as they were around the corner I resumed my journey.

I passed a layby. Another saloon pulled out some way behind me. Damn! I had been picked up again. This guy stayed back. I hit the gas, came into a village, swung in behind a warehouse and stopped, again killing the lights. A minute, it seemed like a year, passed. He pulled into the side road I had just turned down and stopped some 70 yards behind me half-way around the corner. He had seen me and I had seen him. He was alone. I resolved to play the psychological game. I knew he would call for back up; he would not risk taking me on, one on one.

I started my engine, put my lights full on and backed up alongside him. He was young, very young. I knew at this point he was probably calling for his brown trousers. He ignored me but started to bend down and reach under his seat. I was off with a roar of the engine and squeal of the wheels. He'd killed his engine on stopping but didn't restart it quickly enough to follow.

Two side road junctions and I hit the main road. Not a soul in sight. I gunned it at 90 mph away from the deserted area. I passed no one. It wasn't too hard to find another remote olive grove in this area, so I left the car camouflaged by the gnarled branches of the low olive trees and walked to the overlooking hill. I hid in the bushes from where I could watch both the car's location and the road and breathed into my coat to counter the cold. It started to snow. Thank God, now so my tracks would be covered. A problem if it had snowed before.

I hung out for three days. The dawns were lovely and the bird song but a more dangerous time as people could be about. However, it was not a time when farmers had much to do. No one came. Hardly any traffic used the road below me and there was no sign of planes or helicopters. This told me the crew that was after me had not engaged the local police or law enforcement. They were working on their own remit.

With a day in hand, I made my way overland and off the roads at dawn to the other safe house and was greeted with surprise and coffee by trusted colleagues.

"Who did that to your lip?" quizzed my mates.

"Lucky to be here," was my response. "When are you leaving?'

"Tomorrow at dawn. Get some sleep it's a long ride east."

11. Over the hills and far away

"We'll get you as far as the port. Then you'll have to board alone. Do you have enough cash?"

"Yes enough," I replied.

"Good, we'll see you on board. Your next link will meet us on the ship. See you in the bar."

It had been a long journey, the drivers changing every few hours. We never stopped. Land Rovers are not very comfortable vehicles, but what else would they drive? The boys had made it clear that I was a priority. I just hoped to God we did not get pulled on the way, as these chaps were the elite of the old regiment. If one of their own was in danger, there was no hesitation in them taking 'executive action'.

You may be confused as to why I trusted these chaps so completely, why they were with me and I with them in such complete unit security. Let me explain how it works in the real world. In your Hollywood film fictions, you may assume various departments even from the same government work in close cooperation with each other. This is far from the truth. The system is called 'compartmentalisation'. MI6 does not necessarily co-operate with MI5 or even Special Branch, within which even offices from different constabularies don't inform each other of their presence in each other's manors.

These chaps were from the 'Inner Keep', now all redesignated as sub-contractors. They knew each other very well, worked in close knit units and were not officially part of any 'official unit'. However they were all ex-SAS, SBS or MI5.

5 does not get on very well with 6 and neither does 6 with 5. 6 is public school mostly, lots of diplomatic connections and people in embassies. 5 is much more down to earth, red-brick education and deals with real British interests as opposed to 6, which plays the international game and tends to lick arse to the 'partners'.

MI5 works also in Europe, not just in the UK, although you are not supposed to know that and it pisses off 6 who think they have sole rights outside the United Kingdom.

As for the 'other capabilities', as I said they are technically freelance and that makes them very independent as they do not officially exist. Hence they do not pay tax or national insurance stamps in the main and can find themselves somewhat disenfranchised by their masters if they so choose. This is also the case with chaps like me who are working 'legends' undercover and are oft living a double life.

So although I was as safe as houses with my own chaps, that did not mean that some other band of brothers would be automatically on our side if they came in contact. The chaps I have worked with have a certain reputation. They do not take prisoners and you would be well advised not to take them on. They have friends in both low and high places as opposed to the piggies in the middle who work on the banks of the Thames and only need to know two words, "Yes Sir!"

The other characteristic that you may find surprising is that all men are considered of equal rank. Situations and lightning response is what governs actions in the field, not the pecking order of pips on shoulders or scrambled egg. Most would be considered commonly at the rank of sergeant, although 'team leaders' may be chosen in the course of planning. In field though, men must act entirely on their own initiate and in fact often work entirely alone or with only arm's length back-up. You do not do this kind of work for money or career benefits; it is a vocation, a term the geeks at their screens at the known HQs sometimes do not fully understand. We are old school and although some would say we're becoming dinosaurs, we still have very sharp teeth.

Obsessively loyal to the crown, they stand no truck from politicians who often abuse their trust and devotion to the national interest of the United Kingdom and real national security, as opposed to party, personal or even corporate interests. End of rant!

Various politicians have, over the years, co-opted operations from the units to go overseas and break their wayward teenagers out of jail when they found themselves banged up in foreign lands, mostly for drug offences. This has happened a number of times although less so these days and is always 'off the books'. That is if you can't simply bribe the local goons into leaving the cell door open overnight. My mates know the Atlas Mountains well.

You might think these 'super-soldiers' are like US Marines, six foot four inches tall and three feet wide. Nothing could be further from the truth. No man is more than five foot ten and a half inches tall, light, wiry and with incredible strength. They work out all the time, even when they 'retire', although you actually never retire mentally from such service.

Perhaps my most concern for these guys and gals, is they can hardly ever be acknowledged for what they have done, even saving the lives of hundreds of people. They work without public recognition and must keep this life separate from their families who remain in the dark as to their true achievements.

Why am I able to write even this highly sanitised work/book? That is because some bright spark working for the DWP (Department of Work and Pensions) was spiked, fired up to 'out me' on the basis of some technical anomalies which resulted in the crossing of the line of some aspects of my work over the past fifty years. As a result, I have decided to set the record at least partially straight, even if it does cause a few red faces in the ranks of elected officers of HMG. These are people who should remember who they serve; the people of this old and venerable country of ours, Great Britain, not their own personal interests or bank accounts or political theories, or should I say hypotheses, which is spelled 'prejudices'.

Am I political? No! I am looking at the world with a historian's perspective and wishing people would learn the lessons of history, rather than marching troops slowly towards the enemy lines in order, perhaps, to 'confuse them.'

The mistakes of the leaders of all factions and nations seem to be boringly repetitive over the millennia and seem vested more in the primitive origins of their alpha male DNA. Even the dominant women, such as Margaret Thatcher, seem to mimic men rather than bringing to the office true feminine qualities of caring, guardianship and, dare I say, trust.

It is not good enough these days to have gone to a good public school or have a qualification in Latin to join the FCO. What we need is real people who can relate to the real world and have on-the-ground, grass roots experience from all walks of life.

Back on scene and some hours later, I stepped off the ferry to the pre- arranged meeting spot. There was a classic, nondescript, 'white van' where my contact was waiting in the dockside car park.

"Where do you want me to take you?" he asked.

"How far can we go?" I replied.

"Anywhere. Do you speak Greek?"

"I'm learning," I mused. "Let's go north, I will tell you where when we've left the port area. Do you have a map?" After 6 hours in the not-too-comfortable passenger seat, stopping only for coffee and comfort breaks, we arrived at our destination. My driver spoke little? Was happily silent so I could recover from my rather tense journey over the last three days.

The villa was familiar to me, the stone walls, the smell of wood smoke from the hearth and the peeling white paint; little changed from when I had been there years ago. Just a little more crumbled, a little more derelict, bathed in the late afternoon setting Sunlight. Rather like the folk who staffed it, whose faces were now more lined and they were perhaps more mellow. The tragic memories of their past faded back into nostalgia of their youth post-Nazi occupation.

I was to stay here for some months, no contact was to be made, my family were by now used to this, they were safe in a more stable location, nothing was to be done, no questions would be asked. Time would fade the memories, history would wait, just as with the gardener and housekeeper of the villa in the hills.

Others would take care of the business of cleaning up the former operations. Paperwork would be gathered and burnt. Vehicles would be scrapped, several thousand pounds' worth of them. The safe houses I had left were no longer operational. Everything would be stripped out, the kit given away, generators, kitchen gear, basic electronics. Only the comms, being secure, would find their way to some disposal facility. I was posted as 'missing' a status I would keep for some time until people forgot. People always forget, they have lives to lead.

12. Sunsets & Sails

FIRESTORMS IN THE MED

I was enjoying yet another peaceful day when I noticed the white Fiat drive past the villa. My position on the roof terrace, where I was sipping a local white wine, terrace, was somewhat obscured by the barbecue chimney so I couldn't be seen from the road myself. I was missing my family and they too would be missing me, but procedures are procedures and it keeps everyone safe. My inner sense of awareness signalled that tranquillity could be changing.

The Fiat stopped a few tens of yards down the track. An older man got out and took a GPS reading. Curious, I thought. Such things do not go unobserved in my world. Was he a surveyor of some kind? It did not make much sense. I was not aware of any building works to be planned in the area and no one ever repaired the roads. That really would be a waste of money.

I filed it in my memory, but did nothing about it at that time. Days later, another vehicle stopped by in very much the same position. This aroused my attentions even more, as it pulled up under some trees pointing away from the villa and remained there for 35 minutes with the engine running. Really odd, I thought, as locals do not waste fuel like that. The occupant, another guy in a pale blue shirt was obviously observing the villa though the wing mirror of the car. To my suspicious eyes, it seemed like standing up in the front lines of WWI and painting yourself green. In other words, the villa was under surveillance from people who were not very good at the game. Naturally, I was now on alert for any other anomalies. I kept my side arm close at hand and with the safety catch off. It's nothing special, just a regular automatic. Never had to use it in anger yet.

The secret of operations is to stay under the radar. If it comes to a fire fight, you've blown your cover and the game is up. I remember Major Reedman recounting a yarn about when he was keeping tabs on an American agent, all those many years ago, who was in the process of breaking into a factory office of what later became British Aerospace. This was before the days of electronic eavesdropping and when challenged by my old friend, the Yank fired off a round in his direction. Not a very friendly thing to do. The Major let him get away; shooting Yanks on a creep is not very good form.

Two days after the rather obvious eyeballing of the villa, I was again on the roof terrace enjoying the afternoon Sun. It was a good observation point, with 360-degree vision on the countryside and local forests from the low hill upon which the villa sat. I now had a scoped rifle by my side, more for looking at distant points than defence. Even so, it was loaded.

Out of the corner of my eye, I detected a brief glint of red laser light in the far woods. I hit the deck. The bullet passed inches away as it whistled past my ear. From behind the protection of the rampart wall of the terrace, I let off a couple of rounds into the air just to indicate that one was prepared to return fire if necessary. I had no intention of taking on whoever was out there and I couldn't see them anyway. I was alone in the villa and assistance was not to hand. If you cannot win a battle, don't even consider engaging the enemy.

It was a few minutes later that I smelled smoke. Carefully using a mirror, I peered over the parapet and yes, there was smoke rising from the nearby forest in the direction of where the shot had come. The wind was blowing my way. Damn!

Then the sound of a car engine from a track over there behind the trees, which kind of circumnavigated the area. A few minutes later and further to the east, more smoke started to rise up. The bastard was encircling me with a forest fire. What to do?

Breaking radio silence, I called my mates for help but it was hours away. No time to wait for that, the fire was getting going under the light breeze and jumping from one bunch of dry scrub to the next. These fires can travel with unbelievable speed in the arid conditions of that part of Greece. The grasses came right up to the edge of the property. What was my opponent's plan? Was he trying to smoke me out or finish me off?

The fundamental question was to either sit it out, if it remained safe to do so, or make a break for it. The latter seemed the better choice. I had minutes before the fire would completely cut me off as the tracks from the villa went through dense Scots Pine trees which could easily fall and block the tracks if they caught fire and exploded in a ball of flame as I had seen before in such forest conflagrations.

Running around the villa, I made it as smoke-proof as I could, closing the shutters and doors. I figured my friendly assassin was too busy setting fires to be taking pot shots at me right now, so I had a few seconds.

Fortunately, the 4x4 was around the back and out of sight. Grabbing my laptop and couple of sensitive files, I ran to the jeep, gunned the engine and slewed it around to exit away from where I figured the opposing force might now be.

"Calm down," I thought to myself. I knew it was much easier to defend than attack. "Don't drive the bloody thing off the road. That wouldn't be very smart!" Into the hills I raced, just clearing the fires as they swept through the bone-dry timber. Just made it. I kept low in the driving seat and kept abruptly changing speed and road position as the track allowed, which was not a lot. I headed for a back-up safe location, satisfied that no one was following me, as there were no dust trails on the tracks behind me.

I rendezvoused with my mates coming the other way and we swiftly conferred. One joined me heading west, while the other two returned to secure the villa and alert the forestry fire department. They figured the enemy would have cleared the area, knowing that forest fires bring in resources quickly including aircraft to fight the fire so it would be getting too hot for them, in both meanings of the word.

Reaching the port; the Gulet was still there but about to depart. Thank God, what a welcomed surprise, as I feared she may have already left on her re-location Westward. The gods were on my side and suitable thanks was in my heart for yet another 'coincidence.' We always had a back-up plan B and kept informed of options.

The gulet was a beautiful little ship. Two tall, majestic masts, teak decks and polished varnished wood interiors like a London gentleman's club, as well as a very obliging crew. I felt a hint of the surreal as I sipped a cooling glass of wine on the forepeak and reflected on the past 24-hours. Here I was, sailing away from the drama in the smoke-filled hills into the welcome off-shore breezes and the security of being separated from land by half a mile of azure sea.

My heartbeat had returned to normal and after a bath, the earlier events of the day seemed in a completely different world, even though just a few hours and under 50 miles away. I thought I could see distant plumes of smoke rising over the mountains, but it was probably my imagination. It was hard to miss the bright yellow fire department sea planes though, as they roared overhead. They would skim the surface to scoop up water refills for quenching the forest fire. I worried for the wildlife that would be harmed; such a selfish and pointless waste.

A colleague joined me on the foredeck. He was more a beer man and he gripped a suitably filled tankard.

"This baby is being repositioned westward. Good timing that you made her departure", was his reassuring comment.

"Angels on my shoulder," I replied, without being more specific as to their actual reality to me.

"I could do with a few of those," he joked.

We sat and recollected former gambits we had been on. Only in such company can one really relate such anecdotes. Being a spy or special forces can be a very lonely occupation; the trust and bonding which is exclusive to brothers in arms.

"Who was after you?" questioned my mate.

"God knows, but it looked like 'friendly fire'!" I quipped. "Ever had that situation yourself?"

"Yes", returned my chum. "I was on this job in the Middle-East. I won't say where, but you can guess. I was dropped in by the chopper, infiltrated a half mile to the pre-selected hit point and set up. It was a long shot, just about at the edge of my range. So they get this target out on the balcony, these 'colleagues' of his…only had seconds to calculate the shot….and I got lucky and took him out with one pop. Head shot."

"No luck involved. You are one of the best!" I lifted my glass to him.

"Well, had a little practice over the years. And this other Army officer, bloody captain, comes up to see how it's gone. So having established business is done, he starts to go for his gun. I knew where that was going. Just knocked him out and carried him back to the extraction. "I thought it was only one out," says the pilot. 'No two, you bloody idiot!' That was that!"

"I've moaned about this before," I returned.

"So since then, they've been sending me on these fucking doggy missions, not expecting me to return. But here I am, still here. Fucking bastards, just because we aren't on the pay roll anymore they think we're fucking expendable. I'm coming off with you at Malta and quitting the unit now. I've told them, if anyone comes after me they will not be going home. Where are you going from the island?"

"The Knights are looking after me for a bit up at the fort and then they want me back on something to do with royal protection for a while. I've been tasked on something safer. The run up to HM doing a lot of public exposure. Some whiff in the air about some evil plot to have a go. That's all I know at the moment. I think they are buying me off."

"Why don't you quit if they're nervous of you?"

"Well you know the way it is, it gets a habit. I'm safer inside the unit than outside. I thought of setting the record straight a bit with a carefully crafted book. Nothing too accurate, but just enough to stop some of these snow job clean ups that have been going on. How many is it now? 16 or more? Makes me bloody sick considering what we have done for crown and country."

"You be careful my friend!"

"Well, you know when you have a horse that might kick you. You stand right against its flank. Then it can't get its leg up to belt you one."

"Know about horses, do you?"

"Had eleven. TB's and Arabs, flighty bits of kit. But ruined my finances. Just a black hole in vet's bills. I am sure they charge by weight."

"You know this trainer had this horse that kept losing on anti-clockwise tracks. So this little Irish guy says, 'Ah! I've seen this before; she's off-balance. 'Needs a bit of lead in the left ear'. 'And how do I get that in there,' asks the Owner. 'I usually use a revolver' says the little Irishman with a straight face."

"Do you think I am an awkward off-balance horse myself?" I joked.

"No, you are an old fox, Peter. If anyone took you on they would be fucking mad with the people you have been with."

"That's probably why they want me for this royal job. Keep me out of trouble. My family has been serving the great and the good for over a thousand years. Started before the Norman Conquest."

"A little blue blood never goes amiss."

"More a question of who you know these days. Never trust the new boys. Just bloody civilians. No idea of theatre."

"The only 'theatre' they know is a bloody stage show. A media circus! Where the hell has national security gone? Now it's mostly stunts."

"It's called 'social engineering'. The soap opera of political life."

"It wasn't such a soap opera when they dropped me in from a chopper though that skylight only armed with a fucking knuckleduster to take out the prison riot up North."

"Well, that's what you are good at."

"Did you kill anybody?"

"No, that was forbidden. Wanted to though. The last time I was given an insertion kill remit was directly from Maggie on the embassy siege... some time back you, remember. She did not want any witnesses to the

Fletcher hit. Bloody politicians."

"She's with the angels now – Bless!"

"Or the other place? Depends on your point of view?"

I gazed out to sea and wondered how many other politicians might be there to keep her company.

"The Fort's got a swimming pool and they keep insects in it, that like row about underwater to eat the mosquito larva. Saves on maintenance."

"Could do with a few of those in the Thames – perhaps they could consume the parasites that live on the river bank."

"Don't suppose they would. Only get indigestion. They say our Tone is going to work for the Yanks out in the Middle East."

"Tell me something new", I returned philosophically.

My companion began to reminisce about his own turn doing royal protection duties with The Prince of Wales when his charge wanted to stop off for a quiet drink on the way to Portsmouth.

"So we stop and I go in and brief the owner very discreetly. 'Look I've got this very special VIP with me. He just wants to have a quiet drink, so over in that corner make that table available, give us a bit of space and don't 'recognise' him when he comes in, but keep my line of fire clear to the door, just in case."

"You nutter", I responded.

"So in comes Charlie Boy and we go over and sit down and the bloody landlord's wife comes over to serve us and fucking curtsies. So of course some of the locals clock who is in their local, no bother. The lad got a bit pie-eyed. We had to help him out to the Land Rover. Quite funny."

Then he asked me about another dead prime minister, Edward Heath, a man who never married and who has, in recent years, been the subject of investigation relating to the long-running child abuse inquiry.

"What about Heath and his little boys?"

"No! I am not going there," I said. "The subject is just too sensitive. How many children's teeth did they dig up on the Isle of Wight?"

The conversation moved on into safer ground. Some things you just do not want to know. It could damage your faith in the human race. All I will say is Savile is the tip of the iceberg. You cannot libel the departed, but some things are best not said. Let the demons die with the devils, no doubt they have gone to join their kin in a darker if hotter place. Perhaps alongside the politicians!

The men I have known have, over the years, been tasked to take out what they were told were the 'enemies of the state'. However, of late, the last 15 years or so, it would seem there are as many 'enemies within' as 'enemies without.' You cannot always tell the sheep from the goats. Perhaps we should insist that all politicians take psychological screening and lie detector tests. No, let's be fair, they would never pass any of those, would they?

The military, for their part, just do as they are told in the UK. "Defending the realm," is the phrase used. They do not have executive powers, as Joe Public would like to believe. They work by the rules, although the political and cabal elite see no reason to be constrained by such inhibitions unless they are caught out. Then they suddenly become 'as pure as the driven snow' and beyond reproach.

Am I cynical? Not originally, but I have grown that way.

"How's Reedman these days?" queried my chum, as we topped up our respective drinks.

"I don't know. I haven't heard from him for a long time. He's probably dead by now. Must be getting on."

"He was your first handler wasn't he?"

"Yes. I remember him telling me about being on a NATO exercise when he was in the Paras. They were flying over to Holland for a drop in a Yankee DC3 and the green light comes on. So they all pile out of the door and pull their cords and there is nothing underneath them except miles of fucking water. They're being dropped over the middle of the North Sea. So luckily, it's summer and they get picked up by air sea rescue. No casualties and Reedman gets back to his barracks in the UK and is fucking livid. Tracks down the Yankee pilot on the phone, out of Mildenhall, and gives him earache and the Yank says, "Gee, Limey, I'm sorry I was reaching for the cigar lighter and I hit the wrong button!"

'Ha!"

"Reedman said if he ever caught up with him, he would kill him!"

"Fucking right. Stupid bastard!"

"Yanks. I tell you, unbelievable. Ah! but they are all heroes!

"Excuse me while I throw up! Is that why they get us

to do all their dodgy jobs then?"

"Exactly; it's called 'outreach'."

"Deniable responsibility. Like we listen for them at Doughnut and they listen for us at Menwith Hill. Me, Sir? No, Sir! Not me!"

"Oh, it's just all a game. Keeps people employed. They say 15,000 these days."

"We should complain? Pays my bills now and then."

13. The Great and the Good

ALL MEN ARE BORN EQUAL ... NOT!

Malta is a barren little island.

The Fort, dating from the times of The Knights Hospitaller, or The Knights of St. John, as they were known, was not overly large, but amazingly well defended with its massive, high thick walls. No one could see inside and access was restricted. It was not on the tourists' map, maybe not on any map. These places sometimes 'get lost.' Rather like when the old USSR used to produce maps where cities that were sensitive areas were displaced by up to a couple of hundred miles from their real locations. This was before the days of spy satellites and the internet, let alone the U2 spy plane.

Now you can look up Area 51, in Nevada, on Russian satellite pics. The Americans still obscure it on their photos. Pretty pointless. But then again they are still blurring out photos from their NASA satellites that occasionally show what the general public are not supposed to see. Or recolouring their Mars photos to obscure the blue sky and moss green and brown terrains. Can't have too much information out there. No, that is all classified, like the pictures of the domes of the old moon base around on the backside of our lunar companion. As the astronauts said as they first came back into radio communication with Houston, "We can confirm 'Santa Claus does exist'!" That was their pre-arranged code word for a base identification eyeball. They could see it clearly from their low trans-lunar orbit. Then they switched to their encrypted closed comms circuit. Say no more. I've seen pictures of it, very clear. That came from my Florida contacts and I hesitate to say more as some of those friends still work for NASA.

Geometrical structures have been seen on the moon. Looks much like any modern airport terminal. There is also a long disabled cigar shaped 'mother ship', damaged but probably been there for centuries. Not 'one of ours', I assure you. Part of the lunar facilities appear to be abandoned, damaged even, whether by natural causes or otherwise, one could not say. Insider speak has it that after the last official lunar landing, there were other trips that are not in the public domain. These took a looksee at the facilities that 'don't exist', but then the Yanks were 'warned off'; some even say Apollo Flight 13 was a warning? Maybe, who knows? I don't know but Ed said so.

But back in Malta, my time in the hinterland on HMG's hit list appeared to have come to an end. I was no longer in the outback and my demise would be noticed.

I was again allowed to reappear, but under a different name and identity. Standard procedure. 'The King is dead. Long live the King'. I was back in the Queen's service, even if at arm's length, as usual. Keep the old bugger on side!

"The Man Who Never Was," is the proposed title of my next book; a pure fiction (he lied). A lie sandwiched between two truths, or a truth sandwiched between two lies; standard Intel 'double speak'. You have to use your little grey cells. If you know half the key, the message is plain to see. If you do not, then without a 'Rosetta Stone' you are flying blind. Try guessing, you could get lucky but I will not be the one confirming your guess. It is an unwritten rule that you can address up to 150 people in a closed room with sensitive matters without a slap over the knuckles and definitely not say it on TV, an old rule. If you do, then character assassination follows, or worse.

But of course if you go public and then you actually do get assassinated, it only confirms what you said, so it is counterproductive. They learnt that with 'Spy Catcher' by Peter Wright. I don't think they would make the same mistake again. So let's just assume that this Peter - Peter Paget - is a complete nutcase grabbing a few good headlines for personal aggrandisement. That is a good double-cover gambit. Yes, I do play chess; have done so since a child, learnt at my father's knee. I would always be into some complicated strategy and then he would come along and in some damned annoying, piece for piece attack, knock off a bishop of mine and my plan was in tatters. Bugger. Then he would go on to win.

I was not sad to leave Malta, just a chilling out time, rather boring really. The ferry I had boarded sailed away until the island was just a speck on the horizon.

Sunshine notwithstanding, there are some aspects of the Maltese which I find hard to stomach, like setting up bird perches on barren rock shooting grounds, placing a pet little song bird in a cage right by it and when a companion comes along to sit on the perch, to keep it company, blowing it away with a carefully aimed rifle shot. What's the bloody point? The small bird is not for the pot and it only decimates the local avian population, to say nothing of migrant birds in transit. The Swiss do the same with lines of shooters in mountain passes taking out flocks of migrant birds coming back to Northern Europe from Africa. There is a practice of the Maltese that could be gainfully combined with this so-called sport; the habit of rather randomly letting off very loud mortars during the day and night during village fiestas. If one positioned a suitably rotund 'bird hunter' above the exit barrel of the mortar tube, one could have a competition as to how high one could get them to fly through the air! Good sport, what? And perhaps suitable karma, too. Could make more noise than the mortars did anyway.

The Maltese say it is to drive away 'evil spirits'. Yes, my suggested practice could do that too.

After a rather mundane train journey across Europe, I arrived in Copenhagen alone and was met by an exceptionally tall Danish girl. She must have been six foot two inches and would certainly stand out in a crowd. Hardly undercover! Her manner was friendly, but brisk. She was just doing her job and I was baggage in transit, no more. I tried the odd joke but she must have had some German blood in there with her sharp blue eyes as the humour seemed to go unnoticed. Another train journey and a taxi put me on a roiling ferry across the grey and stormy North Sea back to the good old home country. Yet another white van, a transit this time and a rather helpful but scruffy type called Jack. Jack the lad I assumed. I was pleased not to have flown. They have taken down whole passenger jets before now just to take out one man. It is a strange business, rather like being a lion tamer. Dangerous but exciting. The game becomes a way of life after a while, you are always countering the possibilities. Keeps one alive and well. 70 now, must be doing something right.

"Where are we going?" I enquired.

"The usual place," was his somewhat disinterested answer. We both knew where that was. No problem.

Rest seemed the order of the day. Keep your head down and stay out of trouble. They had picked up and cleaned up the old European sites. That was all shut down now. As for any other dramas, no one 'knew anything', a bit like Manuel in *Faulty Towers.*

I got to see my family again. The children had grown some and were now all out in the wide world and doing fine. We had developed this special relationship. No matter what the time gap, we were one family, an old family, duty came first and when together again time was of no matter, everything was the same. Most service families get used to that.

Months passed. I had no viable means of income and logged into the usual support systems that the good old UK offers to folk without much funds, as I was supposed to. You can't be a chap with no visible means of support like some levitating Indian fakir if you are going to maintain the 'legend' you are living. Gaps in stories can lead to trouble for the script if any enemy or group you are tasked to interface should look into it. You will be surprised what you can find out about people given half an hour on the laptop and knowing where to look, so one has to be careful.

Then I was moved into joining a company that was to supply the royal family with food and beverage for upcoming events. The royals were to have a few busy and very public years, including the Thames 2012 Pageant and the Olympic Games. Apparently this exposure had caught the attention of, as Shrub had coined it, "Evil-doers!"

Defensive measures had to be taken and eyes wide open and ears to the ground. The F&B industry has a habit of using a lot of itinerant labour largely from Eastern Europe and the old Soviet bloc. They work hard and for minimum wages, which is about three times what they would get back home, so they all crowd into terraced houses, about twelve to a dwelling and then send most of the money back home to support the remaining family. Checks were not being made too carefully so I, with others, had to keep an eye on them. Polonium sandwiches for tea were not required. Makes you glow in the dark. I did not make this policy; one had to be extra careful as Intel had detected plots. Sometimes you have to engage in defensive measures, after all only a few years ago the Bulgarian Secret Service, working as sub-contractors to the Russians were some of the most lethal assassins on the planet. Then that country was in the EU and we were all friends, but old loyalties stay longer than just a change of government. Espionage is not PC and usually involves money and other rewards. It is only scouts honour and loyalty to The Crown in the UK I have found. Elsewhere it is dog eat dog.

In the course of this long and rather interesting mission some amusing and unrelated incidents occurred, visible only from being on the insider track again. Serving the great and the good is always informative of how the other half live.

At one children's tea party, the usual kind of low-key affair where you have a liveried butler just because you can, I was despatched to obtain some suitable cup-cakes from a very up-market bakery. These actually had edible gold on the top. So back I troll with the merchandise and leave them with the liveried staff. You would think that was the makings of a memorable party. It was, but not in a good way and apparently it was my fault.

I had bought normal size cup-cakes, not the miniature ones, so the little dears could not pop them into their mouths in one bite. Heavens to Mergatroid, how would they cope? And the ice cream was too soft! Tragedy! Would the great and the good pay for such poor service? No, never–apologies were issued, payments were waived. The evil staff had failed miserably. Ah! Infamy, infamy, they've all got it in for me!

Funny really and of course I really couldn't care less. There were only three children at the party, anyway. Reminded me of my own lonely childhood.

And then there were the venues in luxurious apartments with gated entrances and 24/7 security staff. Delivery times are strictly controlled so you must arrive within the approved hour, which isn't always easy in London traffic. The guard says you have no more than 20 minutes to unload and clear the premises. What happens after that? Does the black limo come round with the guys with the banjo cases and baseball bats? So you adhere to these rules, which makes the elite feel they really control their lives and personal environments. Major symptoms of OCD I gather.

Then there was the yearly Royal Ascot, a really grand gathering of the noblest of the land. Top hats, silly hats and Pimms drunk by the jugful until neurological communication with the legs became rather problematical. I have never seen so many stretch limos in my life. I didn't know there were that many in the country. Some filled already with bevvies of girls well tanked up on the way in, let alone during the festival. On the way out it was common to see them staggering into taxis, or not quite making it and hitting the floor instead. I trust for the driver's sake they did not throw up. Perhaps that is where the top hats could have come in handy, after all they are mostly hired; who cares?

In my role, I had clearance to the most secure areas, and helped the high society attendees in a very polite and secure manner. Even the security guard on the door, ex-Army, was wearing a penguin suit. We joked about it. 'On-side' staff, always recognise other 'on-side' staff. The odd insider word, the query of, "who were you with?" The half-disguised salute. All these are quickly picked up. I've even had uniformed guards at the royal palaces present arms. They know how to be polite and respectful and so do I, we are on the same side. It is what makes this country the place it is, traditional and with good manners in the main. I confess, I like it that way.

The ex-Gurkhas on duty at various sensitive sites always snapped to attention when I passed through their gate. The odd 'Namaste' would secure an enduring respect, plus I would slip them the odd spare cookie when they were over-ordered. These guys worked 12-hour shifts for minimum wage, and I felt their life-long loyalty was rather taken for granted by their British employers.

I did meet the occasional Arab head of state. A subtle salute would bring a polite acknowledgement and a respectful and quiet, "Thank you." I do enjoy people who know how to behave. Probably went to Eton I expect. Manners matter, in my book, they matter a lot!

As they say of the French, it doesn't matter what you say as long as you pronounce it correctly. Having studied at the Université de Nice for a year, I not only spoke poor French but also with a Provençal accent, so ordering a cup of café in Paris nearly gets me thrown out of the venue as a lowly southerner. At least my accent is not Marseille. That would brand me forever as an almost untouchable in French society.

My principle tasks in my little day job were transporting logistics to various events of the great and the good, including prodigious quantities of champagne, wine and other goodies to weddings and events all over the South East. This included on one occasion to a country estate where I recognised one of the principal London mafia bosses who was clearly enjoying the fruits of his criminal activities!

I also came into contact with a colourful character known in the press as 'Flash'. The story goes that he'd had acquired a prestigious address in London for £50,000 from an African diplomat, who offloaded it when his country was going through a coup d'état. It's is now worth about £23 million, not such a bad profit for being in the right place at the right time. Many a party was held there and they also shot "The King's Speech" film there as well. It's a beautiful listed building that included a sliding hydraulic wall, the first of its kind, dividing the large ballroom on the ground floor. Flash got banged up for a few years for being a naughty boy by the serious fraud squad, over offering to broker bank loans that he didn't actually have access to. He got early release as he was in poor health.

I was tasked with keeping an eye on logistics around the Thames Pageant when the Queen and Prince Phillip were to proceed down river on a made-over barge complete with thrones and much regal bling. There were apparently five plots in train to take out the royal party on this event. All were interceded and no one was any the wiser. That was why all the bridges were closed off for the transit as certain undesirable types planned to drop some bombs on the barge as it passed underneath. It just didn't happen.

I lip read a bit and in the final stages of the journey on the close shot TV pictures, I saw Prince Phillip turn to the Queen and say, "Shall we sit down?" They had not used the thrones at all during the journey. "No!" said the Queen. Prince Phillip was getting tired and a little cold in the sharp wind but I believe the Queen had been briefed that she would be literally a sitting target if she travelled downstream seated on the thrones towards the prow of the Royal Barge. Phillip was ill the next day.

Her Majesty, had also been briefed that she was in the front line at the opening of the Olympic games when she and the royal party looked very on edge and uncomfortable. I understand there were three plots to assassinate her during that period. Again, none of this made the daily papers. Need I say more? It did appear on the internet but was never confirmed. Bad press around the royals is always controlled and suppressed.

Life had become rather trivial and mundane compared to my former missions. One day I had to travel 15 miles to deliver a single knickerbocker glory spoon to a National Trust event, which had been forgotten in loading. Another time it was 20 miles to collect a dozen miniature flower pots for the chef's specialist baking.

However, everyone was safe and happy and business continued as usual in the home country. Even if it did feel somewhat detached from the real world out there where people were still dying and starving in considerable numbers. That is the prerogative of fame and fortune. The elites can just look the other way and their only worries are the FTSE index that morning.

I attended several bankers' meetings in a supportive role where matters such as how to maximise profits was the order of the day. No international crisis was missed in its potential to produce the extra few millions. Always see the glass half-full not half-empty. The potential demise of Greece or the Cypriot bank crisis all offered opportunities to make a killing, apparently buying up assets ten cents on the dollar. Am I implying that American money was involved? Americans never miss an opportunity to take advantage of such events. On occasion they might even have helped created the crisis in the first place, I suspect. Such is the objective of taking a major market share. *Greed is Good* is a phrase I have heard used more than once aside from in the movie it came from.

14. Exposure

GOOD MORNING YOUR HONOUR

2012; it was 07.50 am when the polite young police constable knocked on my barn door. The building dated from 1760 and was part of a secure estate that I was living on in West Sussex. The gardeners were all ex-police and helicopters landed in the grounds, but none of this was known to the goons who now came calling at the behest of those who saw me as a threat that needed to be kept on the 'backburner'. Rumour had got out that I was writing a book and a necessary character-assassination was called for, it seemed.

In train to the raiding party were two 'investigators' for the Department of Work and Pensions, a council official and a second police officer. They all wore latex gloves and it looked a little OTT.

"Come in chaps," I beckoned, "Have you all signed the Official Secrets Act?" They looked a little confused.

"Anyone for coffee or tea?" I had been briefed they were on their way so their appearance came as no surprise. In fact, they were a little early. The police officers had only been told they were on the raid 30 minutes earlier so they knew nothing, but the DWP boys had been spiked for several months and had been fed all kinds of detailed junk on legends, second identities and the like. This was in order to put me on the wrong side of their line of definitions of what you are allegedly allowed to do in the European Union or the UK. It appeared they were alleging, that I had contravened the rules of 'habitual residency' while I was receiving a disability benefit, legitimately awarded because of my Multiple Sclerosis.

This definition of residency happens to mostly be in contradiction to the rulings of the European Courts, to which we are (then, at least!) supposed to be subject and it had been suitably skewed to make me look the bad guy. Here they were, ready to be very official and look for misdemeanours anywhere they could find them. However, when HMG wants to bend the rules for its own purposes, it will. I knew that.

The police officers said they needed to search the premises.

"Sure, no problem." Nothing had been lost, shredded or moved. It was all there. I was quietly bemused as to what they would find. They were very thorough. All my domestic appliance owner's manuals were examined, the underwear drawer, under the bed. I was very helpful and took pity.

"You need to go up there in the loft," I guided.

"Don't bump your head and be careful of the cobwebs. You need that red case and the computer bag and you had better have those achieves as well."

He opened the voluminous files and started to sift through.

"No, no. You haven't got time to read them now. You'll be here all day. Take the whole lot and just let me have them back later when you have looked through them all."

It took them over a year to do that and they did not all come back. The Stateside classified technical stuff on anti-gravity drives disappeared. 'Of no defence significance,' was the public MOD line. Really?

So, off to the local nick for a bit of a chat, under caution of course. It took all day. The second investigator was looking tired and wanted to stop, but the main guy, (I called him, Woody after the *Toy Story* character), was persistent. He had been commissioned to find dirt and he was digging, scraping the barrel. You have to play their game, avoid the loaded questions, the ones that try to put words in people's mouths. You have to ignore the self-righteous attitudes they assume while they think they are addressing lower pond life, the criminalised, the itinerant scum whom they are commissioned to destroy. God help any single mum, disabled teenager or other persons who might find themselves in the hands of these big burly goons. I kept it going until they finally tired of getting some ultimate confession that I was in fact the devil incarnate, hell bent on world destruction, total depravity and the end of civilisation as we knew it.

These guys were there to 'save the government money' or just persecute the under privileged whenever they stepped over the line, it seemed. I knew their game. When they switched off the tape recorders the number two confessed he hated the job, could not wait to retire. Still, he had his mortgage to pay like everyone else and if the government needed scapegoats to offset its poor decisions then the 'benefit frauds' and illegal immigrants would do nicely. I knew differently, as I had been privy to their own nasty misdemeanours for a very long time, hence why they had every reason to be nervous of me and my kind, as we have access to most things that go on behind closed doors. The things Joe Public does 'not need to know'.

So police bail was granted, no problem. I was very polite. No threat to society, though maybe a threat to the halls of power, if they could find something to stick on me. They had seized all the laptop computers but of course all my real data was backed up at secure locations with people who did not jump to their tune, the old guard.

These were all new political kids on the block as far as we were concerned; the kids, be they in their 50s, who needed to arrange 'stunts' as we called them, to keep them in power. Keep the mass populations in fear and dread needing their protection and defence. Why else would you need them at all, what did they do for you? As one of the candidates for The Monster Raving Looney Party had said, "I am going to do for you, what all other politicians will do. Precisely nothing!"

Some parties do less than others, they have more experience in building duck houses or cleaning out moats. They would need those to keep the unclean at bay.

Ah! The great unwashed, the mob of Rome, the people who the halls of power are really afraid of! Keep them in the dark and throw shit on them and, like mushrooms, they grow just beautifully. Once every few years or so, when their vote is needed, suddenly they become really important. Babies have to be kissed, flesh must to be pressed and the constituents promised the sun, the moon and the stars, which of course has not happened so far because they've been too busy cleaning up the mess left by their predecessors, whoever that was.

We voters are expected to swallow this rubbish decade after decade while business proceeds as usual, money is made and the elected politicians pay off their sponsors or lobbyist who got them into office in the first place. Just so they can rule over us all with wisdom and superior, moral ineptitude. Make prodigious mistakes, engage in grand unnecessary projects and spend other people's money. Yours.

Of course we need more nuclear submarines, after all if we don't have them the Russians would annihilate us tomorrow, wouldn't they? The fact that as Europe alone we are one of their main sales markets should indicate to you that they would not destroy one of their best customers. No, but hang on it's not the Russians you need worry about; it's the Chinese. But just a mo? China owns most of the bond debt of the United States so if you go to war with China or China with the USA, both are financially destroyed in the process. I'm sure you've worked out by now that these big defence expenditures are just to keep the good old armaments industry going, building weapons that no one needs, achieving nothing except profit. Should I object? No, of course not, even my own family makes money out of this, and lots of it, so it's the pot calling the kettle black.

'Beat their swords into ploughshares' was a fine, if unlikely, phrase put forward by some former religious prophet I recall. But then we have the saving grace, the grass fire war, the religious rivalry, a different interpretation of the Koran. Something you would absolutely have to kill for. Yes, the misunderstanding of your near neighbour is something that has to be a capital offence. Your view has to be held supreme and all others must pay the price for your assertion that you are right, God or Allah said so, and as we know God can be pretty dominant in asserting that only his followers should inhabit the Earth, then all others must die!

Have I got that right? Is that logical? Is genocide built into the DNA of all primates or indeed all animals? Ask the Robin in your back garden when he is kicking shit out of his fellow male companion in order that your garden is his and his alone. But of course we humans are above all of that, a higher evolution of species. Not! Did Darwin get it right? Survival of the fittest?

Perhaps Peter Cooke and Dudley Moore were right in their sketch when they had a long line of old and infirm folk queuing up to jump off Beachy Head to their doom, under a banner proclaiming, "Jump for Britain!' That would save the NHS a lot of money. Now who had that idea last, let me think, was it Adolf Hitler? Not the most popular of fellows, got rid of a lot of the Roma people and the mentally ill or disabled. Oh, and yes, a lot of annoying business and property owners who were in the way – known as Jews. That was very unpopular too, got very bad press. Caused a lot of war and mayhem. So no silver bullets for these sociological and resource problems. Better yet, just allow two thirds of the World to starve and funnel most of the resources into the developed nations. That works.

Then we can solve our conscience by giving lots of charities helping the developing world, holding dinners and events at high ticket prices, say a $1000 a seat, so we know we have done our bit for the poor and homeless. I became aware that one charity raised £13 million and put three nurses and two Land Rovers into the troubled areas, that was good value for money!

And then the Haiti Earthquake funds. So much of that is still in bank accounts in the States. Why? Because of course the Haitians are not capable of administering it themselves. Sounds logical to me, Bill. Work it out for yourself.

While we are in very non-politically correct territory, where did the Nazis get their core philosophy from? The Odessa Society, and who were they? A combination of European Freemasons, The Knights of Malta and a couple of female mediums purported to be in touch with the 'Nordics' alien race, who just happen to have blue eyes and blond hair, like me.

So you cosmic types out there are between the rock and the hard place. The Pleiadian Nordics could be described as fascists, while the little Greys could be characterised as communists, according to Forrestal, way back when.

No wonder Eisenhower could not do a deal on nuclear disarmament with the first alien contact, the Nordics. He would have been getting into bed with the crew who had just tried to take over the Earth via the Nazi party. No, he did a deal with the Greys. Kind of a no win, no win, I feel. And what was that deal? Simple. They gave a certain amount of technological assistance and he allowed a few thousand humans to have their DNA genetic material borrowed to help a 'dying race' – sound familiar? A bit like the origins of 'Superman?' Except the few thousand became over 250,000, all RFID micro chipped as well.

When a young boy I used to take a very innovative science comic called *Rocket* edited by ex-RAF Spitfire Ace, Douglas Bader. We wrote to each other, it was 1956. It was great stuff, very good dialogue on space exploration and also features like *Flash Gordon*. It only ran for 32 weeks. In the final editions it started to run a strip cartoon about an ex-Nazi moon base and in the very final edition about a disabled spacecraft, as the helmet of the occupant was about to be taken off. Edition 33 never ever appeared and *Rocket* folded suddenly, gone without trace. I wondered if the being inside the helmeted suit was in fact a girl who had blue eyes and blond hair. We may never know. Douglas maybe knew, but it was not PC to say so.

Am I a fascist? No, it would be far too much of a cliché. We should not, however, debar the very wide range of beings and philosophies of potential denizens of other worlds who may be visiting both now and historically our little island planet Earth. I know only too well that we are far from the only intelligent life in the billions of stars in our galaxy alone. The Pope doesn't think so, why would you? Charles Fort, the America writer of strange phenomena and the inspiration for the Fortean Times magazine, speculated that someone owns this Earth and all others have been, "warned off."

Myself, I see it as I kind of cosmic natural park, wherein many species reside, left to their own evolution and random outcome of survival. Attempts do seem to have been made over the millennia to upgrade, educate and pacify the human population.

All have failed, with the favoured group then assuming they are the chosen ones with outright domination rights over all the rest. Many groups have fallen into this trap. It's called colonialisation, perhaps a word that now should be understood in the context of a colonial power implanting its culture and standards on another land and the races that inhabit there, the indigenous people. Results vary.

On a planetary level, the British had the Raj in India when a quarter of the world map was coloured the pink of the British Empire. That left behind overtones of British culture from that period. The Canadians still speak old French in some territories, so different that when they speak on French TV they get sub-titled. Many other countries speak English, French, Spanish or Portuguese depending on who 'conquered' them first. Communities move around, so the Italians are not Roman and neither are the Egyptians the original stock in the main. The current majority of the Chinese population do not want to admit that much of their great and ancient history was down to Indo-Europeans, which is why they suppress a lot of their archaeology.

Meanwhile, back at home, I was still under suspicion of defrauding the system. It took two years to get me into Crown Court through numerous delays involving the Crown Prosecution Service simply saying they could, "not proceed". They wrote to GCHQ, MI6, MI5 and Special Branch. The answer was always the same, "It is Her Majesty's Government's policy that we can neither confirm nor deny the connection of such a person so enquired of." In other words, we are not going to admit anything at all about the security services and their sub-contractors and the way it all works.

Obviously various road blocks had been thrown in the way of the investigation and certain enquiries were a no go area but they allowed it to rumble on. My name needed to be blackened in case I published not only my own stories, but the rather more sensitive stories of others who had been within my care. No one trusted my sensitivity or loyalty to the crown, even knowing I had, in effect, been a censor myself over the years. But it's the nature of the beast. No one does trust anyone in the intelligence agencies anyway, evidenced by the tasked investigations I had been put on myself looking at the grey men, the suits, in the various sensitive areas around Q and the obsessive compartmentalisation that goes on to this day. The right hand is not supposed to know what the left hand is doing. This also unfortunately allows a lot of manipulation and shielding of both agency people and the power elite if they have been 'naughty boys', enabling them to hide behind the cloak of 'national security'. Bullshit!

It is unconscionable that this has involved the exploitation of vulnerable children over the decades, by very senior politicians, military and police alike. If an agency has the power to hide anything it wants to, it is a power that is very liable to be abused.

As for the oversight of the Parliamentary Intelligence Committee, then excuse me while I reach for a brown paper bag. The term the 'fox guarding the hen house' seems appropriate, as mostly they are protective of their own domain rather than asking pertinent questions. Two of them were in the control of US intelligence anyway and had their balls in a vice so to speak, pun intentional.

As for vested interest, say no more, referring back to the historical Lord Manchester again, "If you cannot take advantage of being in the House, why are you there?" Ah! 'The greater good, the greater good," of course; silly me.

The crown had to change its charges three times, along the way dropping 14 counts offering 'no evidence', perhaps because no evidence existed. One charge was dropped on the basis that it had no foundation whatsoever and had crept onto the charge sheet just because the 'American' barrister conducting the case had been thinking of the 4th of July celebrations.

In the end, the presiding senior judge accepted the apology of the crown on this charge, commented that it was, "a very messy prosecution" and sent us all away to find some kind of 'plea bargain' deal that she could agree to in court.

So after lunch we returned, further negotiations occurred with the CPS and a 'suspended sentence' ensued, the case was never heard in open court and lots of very sensitive material was saved from hitting the fan. As the crown barrister herself had advised, "You can only keep that out of court if you plead guilty." So in HMG's best interest that is what I did. The two MI5 observers in the public gallery slid off happy that matters had been resolved and life returned to normal in the corridors of power. All was well, other than claims made in certain circles that because I accepted the deal, I must be guilty.

The book you have just nearly finished reading was heavily sanitised, made nearly politically correct and most of the people who did wrong are either dead or nearing the 'pearly gates'. Current bosses and politicians can say, "It wasn't me sir, no sir," in the realm of previous British or American governments.

We have all moved on". Even Dame Butler-Sloss seems to have had an epiphany on the road to revelations and after standing down from the ever-widening (as of date of publication) and increasingly chaotic child abuse enquiry, seems now moved to have the truth come out eventually. We shall see?

Before I close, I want to mention some matters beyond the timeline of 'previous regimes' and briefly into the domain of more current 'mysteries'. Has anyone noticed that it is very difficult for modern civilian airliners to 'disappear'? Many residents of the Maldives saw Malaysian Flight MH370 fly over their islands before heading south into the wide blue yonder. The fact that cell phones on the flight were receiving calls from relatives after the fuel would have run out and one of these established its location by GPS as being on land at Diego Garcia, which is a highly secure US base leased from the British.

It has been established that the passengers included a specialist team of computer engineers who worked for Freescale SemiConductor taking a new and very, very special microchip to be manufactured in the Peoples Republic of China. This chip's applied-for patent was owned by some of these engineers and registered days after the plane went missing. Its ownership is now believed to be in the sole hands of Freescale. The chip is a major breakthrough in surveillance technology and is planned to be installed into every possible electronic device known to man, thus giving the super-computer systems (that includes NSA Utah) the enhanced capacity to snoop into every home in the world as they become infested with new "smart" pieces of wifi-enabled domestic equipment.

The insatiable need to know your every move is an obsession with those who have much to fear from 'the mob of Rome', the general public. Those whom one day might wake up and start thinking. They call the general population, 'milch cows', meaning those to be 'milked'. It was also the name of a WWII German U-boat class used to supply the wolf packs at sea, but it means any source of easy profit. So the new chip stayed firmly in American hands, as was, I am sure, considered necessary for US Security and continued commercial corporate domination of world markets.

The CIA's principle role is commercial superiority for the USA. National security is now taken care of by darker agencies in the States who report directly to The White House. There are 17 security agencies run by the United States, one of the most significant is the NRO, The National Reconnaissance Office, who happen to take a keen interest in UFOs, as I know from my personal connections with colleagues in the past.

As for the 'darker agencies', ask the US President, who has himself said that every week in the White House situation room, he sits down with security officials in the weekly counterterrorism 'Terror Tuesday' meeting. He's presented with weekly drone-strike hit lists of identified insurgents, terrorists and other undesirables upon which he deliberates and signs off termination orders. These are people who mostly live in Yemen and Pakistan and Afghanistan, who allegedly pose a threat to the security of the US of A. Presumably the lives of those unwittingly caught up in the impending, lethal 'surgical' strike – the collateral damage - don't matter.

War by proxy. Operators sitting in air-conditioned cabins in Nevada killing people on the other side of the world. Gallant stuff, the work of heroes, methinks.

I trust they all get medals and pass their eyesight and intelligence tests, as you have to be able to identify an insurgent from 15,000 feet via the on board videocam and have local intel of their intentions. Problem? That means people on the ground.

Which is where me and my kind came in before the day of the intelligence nerd; the super-geek sitting at a screen breaking mega-encrypted code transmitted by some insurgent in a cave to his evil surrogates world-wide, bringing destruction to all you innocents out there. Am I being cynical? What do you think?

Reservations and reducing numbers, as was done in colonial days will not work in these modern times. Neither will drone attacks, they just produce yet more angry families and allow a grass-roots rebellion to gain strength. Iraq is a clear example of this in the year 2014.

They held a competition recently on 'Blue Peter' at the BBC to find potential 'spies' for the security services. The kids had to break codes and shown they were nerds in the making. Bless! I wonder if they could speak five Indo-Chinese dialects, dress as a local, fire an AK-47 with some accuracy or know much about central Asian traditions. Probably not, but why would you need to when you could Google it?

Those who could pass, might be invited to join the 15,000 upstanding souls whose mission it is to track, listen, snoop and intercede the affairs of others from their desks in Cheltenham, Yorkshire and Cyprus, to name but a few.

Of course, I am not too cynical to accept that we do need these people. It all started at Bletchley when they cracked Enigma and it was realised that you then had to disguise the fact that you had the drop on the enemy. Thus enemy actions had to be allowed to proceed, otherwise you gave the game away. The game started then of controlling history, of actually trying and succeeding in controlling the enemy's actions, of staging false flags, of creating crises which had advantages to your own position. In those days it was national interests, but now nations are run and owned by the corporates and they are guided by 'the bottom line', the profits that can be made at the end of the day.

National boundaries are a thing of the past, only to be used as PR when trying to get a project approved through the legislators by making some nation or group the new enemy who wishes you ill. Unfortunately, as you demonise a new 'enemy', you create a side-effect of home-grown angry young sympathisers who, inculcated by this insidious propaganda, are motivated to form their own under-the-radar cells of like-minded people, hell-bent on making their own mark from a close vantage point. As well as these, the British Foreign and Commonwealth Office (FCO) has said that there could be 4-500 radicalised British young men now fighting for Allah in Iraq and Syria. Many of these men, hardened by conflict, could return to the UK with savage plans. I flagged this up a decade ago when we were keeping tabs on such endeavours in the London Mosques. They didn't listen then and they are reaping the results of that now.

Thus we get madness like the Woolwich murder of a mild-mannered medic and musician, who was just walking back to his barracks. The Royal Regiment of Fusiliers is a company of men with whom I have had associations and they command my highest respect for their professional and measured discipline in theatre. The British armed forces are the very best, always have been and that is why when there was a particularly difficult or dangerous mission, our American friends would pay the British to do it for them as I know only too well. Don't get me wrong, I have many American friends I like very much, a sociable, fun, kind people in the main. Just young.

I laugh when they say, "You're from London, that's London, England?" I recall when voting as a local tax-payer in Florida, I strolled in and was confronted by a much-aged and diminutive lady at the voting reception desk.

She eyed me with suspicion. "You have a very peculiar accent," she said accusingly. I could not resist.

"Yes," I said, "It is The Queen's English. We invented this language!"

15. Epitaph?

THE END IS NIGH?

The hate mail was a little unexpected. What exactly had I done to deserve this? Water off a duck's back to me, but I had to protect the people around me. Sensitive souls and regular church-goers who believed God was in His Heaven and all was right with the world. But that it was so!

I got fired from my logistics oversight job. The royals would just have to rely on the other filtering measures to secure their safety. Most of my mates and colleagues were now either dead or somewhere off the radar in foreign lands living under new identities or even their real names, which they had never used. Some were well-fed, others were struggling, but they were no longer my responsibility.

The director of my parent organisation, NAIG, fell ill and retired so they made me director. We had once been 132, now we were five. 'Give me four good men'. The phrase seemed appropriate.

If you publish they will kill you, advised my peers. I sought the advice of friends at the NSA and at home in 5. No advice was forthcoming. All over, on the run up to the 2015 General Election, shit was hitting the fan as one party and then another attempted to sling mud around. Even Tony Blair re-emerged to put in his two-penneth. It reminded me of Churchill's comment on being told by an aide, with great concern, that the Italians had joined the Germans.

Churchill replied, "It's only fair, we had them last time!"

I recalled the words of others. "If I don't tell them no one will know. The secrets will die with me."

Well, dead men talk.

The phone rang. "We have a new job for you. They need an old fox. Are you available?"

16. In Retrospect

BRAVE NEW WORLD?

In final summary, over the years I have worked for five Constabulary Special Branch Offices, GCHQ (two compartments), 5 (via a handler), occasionally Uniformed Branch (Help Desk Scotland Yard), NAIG (consistently, which is a privately funded NGO), the Cabinet Office and two American agencies, always as a 'sub-contractor'. Thus, I have always been off the books and in a comfortable position for governments giving deniable responsibility. I am proud of what I have done over time, wish I could have done more, but I believe I have saved lives, many lives, and contributed to the UK National Security at sometimes critical moments in history.

I apologise to the reader that more detail has not been possible to be given in these carefully sanitised pages, but where there was any question of 'blow-back' to the service or people or the families of people still alive, obscuration has had to occur so as to protect their identities and actual locations. At times, I have had to skate along the line of complete veracity at times and refer to events in oblique terms and so some with insider knowledge will understand while others, I hope, will be able to surmise the truth. Intelligence works like that; you have to have some inside knowledge to understand the format and information that is being conveyed.

Over time I have been allocated different 'avatars' for purposes of infiltration to various targeted people or groups. I have always tried to bring out of the mission the most positive result. None of what I have investigated has ever been casual or malicious. If a mission did not seem ethical I declined it and it was always with the best interests of the Crown and the British people at heart. Sometimes partners' interests were the driving force, but I would only undertake these missions if they did not contradict British interests.

I, and my family, have served the crown for over a thousand years one way or another and my forebears litter the pages of history to that account. That heritage is a strong influence on my moral code. Nothing will change that and I knew where we are coming from. In my duties, I have sometimes had to call to order individuals in various departments who were not working in the best interest of this sceptered isle.

I have never harmed anyone personally and my intelligence findings have been the basis for four decisions made well above my level, to neutralise four enemy agents or their sub-contractors.

Although these decisions were never mine, I was aware of the rules of engagement when we were at 'war' with the enemy. These are, by their nature, matters that could not have been dealt with by the normal legal process, which I absolutely respect, but British lives were on the line and the enemy under those conditions does not respect your moral code or due process of law.

People would have died for sure if those executive actions had not been taken and I back and support those who took those decisions, even though I do not know exactly what that chain of command would have been.

You never know who is above you by more than one level. Figureheads, directors of agencies, are for public consumption, everyone uses codenames and alternative identities. If you are taken, you therefore cannot endanger others in the field if you are forced by torture to talk.

Over 50 years, I got to know many things and string many others together. Be assured nothing in this book is without known foundation that has been checked and cross-referenced with other sources of data. I do not need to make anything up unless it is obviously to protect fellow agents and their families. I never knew the real names of many of these chaps and gals. I never needed to and we were not allowed to keep in touch after they retired and returned to their 'normal' lives.

It is difficult to return to a normal life when you have been 'somebody else' for a while. Many find this very stressful, as you can never tell even your own family what you have actually been involved in or where you were. I know my friends and other undercover agents will be able to relate to that statement. Ordinary civil servants and regular government people do not have the experience to understand this. Those of a more normal lifestyle may consider that many of the processes and procedures to which I have referred are unnecessary and even a breach of the rights of their fellow citizens, either in the UK or abroad.

However, the enemy, and yes UK and America do have enemies, I assure you, have no restrictions on their use of totally ruthless and immoral methods to achieve their ends and objectives.

This is a game in which the rules are often made by others, and we have to respond as ethically as we can. Inevitably, we also have to be pragmatic or we will not survive the integrity of this nation of ours. We try to cooperate with our partners both in NATO and the wider world, but we do not always agree with their policies or decisions and I and my kin have always tried to influence them with the best of traditional British values. We are a fine nation and a fine people with hundreds of years of diplomatic and world experience.

I ask you, dear reader, to try to understand the difficulties of both the history of the past 50-odd years and the current world situations in which we remain involved. Be assured that as for myself, and my 'old guard', we cannot be bought. Our interests are your interests and we try to take the moral high ground without being hypocritical.

However, I am aware that mistakes have been made over the years. Poor decisions have been taken on sometimes critical issues, where those in power behind closed doors have taken matters into their own hands and tried to make it right. As my most aged relative, now in her 90s would say, "They meant well." It is not for me to judge their actions or decisions now as I enter my own twilight zone of life.

I trust these pages have helped inform you of things some would not wish you to know. You will have to be the judge of that, not I, nor the media, which is merely a bought and paid for PR department of others.

Right now, February 2016, proxy wars and grand games are being played out in Syria with a very complex mix of players. One tries to stabilise these situations while certain parties seek to create as much chaos as possible. One would like these players to grow up before the Mandate of Heaven decides to intervene.

EPILOGUE

THE MAN WHO NEVER WAS

If you have heard me speak or seen my videos on
YouTube, you may wonder why I haven't referred in
detail in the body of the book to my own
communications with extra-terrestrials.

I have lived not just a double, but a triple life, in
many respects with the third part made up of these
contacts and, through the nature of my work, it has
been even more secret and deeply personal. To
maintain focus and sanity, it was necessary for me to
compartmentalise my inner self, but these
connections have been what, in the darkest of
moments, have kept me going.

I was planning to devote another volume, *The Man
Who Never Was* to this, but it is necessary, of course
to address it here so you can see how it fits together
and why it would have been too confusing to write
about in one book.

As I write, in November 2016, the world is on the brink of some major changes and revelations and you all need to know some of these things now rather than waiting another year.

The ability to compartmentalise his triple life – family, HMG and other-world, is indeed what made me so suitable for the Intelligence work. It is a special and peculiar mentality which does not always sit easily with most people. It is why there are so few successful field agents as opposed to the desk-jockey analysts who get their information from trawling through data, snooping on your personal e-mails and communications via super-computers, mapping your movements and connections. That is intelligence with a cup of coffee in your hand, a fully-equipped gym downstairs and virtually no risk or exposure to being in harm's way. Bless them, they do a good job, but I believed in shoe leather and infiltration as the way to go. The sharp end. The rules of engagement, where if you got it wrong you were at risk of dying.

So let me bite on the bullet and allow you to merge my other-worldly connections with what I have been allowed to tell you of my Intelligence work and life over the past 53 years. The other side of my personality may be more difficult for you to relate to, as it requires perhaps more of a leap of faith than just detailing the factual and physical events I have navigated.

First of all, I am not entirely human, that is, homo sapiens, homo sapiens. Then again, neither are you. You were all created by off-world entities some 250,000 years ago by merging primate DNA, splicing the 24 pairs into 23, creating humans. This DNA structure is also the format of those off-worlders.

Primates have 24 pairs, so they cannot breed directly with either off-world entities or humans without genetic engineering being involved. It may occur to you that by definition, you as humans could not have evolved from Apes without some help because of this fundamental fact.

However, whereas you are 98.4% primate and 1.6% alien, I am 51.6% alien and 48.4% primate. However, it is even more complicated than that because my alien mother's cell was itself a hybrid construction and that is too long a story to analyse here.

How did that happen with me? As I and others detailed in my previous books, foetuses are extracted from human mothers, genetically modified and then returned. Later they are usually extracted once again and brought on in the incubation chambers that many have witnessed when taken off on these 'procreation abductions'.

So although my human father's DNA is in me, my mother was the unwilling and resistant subject of an alien implantation. Her DNA was replaced in the fertilised egg, from which I was born. This may explain to you why she was so anti-sex, anti-me and against my father, who always had a deep and close connection with the 'other' side of life.

My mother tried to love me but she knew I was not hers and deep down that rift was always there. I could not have done what I had to do with only the normal human DNA mix. There are many others out there like me, some of you may be reading these words, knowing you are Star-seeds. You don't easily fit in. You are living a lie or acting a role, which is where the title, *The Man Who Never Was* comes from.

For those who have delved into my hidden

intelligence past, you may be detected that 'Peter Paget,' although a legitimate historical family name, was not the name I was born with, no more than some of the avatar names I have been issued with and used over my life. The film, *You Only Live Twice,* contains an amusing joke when Bond is undercover in Japan and that maybe was more than a coincidence, who knows, as intelligence folk often have a bizarre sense of humour and in the Americans' case, it is often rather obvious.

Other-worldly entities have been working with human culture and the human mind for many thousands of years. Although there is still a huge disconnect between their cultural awareness and understanding and that of current human civilisation, they tend to repeat the same interface patterns they have employed over the centuries and millennia. So, when the very first direct contact physically was made with me as a child, it was through a bird, yes, that talking magpie that kept me company as a sick child. It was used as a soft mechanism to first introduce this innocent little boy into matters far beyond the mundane world of which he was aware in the mid 1950's.

As I mentioned in the first part of the book, the magpie cracked jokes, actually quite clever jokes. That same magpie, or at least his slightly croaky voice, was the help that got me through the 11+ exam whose results divided British children into those destined for grammar school who passed, while those who failed ended up at the local Secondary Modern school. My magpie answered some questions in mathematical calculus, which I had neither been taught in primary school nor by my private governesses while in that vital off-school year when I was ten years old.

The magical feathery input placed me third in the County of Devon and in the potential genius programme. As I said earlier, my results sent me to a very special school for scientists, where I was never less than third down the class of 26 and usually top. Off-world help gets you a long way, just like Nicola Tesla where he was the conduit for their science and knowledge that needed to be introduced into a fledgling society that was then using mostly steam.

The magpie talking physically in my garden evolved into the voice of the bird helping me in my head. That was a clever and comfortable way, almost cartoon-like, to get that telepathic communication going and working. It helped that I was brought up almost monastically in complete isolation with no friends allowed, no siblings, no competitors except in school where I had to avoid the bullies as they knew I was not one of their herd.

I was the odd one out, to be singled out for rather cruel treatment, with little or no help from either school or my physical parents. My instinctive ability to dodge and duck and dive and keep out of the firing line was instilled then, and stood me in good stead ever since. Most of my friends in my latter teenage period were elderly, wise ex-military types, with whom I had endless conversations and instruction. These were eminent men.

So are some ETs avian? Well, I think their conscious intelligence can inhabit any life form they choose, from a beetle to an ape to a horse. The spark of intelligence and soul can be anywhere it chooses to be after a certain level of evolution and experience, hence why yogis can instil plants to grow and command animals at will. You might say horse whisperers are in the same tradition, talking to animals and understanding their thoughts. I speak fluent cat and have even spoken to tigers in my local zoo. I drove the howler monkey alpha male a bit crazy when he thought I was coming on to his territory on the island they inhabit at the zoo. He was the only bloke on the island and feared for his rights with the females in the group. Bless! Some human men are similar. Food, territory and sex are pretty strong drives in the primate brain.

My father was very into the spiritual life. As practicing spiritualists, I was taken willingly along to the Spiritualists chapel every Sunday from the age of seven to eleven, after which age my school homework got in the way. The other side of life, the spirit world, was as familiar to me as the local tuck shop, where you could get one of my favourites: sherbet flying saucers.

It was not until my father introduced me to the stories of George Adamski and his photographs that I had any interest or understanding of matters actually off-world, but when I did, I embraced it like a duck to water. I may have been a fledging but I was flying in familiar atmospheres. There was a recognition, of no known origin, but when I saw the negative that had been returned from his contacts and that picture occurred in his first work, 'Flying Saucers Have Landed' I found I could read and understand the message therein contained. I do not wish to go into detail here, although I have mentioned it before, but by the age of 17, I was building anti-gravity machines and other devices. These I disassembled, as I was of the opinion that humans were too violent to merit these sciences and although I much later realised that similar instructions had been 'downloaded' to, amongst others the Thule Society in Germany many years prior, I had no knowledge of that at that time. Many years later I would build 'lifters' which in fact are built by French sixth formers and demonstrated online. They are quite dangerous with their very high voltage, which can easily kill you if you don't know what you are doing.

I suppose again in my late teens was when a more direct contact came in to me. George Adamski, who was also off-world, not Polish and human as you might think, died in America and then on Dartmoor just 18 miles from my home in Torbay, Devon, he came back, landing in a classic 'Flying Saucer'. Yes, the 'Scorriton Mystery' story is true! With his two cat-eyed pilot companions, he instructed Arthur Bryant in all manner of things. That contact and information came quickly to me and also in part, to my one and only trusted school friend, Chris who was also a rather special lad. Chris was also the subject of a Close Encounter but he did not want to talk about it. He valued his position in polite society, as he was dating Miss Torbay, whom he later married. He bought a run-down stately home, drove a 1934 Bentley at aged 17 and moved in suitable circles. Flying Saucers and off world contact was not for polite company.

The whole oil pollution clean-up technology that I gave Sir Solly, was a direct download from 'upstairs', my off-world connection. It worked; of course it worked. By this time, I had had direct voice communications and diagrams in my head, been saved from a lightning strike on my parents' property and various other helpful input that I had got used to.

I did not really question where this came from. The source was kind of irrelevant, it was just part of my daily reality. They did my school exams and helped with my life. It was not part of an ancestor thing, like it was my deceased grandfather helping me, although he was a marine electrical engineer. No, this talked in a much more logical and surreal manner with concepts way beyond human ken. I felt more or less completely detached from regular human society by the time I went off to university to do Computing Science, which was in its infancy. I did find, like Uri Gellar, I could interact with the computers, knowing when they were about to fail for instance.

I craved for human contact but it rarely came. My world was not for discussion with regular folk. They would probably think I was mad. I did have a beautiful mind but I was very sane and kept my private world of telepathic input very much under wraps. I called my main mentor, "Geoff" and thought he was a male. Later, much later, I realised that entity was in fact female but could display both attributes as was required. This was inter-dimensional, which I did not fully understand at that time. I was only 18. I hadn't even had a girlfriend, let alone much worldly experience. That all came later.

Synchronisations and other playing with my event horizons happened constantly, rather like in the film, *The Matrix*. My off-world or spirit friends could play with time, make things happen or have situations changed or avoided. The support was constant, if not continual. Conversations occurred when needed but the surrounding support was always there.

Why me? Simply put, I was and am one of them. I had work to do and needed protection 24/7. There were not many of us here on Earth, maybe 3000, I understand and that is not many to influence a population that is now around seven billion in 2016 although it was quite a few less back in 1946. Why had we come? The atomic bomb explosions in Japan in1945 had set off alarm bells all over the cosmic sector. The Earth is in the Solar system of Sol which is sun 129 down the line of the Pleiadian's arm of the Galaxy. We had direct oversight of the domain and responsibility to maintain the planets and solar systems viability to continue as a biological area for evolution and environmental continuation into the futures (plural).

I have seen many 'UFOs', mostly high up and moving as they do in ways that sets them apart from satellites and meteors. I could request a manoeuvre and they would oblige. Elementary stuff, really. Why did they not come close very often? It is to do with the cosmic radiation the drive mechanisms transmit. Not good to get too much of that. I gather that was one of the reasons why some races from those domains are virtually sterile now. Take note, microwave cell phones and towers are probably in the process of doing the same down here over time. Radiation is time critical, hence I rarely carry a cell phone and when I do it is shielded from my bone marrow by a simple aluminium shield. Your pelvis is vulnerable and ladies, never carry your cell phone tucked inside your bra if you don't want to get breast cancer.

As well as saving me from death by lightning strike, there were other times my connection has prevented me from harm. "Lucky" near-misses, such as avoiding traffic accidents when I was delayed for a few seconds, or being 'told' to pull over, then continuing on to find there had been a pile up that I would have otherwise been in. During my time in the States, I was briefed on the arrival of a magnitude four hurricane, which probably saved my life yet again, and that was by some 14 days; better than the National Hurricane Center can do.

I suppose another helpful, critical time was when certain mercenary types were given the remit to assassinate me. They did not stand much of a chance, as 'upstairs' knew where they were all the time and moved me about accordingly. That is why in the narrative, apart from me knowing their moves and modus operandi, I was also being given direct instructions on where, how and at what speed to navigate, both on foot and in a vehicle. When the police and the Works and Pension boys came visiting that time, I was already briefed by both physical Intel and upstairs. And when I was raided because we were curing terminally ill patients, I knew they were on the way. Big Pharma does not like you stealing their drug business and in no way wanted cures for cancer. Far too much money to be made; about £60,000 to £90,000 per patient per year, I understand. For someone without an MD qualification to be taking people off their patient books back in the late 90s was a real threat to Big Pharma's bottom line. Most of those companies are controlled from Switzerland and the USA. Need I say more? Money rules OK. People dying? Well who cares, they would never meet them and the irony is the directors used alternative methods themselves. Giving money for research for the cures for cancer is a tragic con. The answers have been around for over twenty years. I was told, off the record, by the police that we had made some powerful enemies and to close the clinics now, or potentially go to jail. What can you do? Some others have taken up some of the natural methods in overseas locations, but they are all at risk, as the big money only considers profit, never your well-being, I assure you. I healed a lot of people, when it could be legal. That is why I became ordained in the States, as it made it legal to work with people that way.

Having this connection didn't really affect my younger self as I had learnt years back in my teenage life that to even mention it lost friends and killed any female relationship potential. Girls in those days conformed more than boys. Just go and play with your dolls dear, and get ready to have babies, was the order of the day. Brain, my, you don't need a brain dear, just be 'arm candy' and you will do fine. Not the situation now, I am pleased to say. Well, most places, except certain Muslim countries where if anything, it seems to be worse. The other week I understand a panel of academics in Saudi Arabia declared that they had established that women were in fact mammals; I found on scientific evidence that many men were in fact animals; just beyond pond life. Not wishing to demean pond life; I think frogs are cute, but toads gang bang their women, so no change there then.

As to my relationships with my wives, although many things were shared where we had a history, others were kept under wraps. Two of my four wives knew and remembered our relationships in former lives, Jane in Egypt and Rome where I was assassinated, and also my current (and final) wife of some 28 years too. We were in Egypt, members of the last Royal House. I was an elder brother and was bumped off first, as my younger brother was young enough to be manipulated until he too was despatched when he got a mind of his own. Dad had the dumb but accurate idea of making Amūn the Sun God, the one and only, and taking away power from the priesthood. They did not like that much and just progressively did away with us all. Took the power back. Business as usual. A sort of Egyptian 9/11 really. Nothing changes.

We also remember the times prior to and during the great flood. Building and sailing great ships; Noah was not the only one. Looks a bit familiar now with the coming of 'The Crossing' and all that 'Planet X' stuff.

None of this is very good for making money in a mercenary world. The idea that contactees and other UFO types are in it for the money is farcical. It usually ruins their lives and has lost them both jobs and friends. My God, another delusional soul. Stone him, works of the Devil, heresy at the very least, a candidate for the funny farm. Mankind is the only life in the Universe, God's crowning creation, the cleverest and most knowledgeable creatures ever to walk on this planet. In your dreams! Have you ever worked out how many galaxies, let alone habitable planets are out there? You could not get all the noughts on this page if you counted them. Even Brian Cox will tell you that.

Upstairs also helped intercede on a couple of very dangerous overseas attacks on British home shores, for which I was commended for Intelligence Excellence and been mentioned in despatches as rather special, to say the least. Do I have an ego? Sure, so does everyone, but I am not special where I come from, just normal.

In a former incarnation, I was second in command of the M86, a sort of cosmic fire engine engaged on crisis management and rescue. Then I moved to be a Fourth officer on the M89 a much larger ship of around three English miles long, which also engages in solar management. On the Suspicious Observers website, you may have noticed something called, 'Earth facing quiet'; well that's partly management. One function is sun-diving torpedoes which blow off excess energy build up, so that it is not directed against Earth. Behave Earthlings, if you don't want a large CME heading your way, which could produce a major EMP. That could spoil your whole day or even your whole year. (For those asking, a CME is a Coronal Mass Ejection and an EMP is an Electro-Magnetic Pulse – kills computers. In fact, damages lots of technical stuff). As I have also explained before, the sun is a brain. It is electromagnetic in function, not just a big nuclear ongoing bomb in the sky. Humans are obsessed with things that go bang. You can interact with the sun by an analogue effect. I am not going to explain that unless you are prepared to do about 30 years' initiation studies. Took me that long, so no free lunch.

Well that's about all for now folks. The next volume will cover this in more detail, so let this just whet your appetite. Until then, you can find me, in person, on my Facebook profile and page, links follow at the end, and also on my website. I'm also on various YouTube channels with different presentations I have made, including Miles Johnston and Kerry Cassidy who, if you are familiar with the UFO field, you are likely to know of. If not, look them up. Giving talks in different locations usually costs me money to do rather than making any gain. I also have a fledgling YouTube channel of my own, again, link to follow.

I wish you well. May your God go with you. You can message me on Facebook for specific questions or whatever I know of where you are located and help you survive the great changes yet to come about here in the solar system at large, and on that mud ball called Earth.

Blessings,

Peter Paget

7th November 2016

Find Peter Paget:

Website: https://www.PeterPaget.com

Facebook Profile:
https://www.facebook.com/peter.paget2012

Facebook Page:
https://www.facebook.com/PeterPagetDisclosure

YouTube
https://www.youtube.com/channel/UC5F6bubEpRDs
2p-IHPP9RhQ or search Peter Paget, Disclosure
Advocate

Based on a True Story.

Other books by Peter Paget

"The Welsh Triangle" 1979, 5 reprints to 1989
Granada/Panther/Grafton/Harper Collins Distribution.

All Rights held now by Author, © 2011

"UFO-UK" 1980 New English Library, one edition.

All Rights held now by Author, © 2011

Both these previous books coming to eBook and in
reprint in 2017

59777358R00173

Made in the USA
Lexington, KY
15 January 2017